ANTONIO
BUERO-VALLEJO

THREE
PLAYS

ANTONIO BUERO-VALLEJO

THREE PLAYS

The Sleep of Reason
The Foundation
In the Burning Darkness

Translated by
MARION PETER HOLT

TRINITY UNIVERSITY PRESS

Library of Congress Cataloging in Publication Data
Buero-Vallejo, Antonio, 1916-
   Three plays.

   Bibliography: p.
   Contents: The sleep of reason – The foundation –
In the burning darkness.
     1. Buero-Vallejo, Antonio, 1916-   – Translations,
English. I. Holt, Marion Peter. II. Title.
PQ6603.U4A24 1985   862'.52   85-1198
ISBN 0-939980-09-6

Printed in the United States of America

Contents

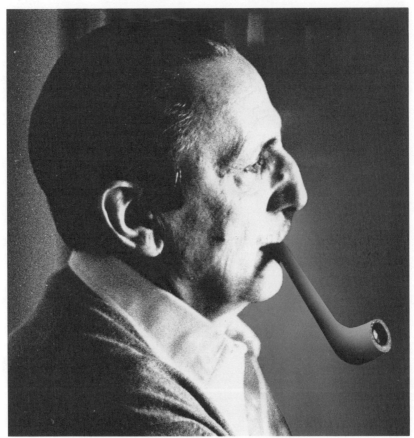

Antonio Buero-Vallejo. Photo credit: OLAF VALVERDE MORDT

Introduction

Antonio Buero-Vallejo was virtually unknown outside his small circle of artistic and literary friends when he won the prestigious Lope de Vega Drama Prize in 1949 for his second play, *Story of a Stairway [Historia de una escalera]*. The subsequent production of the work in Madrid's historic Teatro Español ran for an impressive 187 performances and inspired almost universal critical praise for a young former art student who had turned to playwriting after six years of imprisonment for support of the Republican cause during the Spanish Civil War. Although the play was in no sense radical in theme or staging, Buero's uncompromising treatment of the struggle of three generations of Madrid tenement dwellers against economic deprivation, and his effective opening up of the dramatic space by placing the action on a symbolic stairway, signaled the arrival of a dramatist who might provide a new direction for the stagnant Spanish theatre.

Today the play is viewed as a landmark; its importance in the annals of modern Spanish drama is comparable to that of *Death of a Salesman* or *A Streetcar Named Desire* in the American theatre. But unlike his American contemporaries, Buero-Vallejo did not reach an artistic plateau early in his career;[1] his full maturity as a playwright came in the 1960s, and only after the staging in 1970 of his astonishing multimedia drama *The Sleep of Reason [El sueño de la razón]* did he begin to gain the international attention that had eluded him for two decades.

The success of *Story of a Stairway* created an immediate interest in Buero's work and led to the staging of an earlier play, *In the Burning Darkness [En la ardiente oscuridad]*. After his provisional release from prison in 1946, Buero had quickly decided that he could no longer function as a painter in spite of an obvious talent and serious preparation. Over a period of a few weeks he wrote the first version of *In the Burning Darkness,* and later the script was also submitted to the Lope de Vega competition. After revisions, which included the addition of the prototypic "immersion-effect" – a scenic device used to achieve a participatory theatre – in the third act, the play opened on December 1, 1950, a little more than a year after the playwright's first production.

Although *Story of a Stairway* marks the beginning of Buero's professional career and is clearly a superior drama of its type, it remains in some respects atypical among his more than twenty works for the stage, while *In the Burning Darkness* is a seminal play providing examples or suggestions of themes and metaphysical concerns that recur in later plays. It also tentatively employs scenic techniques that have become fundamental to Buerian concepts of total theatre. We find the first use of a struggle against a physical defect as a dramatic parallel to an intellectual or spiritual struggle, and Ignacio, the rebellious blind boy whose seemingly irrational dream of experiencing light is inher-

IN THE BURNING DARKNESS. *Oslo, 1962. Liv Ullmann as Juana. Photo
credit:* STURLASON.

ited by his murderer, begins the line of alienated visionaries in Buero's
plays. There is a skillful integration of both visual and nonverbal aural
elements (or silences) which become coequals with spoken dialogue,
and musical motifs are used in a commentary function rather than as
mere supporters or effecters of mood. The ironic suggestions of
Beethoven's *Moonlight* Sonata played over loudspeakers in a school for
the blind and the tenuous allusions of Grieg's music for Aase's death in
Peer Gynt as accompaniment for the offstage murder in the final act
may have gone unnoticed by audiences in 1950, but they confirm that
Buero was experimenting with one of his most characteristic theatrical
devices at the earliest stage of his career.

Of even more importance is the initial experiment with a technique
which Buero himself has called *interiorización* (interiorization) and
which the Spanish critic Ricardo Doménech has labelled *"efectos de
inmersión"* (immersion-effects).[2] The momentary dimming of the stage
and houselights to a point of absolute darkness in one crucial scene of
In the Burning Darkness is a far cry from the frequent scenes of silently
mouthed dialogue or the visual and aural bombardment of the audience with projections and amplified sounds in *The Sleep of Reason,* but
it lays the foundation for a scenic device later used extensively to
achieve a participatory theatre. The audience is drawn into the mind
of a character or into a crucial dramatic situation with intensified per-

sonal identification, as the proscenium barrier is bridged and momentarily ceases to exist.

Buero had not turned to playwriting utterly inexperienced in matters of the stage. He had attended performances regularly as a student in Republican Madrid, and his wide readings in modern dramatic literature had extended from Ibsen to Valle-Inclán. Ibsen's influence on Buero's early works has been widely noted; however, his third play, *Adventure in Grayness [Aventura en lo gris]*, with its expressionistic dream interlude, suggests an equal affinity with Strindberg. Had it not been suppressed by censorship,[3] this compelling political drama, dealing with a fateful encounter between a deposed dictator and an idealistic intellectual, might well have found stages abroad and focused international attention on the young playwright early in his career.

The production of Buero's first two plays did not assure him either financial security or unquestioned acceptance. Some other early plays, apolitical in theme, however, had modest success at the box office, and Buero was eventually honored with several of the yearly prizes awarded to outstanding theatrical works. But he also endured on occasion the *pateo* or footstamping with which Spanish audiences express their disapproval. Suspect in official circles because of his participation on the side of the Republic during the Civil War, he was not permitted to travel outside Spain until 1963, although invitations were extended

IN THE BURNING DARKNESS. *Madrid, 1950. Adolfo Marsillach as Carlos; José María Rodero as Ignacio. Photo credit:* GYENES.

as his reputation grew. At the same time, an increasingly vocal group of critics who advocated a theatre of political agitation (regardless of the consequences) began to denounce him as a conformist.

An important turning point in Buero's artistic development came in 1958 when he began a cycle of historical plays, breaking with some of the conventions of his earlier works and placing his characters against a panorama of social or political conflict. While most of his plays prior to 1958 were clearly designed with the limits of the minimally equipped theatres of Madrid in mind, none was without some innovation in the use of theatrical effects and scenic space. Even when the action took place in a setting that suggested (or substituted for) the ubiquitous stage living room, there were visual devices that complemented the dramatic action, or a scenic transformation was effected — as in the visual depiction of the double reality at the end of *Irene or the Treasure [Irene o el tesoro]* (1956). However, with *A Dreamer for a People [Un soñador para un pueblo]*, the first of the historical plays, Buero disavowed the inflexible box set and expanded his action onto multiple sets. He also introduced a Brechtian commentator in the person of a blind minstrel — a device that would figure in more imaginative ways in several subsequent plays. At this point he abandoned definitively the use of traditional terminology (*drama, comedia, tragedia*, etc.) to describe his plays and substituted his own: *fantasía, parábola, fábula, misterio profano*, and *relato escénico* (fantasia, parable, fable, secular mystery, and dramatized case history). This was, of course, a clear notice to his public not to expect plays in conventional modes.[4]

A Dreamer for a People is set in Madrid in 1766 and deals with the thwarted attempts at political liberalization by Leopoldo de Gregorio, Marqués de Esquilache, an Italian minister brought to Spain by Carlos III. This sad historical episode is not particularly well known, but it is easy to recognize parallels between the events depicted in the play and later failed attempts at liberalization in the twentieth century. It was obvious to audiences that the dramatist was making a political statement — albeit an oblique one — and that to a degree he had circumvented state censorship.

But it was in his second historical play, *Las Meninas* (1960), that Buero was able to integrate most successfully his fundamental metaphysical and social concerns with his developing concepts of theatrical representation. He experimented even more boldly with form, allowing his commentator to move in and out of the dramatic frame, employing orchestrated simultaneous scenes, and mingling the arts by using a musical motif synesthetically to suggest the genius of a visual concept. At the same time, the dual themes of social injustice and the struggle of the visionary (the artist Diego Velázquez in this case) in the face of mediocrity and the opposition of religious and political reactionaries were integrated for extraordinary dramatic impact. The final scene of the play, a tableau in which Velázquez is preparing to paint the work that gives the play its name, was perhaps the most startling that Buero had conceived and certainly the most suggestive of multiple levels of theatrical reality. The commentator, acting as a stage director at this moment, leads the viewer into the conflicting thoughts of the principals who strike their historical poses, to be rendered "immortal by light," as Buero expresses it in an earlier passage of dialogue. Unlike the later *The Sleep of Reason, Las Meninas* does not utilize at any point a reproduction or projection of the artist's actual painting. Nevertheless, specific paintings are visually alluded to continually by the presence of characters whom Velázquez immortalized, and the final scene fixes for a moment in time the principals of his most famous canvas.[5]

The inspiration for *The Concert at Saint Ovide [El concierto de San Ovidio]* (1962) – the only one of the historical dramas that is not set in Spain – was an eighteenth-century etching portraying a performance of blind musicians in a Parisian café in 1771, and the writings of Valentin Haüy, a teacher and associate of Louis Braille. Haüy, who actually witnessed the public ridicule of the blind performers, appears briefly within Buero's *parábola* to protest the abuse of the sightless musicians; at the end of the play, he steps forward to deliver a monologue (partly based on Haüy's memoirs) that testifies to the profound effect the mockery had on his life. The play contains one memorable but isolated immersion scene in the final act, in which the blind violinist David murders in total darkness an antagonist whose terror the audience must share. Perhaps a more significant dramatic invention is the "concert" scene itself, a notable realization of Buero's evolving concepts of total theatre.[6] After the exploitative impresario terrifies the blind musicians into submission, the café fills with customers to watch them perform. As their pathetic rendition of an insipid, off-color song progresses, punctuated by a chorus that imitates the bleating of sheep, so does the ridicule of the audience-within-the-play (momentarily interrupted by Haüy's vain protests). In a stunning theatrical transformation, the onstage audience becomes a dehumanized, jeering throng as they echo the animal sounds with increasing abandon.

Buero temporarily put aside his historical themes in the mid-sixties to write *The Basement Window [El tragaluz]*, one of his most successful efforts and the first play dealing directly with the Spanish Civil War to reach the stage during the Franco era.[7] Labelled an "Experiment in Two Parts," *The Basement Window* opens in the distant future. Two investigators (He and She) from a socially and technologically advanced civilization prepare to study the past with holographic projections of events. In addition to framing the principal action, presenting it as a scientific investigation with a potentially instructive message, these objective characters also appear within the play in a choral function to comment on scenes that the audience has just witnessed. Through this device, the playwright invites the audience to join the "experiment" to reevalu-

ate the alienating effect of the devastating war on a single paradig-
matic family.

During this period, Buero also wrote a more controversial drama, *The
Double Case-History of Doctor Valmy [La doble historia del doctor Valmy]*, in
which the torture of political prisoners was a prominent theme. Even
though the play was set in a fictional country, the subject matter was
unacceptable to the Spanish censors, and it was not performed until
1976, after the death of Franco.[8] Returning to historical subjects in 1970,
Buero completed *The Sleep of Reason*, his most acclaimed and most frequently performed play. In the decade following its Madrid run, this
remarkable multimedia drama was translated into some twelve different
languages and produced in as many countries of Europe. In Poland it was
staged by the internationally famous director Andrzej Wajda, in Rumania
by another renowned director, Liviu Ciulei, and at Norway's National
Theatre by Pål Løkkeberg. It is not difficult to understand the appeal of
The Sleep of Reason for such artists, for no modern work for the stage has
dealt more compellingly with the effects of terror and intimidation on the
creative mind in a repressive society.

The protagonist of the drama, which Buero calls a "fantasia in two
parts," is the painter Francisco de Goya. The action takes place over a few
days in December 1823, when the aging artist has covered the walls of
his country retreat with the so-called "Black Paintings" and is living under
the threat of physical abuse or even death from the forces of the auto-

THE SLEEP OF REASON. *Baltimore, 1984. Center Stage, directed by Travis
Preston. Photo credit:* BARRY HOLNIKER.

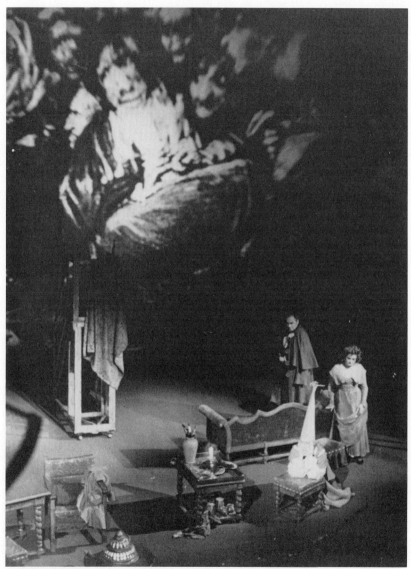

THE SLEEP OF REASON. *Moscow, 1973, Gorki Art Theatre.*

cratic Fernando VII. Goya is seventy-six years old at the time, and his
work has taken on the dark and phantasmagoric qualities that some
interpreted as the product of senility or madness. He is also faced with
the sexual frustrations of his young mistress, Leocadia Weiss, who
remains a loyal companion to him despite his declining vigor. His ulti-
mate humiliation is to watch her violent rape by a soldier of the king's
militia. Like Ignacio, Velázquez, and the blind violinist David, Buero's
Goya is a visionary. Not only is he an artist of genius but he sees beyond
the present reality to a more enlightened future, though his associates
view his musings on benevolent flying men as another manifestation of
dementia.

The title of the play is taken from one of Goya's best-known etchings.
As in *Las Meninas,* Buero re-creates a familiar work of art onstage – in
this instance as a nightmare experienced by the painter just prior to the
rape of Leocadia. Immersion effects are used extensively and intricately
in *The Sleep of Reason.* In 1823 Goya had already endured the agonies of
total deafness for many years, and Buero employs sound and the absence
of sound in the same way that he had used light and darkness in *In the
Burning Darkness* and *The Concert at Saint Ovide.* None of the words spoken in the deaf man's presence are audible to the audience, and comple-
mentary visual actions – such as the silent ringing of a small
bell – underscore the painter's isolation. At the same time, the audience

THE SLEEP OF REASON. *Budapest, 1974, Teatr Vigszinhaz.*

THE SLEEP OF REASON. *Warsaw, 1977, Teatr Na Woli, directed by Andrzej Wajda. Photo credit:* KRZYSZTOF GIERALTOWSKI.

shares the sounds that Goya imagines he hears and the sounds of his heartbeats, speeded up and made louder at times to signal his growing terror. To complete the effect, projections of the "Black Paintings," singly or in varying combinations, suggest the painter's mental state and inner struggle. The demands on the actor performing the role of Goya are enormous; not only must he react to the silently mouthed dialogue and sign language of the other characters, he must also interact with the projections and nagging inner sounds while seeking to maintain a vocal tone suitable for a man who has been locked in silence for some thirty years.

Critics have not failed to associate this play with Artaud's theories and the *esperpentos* of Valle-Inclán; however, granting such influences, *The Sleep of Reason* is clearly a masterly demonstration of techniques that are unmistakably Buerian and represents a definable progression both aesthetically and thematically from *Las Meninas* and *The Concert at Saint Ovide*.[9] Indeed, in this first fully realized example of Buero's total theatre, the only prominent technique of the playwright that is missing is the use of musical themes, which are replaced by sound motifs (the heartbeats, cat cries, or the spoken titles of Goya's etchings used to trigger a visual association).

Buero's next play, a "fable in two parts" entitled *The Arrival of the Gods [La llegada de los dioses]* (1971), was contemporary in setting and dealt with the theme of father-son alienation. Julio, the central character, is a young artist with a modest and uncertain talent, far removed from the assertive genius of a Velazquez or a Goya. He has gone blind after the failure of an exhibit of his work which coincided with the successful showing of watercolors by his father, a conventional creator of popular renderings of pagan deities. Julio has also discovered that his father had been a member of the secret police during an unidentified war some years before and had permitted the torture of prisoners. Not only does the young man struggle with the knowledge of his father's guilt, but he is also intensely concerned with the ever-present threat of ecological or atomic catastrophe. Technically, the play reveals similarities to *The Sleep of Reason* in its use of immersion techniques to illustrate the inner world of a character deprived of a sensual perception. The audience is presented two levels of reality throughout: the naturalistic milieu of the supporting characters, with their casual chatter about business or their involvement in marital deceptions, and the distorted vision of their appearances and actions when Julio himself is a part of the stage action. Links to the two other plays that Buero has labelled *fábulas* are also apparent, for both *Irene or the Treasure* and *The Foundation* (which follows *The Arrival of the Gods*) depict imagined realities that may be the product of mental disorder or of quixotic single-mindedness.

The Foundation [La fundación], first staged in 1974 following a prolonged battle with the censors, draws directly on Buero's own painful experiences in a series of concentration camps and prisons at the end of the Civil War. The work is pointedly set in an unidentified country, however, and the use of character names that cannot be associated with a single nation indicates the playwright's desire to transcend national boundaries and to make a universal statement on human behavior in the face of political intransigence and repressive absolutism.

The four scenes of the play take place in a prison cell that at first appears to be a comfortably furnished studio in a modern research center. Gradually, however, the set is stripped of the illusory conveniences that exist only in the mind of the youngest prisoner, Thomas. Until this point in his career, Buero had used immersion-effects to draw his audience into the special world of a character from a base of "reality" which existed onstage before the initiation of immersion. In *The Foundation* he reverses the process: the action begins from a base of illusion, and the audience accompanies Thomas out of his delusion into the harsh reality of the prison where he and his companions await their execution. A brief section from Rossini's overture to the opera *William Tell* serves as the motif for Thomas's (and the audience's) belief in the comfortable "foundation"; and at the end of the play, after Thomas has been transferred from the barren cell, the theme signals a potential renewal of the delusion for the next unseen occupants of the cell.

Buero's musical motifs are never chosen casually, and they generally comment (at times ironically) on the dramatic situation or contain a metafictional allusion. It is significant that only the "pastorale" section of the overture is heard – complementing the idealized, imagined pano-

THE FOUNDATION. *Stockholm, 1977. Dramatiska Teatern. Directed by Alf Sjöberg. Photo credit:* BEATA BERGSTRÖM.

THE FOUNDATION. *Madrid, 1974. Directed by José Osuna. Photo credit:*
GYENES.

rama seen through a window that is itself an illusion. Thomas hears this
portion repeatedly in his mind, but the music never progresses to the
Allegro vivace section, with its suggestions of conflict or violence.[10] Rossini's opera and Schiller's play on which it is based deal with political
oppression, and Buero has provided an aural signal that may trigger
such associations, while serving its primary function of expressing the
essence of the landscape in musical terms. As in *The Sleep of Reason,*
nonmusical sounds also figure prominently in *The Foundation.* The
chants of the sentries at the end of the third scene, gradually diminish-
ing in volume, and the pounding on the cell doors in the final scene, are
orchestrated to achieve a chilling dramatic impact. In its totality, *The
Foundation* presents a synthesis of the scenic innovations that Buero has
developed over the course of his career and is a seamless melding of a
theatre of images with dramatic discourse.

In *The Detonation [La detonación]* (1977), Buero's first play completed
in the post-Franco period, the playwright explores the causes of the suicide, at age twenty-seven, of the nineteenth-century social critic
Mariano José de Larra. Although Larra has sometimes been viewed as a
typical victim of romantic disillusionment, Buero convincingly supports
the thesis that social and political pressures were the strongest forces in
the young critic's decision to take his own life. *The Detonation* is a worthy companion piece to *The Sleep of Reason,* both in its bold experiments
with multimedia scenic effects and in its continuing investigation of the

plight of the creative individual, the visionary, in a repressive society. Actual quotations from Larra's articles appear in the dialogue, just as the titles of Goya's etchings recur in the earlier play, and the extensive use of masks (both animal and human) reflects Larra's own references to them.

The audience witnesses the events of more than ten years (1826-1837) through the recollections of Larra himself in the moments preceding the detonation of the bullet that will kill him. His altered perceptions are on occasion eerily suggested by a slowing down of speech, and time is also speeded up as a kaleidoscope of historical events flash by in cinematic montage, with crosscuts between personal and public experience. Typically, nonverbal sounds, silences, and a musical motif are integral parts of the dramatic fabric. Since Larra's literary pseudonym for his articles of social criticism was "Figaro," it is the familiar aria "Largo al factotum" from Rossini's *Barber of Seville* that serves as his melodic signature, with metafictional allusions that are explicated to some extent in the dialogue.

Unfortunately, this most complex and most intricately allusive of Buero's works may be destined to semiobscurity, a play that will be studied but seldom performed. One problem is that Larra is not a figure who is widely known outside Spain, nor are the numerous literary and political personages who appear in the historical maelstrom that surrounds him in the drama. In addition, the cast is unusually large, and an appropriate *mise-en-scène* demands resources beyond the means of most theatres.[11] Yet *The Detonation* ranks among Buero's finest achievements and is one of the plays in which his vision of total theatre is most successfully realized.

The Detonation marks the end of a major phase in Buero's dramatic trajectory. His subsequent plays have been more intimate dramas dealing pointedly with timely issues of Spain's post-Franco society. In both *Judges in the Night [Jueces en la noche]* (1979) and *Caiman [Caimán]* (1981), he investigates the inner world of individuals affected by rapid social or political changes, using variations of familiar Buerian scenic techniques to juxtapose two levels of reality or interject scenes of immersion. *Judges in the Night,* which Buero calls a *misterio profano,* focuses on a corrupt deputy who has made a pragmatic transition from the officialdom of the former totalitarian state. In *Caiman,* he analyzes the antithetical influences of a crippled dreamer and a vigorous man of action on a woman who holds to the belief that her lost daughter will return despite grim evidence to the contrary. A striking feature of the play is the use of a narrator who initiates the action from a point in the future, looking back on a story in which she herself participates as a victimized teenager (played by a different actress). In his most recent play, *Secret Dialogue [Diálogo secreto]* (1984), Buero deals with the theme of social hypocrisy through an individual tragedy. The setting in this instance is not specifically Spain, but the associations with present-day Spanish reality are inescapable.

While Buero-Vallejo's relationship to twentieth-century European theatrical currents is clear, it must be remembered that his most important and most direct influences are from a Spanish dramatic tradition that is generally less familiar. He is the most notable participant of the post-war period in the renewal of Spanish drama that Unamuno, Valle-Inclán, and García Lorca envisioned and initiated in the early decades of this century. The existentialist angst of his alienated protagonists (both male and female) has its roots in Miguel de Unamuno's "tragic sense of life," and the scenic daring of his maturity owes some debt to Valle-Inclán's rejection of traditional forms in his search for unconstricted theatrical representation. His use of metaphor in stage directions that sometimes exceed those of most other contemporary playwrights has an obvious link to Valle-Inclán's narrative scenic descriptions. And, like Lorca, he envisions his plays in the totality of their performance, prescribing visual aspects with pointed detail. Yet Buero's precepts for total theatre that unites the arts are uniquely his. He has merged the plastic and the tonal to a degree unapproached by any contemporary, employing painting, music, and movement as coequals with dialogue to further the dramatic action rather than as mere scenic enhancers. He has also reconciled with remarkable skill the Brechtian concept of alienation with the boldest dramatic signature of his own theatre: the immersion-effect.

NOTES

1. Born in 1916, Buero-Vallejo is a year younger than Arthur Miller (b. 1915) and five years younger than Tennessee Williams (b. 1911). The use of the hyphen in Buero's full name in this edition and in all production programs for his plays in the English-speaking world is at his explicit request to avoid the confusion that sometimes occurs between Spanish paternal [Buero] and maternal [Vallejo] family names used in sequence.

2. For a detailed study of immersion-effects in Buero's theatre, see Victor Dixon's "The 'immersion-effect' in the Plays of Antonio Buero Vallejo" in *Drama and Mimesis, Themes in Drama 2* (Cambridge: Cambridge University Press, 1980), 113-37.

3. Patricia W. O'Connor has explored the effects of censorship on Buero's plays in "Censorship in the Contemporary Spanish Theater and Antonio Buero Vallejo," *Hispania* 52, no. 2 (May 1969): 282-88.

4. Buero called his first two plays "dramas." His first departure from conventional terminology came in 1953 with *Almost a Fairy Tale [Casi un cuento de hadas]*, which he called simply "una glosa de Perrault" ["a variation on Perrault"]. For several years, he used both old and new terms. Since 1958, however, he has not used any of the traditional nomenclature.

5. In view of Buero's use of projections in *The Sleep of Reason*, we can imagine a restaging of *Las Meninas* with projections of the paintings that are viewed by the characters of the play but remain unseen

by the audience. In the original production the paintings were suggested synesthetically through a musical motif.

6. In an appendix to his *The Tragic Stages of Antonio Buero Vallejo*, the American critic Robert Nicholas includes a personal letter from Buero in which the playwright acknowledges that Artaud, and The Living Theatre as well, may have exerted some influence on his work. He rejects, however, the direct contact between actor and spectator common in performances by The Living Theatre. Buero was referring specifically to *The Basement Window*, written several years after *The Concert at Saint Ovide*.

7. Patricia O'Connor's English translation of *El tragaluz* has been published in Spain in *Plays of Protest from the Franco Era* (Madrid: Sociedad General Española de Librería, 1981).

8. *La doble historia del doctor Valmy* was actually first performed in an English version by Farris Anderson in 1968. It was staged by the Gateway Theatre (Chester, England) and was later published in *Hispanic Arts* 2 (1967).

9. Similarities between Valle-Inclán and Artaud were noted by Felicia Hardison [Londré] in "Valle-Inclán and Artaud: Brothers Under the Skin," *Educational Theatre Journal* 19, no. 4 (1967).

10. It is the *allegro vivace* section of the popular overture that has become a cliché to American ears, not the slow "pastorale" interlude that is repeated in *The Foundation*.

11. The published script of *The Detonation* lists forty-four characters. In the excellent Madrid production of 1977, this number was reduced to thirty-four, performed by twenty-three actors.

SELECTED READINGS IN ENGLISH

Anderson, Farris. "The Ironic Structure of *Historia de una escalera.*" *Kentucky Romance Quarterly* 18, no. 2 (1971): 223-36.

Brown, Kenneth. "The Significance of Insanity in Four Plays by Antonio Buero Vallejo." *Revista de Estudios Hispánicos* 8 (1974): 247-60.

Casa, Frank P. "The Darkening Vision: The Latter Plays of Buero Vallejo." *Estreno* 5, no. 1 (1979): 30-33.

Dixon, Victor. "The 'immersion-effect' in the Plays of Antonio Buero Vallejo." In *Drama and Mimesis, Themes in Drama, 2.* Ed. James Redmond. Cambridge: Cambridge University Press, 1980, 113-37.

Dowling, John. "Buero Vallejo's Interpretation of Goya's Black Paintings." *Hispania* 56, no. 2 (1973): 449-57.

Giuliano, William. "The Theater of Buero Vallejo: 1949-1969." *Modern Drama* 13, no. 4 (1971): 366-73.

Halsey, Martha T. "The Rebel Protagonist: Ibsen's *An Enemy for the People* and Buero's *Un soñador para un pueblo.*" *Comparative Literature Studies* 4, no. 4 (1969): 462-71.

_____ . "Reality versus Illusion: Ibsen's *The Wild Duck* and Buero Vallejo's *En la ardiente oscuridad.*" *Contemporary Literature* 2 (1970): 48-57.

_____ . "Goya in the Theater: Buero Vallejo's *El sueño de la razōn.*" *Kentucky Romance Quarterly* 18, no. 2 (1971): 207-21.

_____ . *Antonio Buero Vallejo.* New York: Twayne, 1973.

Holt, Marion P. *The Contemporary Spanish Theater: 1949-1972.* New York: Twayne, 1975.

Kronik, John W. "Buero Vallejo's *El tragaluz* and Man's Existence in History." *Hispanic Review* 41 (1973): 371-96.

Molina, Ida. "The Dialectical Structure of Buero Vallejo's Multifaceted Definition of Tragedy." *Kentucky Romance Quarterly* 22 (1975): 293-311.

Nicholas, Robert. *The Tragic Stages of Antonio Buero Vallejo.* Chapel Hill: Estudios de Hispanófila, 1972.

O'Connor, Patricia W. "Censorship in the Contemporary Spanish Theater and Antonio Buero Vallejo." *Hispania* 52, no. 2 (1969): 282-88.

Ruple, Joelyn. *Antonio Buero Vallejo: The First Fifteen Years.* New York: Eliseo Torres and Sons, 1971.

Sheehan, Robert Louis. *"La fundación:* Idearium for the New Spain." *Modern Language Studies* 8, no. 2 (1978): 65-71.

Zatlin-Boring, Phyllis. "Expressionism in the Contemporary Spanish Theatre." *Modern Drama* 26, no. 4 (1983): 555-69.

Translator's Note
and Acknowledgments

This first collection in English of the theatre of Antonio Buero-Vallejo contains his two most widely performed plays, *The Sleep of Reason* (1970) and *The Foundation* (1974), and his early seminal drama, *In the Burning Darkness* (first staged in 1950). The primary aims of the translations have been, at all times, playability and the re-creation in English, insofar as possible, of the quite distinct verbal tones of each play.

The Sleep of Reason incorporates several types of dialogue: the exchanges between Goya and his close associates, including mouthed dialogue and sign language; the more formal and sometimes oblique or double-edged dialogue of the king with Calomarde and Duaso in their respective scenes; and the actual spoken titles of Goya's etchings, which are heard on tape at various moments in the play. Some of the accepted English translations of the titles of the etchings are inaccurate, and consequently I have sought new renderings that are both correct and sayable. While some might disagree, for example, with the title that is repeated with growing intensity at the end of the play, the words are understandable to the audience, and their impact in actual performance confirms the efficacy of the translation.

It must be kept in mind that in spite of their basically realistic settings, in a school for the blind and a prison respectively, neither *In the Burning Darkness* nor *The Foundation* is a strictly naturalistic play. The blind students may engage in a certain amount of student banter, but much of the dialogue strives for a heightened theatrical realism rather than a literal rendition of what we might think of as "normal" speech for eighteen or nineteen-year-old students. In *The Foundation*, Thomas's speech reflects his conviction that he is a young novelist living in a refined environment, and it complements his rejection of the dehumanizing effects of the prison where blunter expression might be expected at one point or another. The dialogue of his companions suggests both their own participation in Thomas's delusion and their awareness of the reality of their imprisonment. In the third scene of the play, when Asel delivers Buero's fierce indictment of human cruelty, we again encounter speech of deliberate theatricalness to evoke the maximum impact.

Equal care has been given to re-creating the special qualities of Buero's detailed and sometimes metaphorical stage directions, which cover all aspects of stage representation. Although the importance of the precise instructions for the integrated visual and aural effects in *The Sleep of Reason* are immediately apparent, the need in *The Foundation* for the extensive indications of physical movements or facial reactions, in addition to instructions for the scenic transformations, is only fully appreciated as we realize that they are essential clues to the nature and degree of the characters' participation in Thomas's delusion. A few stage directions have been slightly abbreviated or eliminated, but only when their instructions are implicit in the dramatic situation.

Since 1960 Buero has restored in the published Spanish editions of his plays the cuts made in the rehearsal process, enclosing these words, phrases, or passages in brackets. In an author's note to the first edition of *Las Meninas,* he explained that his purpose was not to suggest that the restoration improved the play but to protest the constraining custom of two daily performances (at 7 p.m. and 10:45 p.m.) in Madrid's theatres – a custom only partially modified in recent years. With Buero's approval, I have elected to base my translations of the two post-1960 plays on the performance versions, observing the approved cuts except in places where the incorporation of a word or phrase would result in a more effective English line. A notable exception is the inclusion of the opening scene of Part Two of *The Sleep of Reason* (omitted in the first production in Spain) which is essential both to the structural integrity of the play and to the audience's full comprehension of the events that ensue. The English script of *The Sleep of Reason* also reflects a few modifications made in the course of two productions in the United States (at Theatre/Converse and Baltimore's Center Stage). Similarly, the version of *In The Burning Darkness* contains a number of line changes effected during rehearsals for its first production at the University of Missouri-St. Louis.

A great many people have made a positive contribution to the effort to bring Buero-Vallejo's theatre to a wider English-speaking audience. I am especially indebted to: Phyllis Zatlin, Martha Halsey, John Dowling, and Daniel Gerould for their individual gestures of support; to director Hayward Ellis of Theatre/Converse for his artistic daring in undertaking the first tryout of *The Sleep of Reason* and achieving so authentic a realization of the play's scenic effects; to director Travis Preston whose commitment to *The Sleep of Reason* began in Poland and whose efforts were instrumental in bringing the play to a professional stage in the United States; to Warren MacIsaac, dramaturge of Center Stage, for his careful reading of the original script and perceptive suggestions; to playwright Richard Brad Medoff for acting as a critical sounding board for many key passages of dialogue in both *The Sleep of Reason* and *The Foundation;* and to Lois Boyd, director of Trinity University Press, whose editorial sensitivity and imagination lie behind the publication of these plays. To the National Endowment for the Arts, my gratitude for a grant to undertake the translation of *The Sleep of Reason.*

New York City   M. P. H.
November, 1984

ANTONIO BUERO-VALLEJO

THREE PLAYS

THE SLEEP OF REASON

Fantasia in Two Parts

Characters (in order of appearance)

FRANCISCO TADEO CALOMARDE

KING FERDINAND VII

FRANCISCO DE GOYA

LEOCADIA ZORRILLA WEISS

EUGENIO ARRIETA

GUMERSINDA GOICOECHEA

JOSÉ DUASO Y LATRE

THE BAT FIGURE

THE HORNED FIGURE

FIRST CARNIVAL FIGURE

SECOND CARNIVAL FIGURE

THE CAT FIGURE

SERGEANT OF THE ROYAL VOLUNTEERS

FIRST VOLUNTEER

SECOND VOLUNTEER

THIRD VOLUNTEER

FOURTH VOLUNTEER

VOICE OF MARIA WEISS (MARIQUITA)

OTHER VOICES

The action takes place in Madrid, December 1823

Note: All the dialogue enclosed in guillemets (« ») is mouthed by the characters silently, and it only serves the purpose of orienting the actors. The director may, therefore, elaborate on these unheard auxiliary speeches. All of the passages of dialogue in quotation marks are actual Goya texts.

PART ONE
Scene 1

The setting vaguely suggests the two rooms, downstairs and upstairs, of the house GOYA *decorated with his "Black Paintings."* The diagonal doorway at stage left reveals the first steps of an inner stairway; the entrance at right, another room. Near the upstage wall there is a ladder which the painter uses for working on the walls and a chest on top of which are a shotgun, a palette, and a conglomeration of paint pots, brushes, and bottles of oil and varnish. There is a small painting turned against the wall. Downstage right, a worktable with engravings, paper, albums, pencils, a small silver bell, and a table clock. Behind it, an armchair. At left, a smaller chair. Downstage left, a round platform with a cup-shaped brazier, surrounded by chairs and a sofa. A scattering of chairs or stools in the corners.*

Total darkness. The lights come up slowly on a small area downstage to reveal a man seated in a regal chair. He is absorbed in a curious task: embroidering neatly and carefully on a frame. As the lighted area widens, we see another man standing at his right; and at his left, a small table with a sewing basket, a spyglass, and a pistol. The seated man is KING FERDINAND VII. *He looks about forty and is dressed in dark colors. A decoration sparkles on his breast. His overall appearance is vigorous; his calves are notably robust. Dark sideburns frame his fleshy cheeks; a fringe of hair half-covers his forehead. Under the thick brows, two very dark and inquisitive pupils. His nose, thick and flattened, rides over two thin lips which are submerged by the advance of the chin and which are usually smiling. The man who accompanies him is* DON FRANCISCO TADEO CALOMARDE. *He appears to be fifty and is also dressed in dark colors. His hair tousled over a smooth forehead; two shining little eyes gleam in his sheep-like features.*

CALOMARDE. Your Majesty embroiders beautifully.

KING. You flatter me, Calomarde.

CALOMARDE. Credit where credit is due, sir. Such shadings! Such a sense of detail!

KING. I had a lot of practice in Valençay, to calm my nerves when I was in exile. [*Brief pause*] It wouldn't be a bad thing if all Spaniards learned to embroider. Maybe they'd be more docile.

CALOMARDE. [*Very serious*] It would be a good Christian discipline. Does Your Majesty wish me to draw up the decree?

KING. [*Laughing*] You're not a minister yet, Tadeo. [*Stitching*] What are they saying in Madrid?

CALOMARDE. There's high praise for Your Majesty. The summary executions and the banishments have left the liberal Hydra without a head. The patriots think it's as good as dead . . . provided a firm hand is applied.

---

*A list of Goya's "Black Paintings" is provided at the end of the text of the play.

KING. There will be a firm hand. But without the Inquisition. I don't want to restore it now.

CALOMARDE. The country is asking for it, sir.

KING. The priests are asking for it, you mean. If I'm to have absolute power, I don't want a meddling Inquisition.

CALOMARDE. [*Sighing*]   May God grant that 1824 be like an implacable hammer for subversives and Masons of every stripe.*

KING. [*Raising his hand and interrupting him coldly*]   What else are they talking about?

CALOMARDE. [*Softly*]   About the Green Book, sir. [*The* KING *gives him a look.*] Even though no one has ever seen it.

KING. I can assure you it does exist . . .

CALOMARDE. Then, sir, why keep it hidden?

KING. It's an account of wrongs committed against my person.

CALOMARDE. Which therefore deserve prompt punishment.

KING. [*Smiles*]   Time is needed to weave a rope.

CALOMARDE. Your majesty prefers to gather evidence.

KING. Something like that.

CALOMARDE. [*Handing him a damaged piece of paper after a moment*]   Such as this?

KING. [*Taking the piece of paper*]   What is it?

CALOMARDE. An intercepted letter, sir. [*The* KING *reads it, and his expression changes. Then he reflects.*]

KING. Did you witness the execution of Riego?

CALOMARDE. A month ago, sir.

KING. [*Leaving the letter on the table*]   Many accounts of it have reached me. . . . What is your version?

CALOMARDE. It was a solemn day. All Madrid was shouting your name when a donkey dragged the condemned man by in a basket.

KING. One might say an etching by Goya.

CALOMARDE. [*Looking at him, curious*]   Precisely, sir . . . Riego mounted the scaffold weeping and kissing the steps, begging for pardon like a frightened whore. . . .

KING. You saw all this?

CALOMARDE. Everyone in Madrid saw it.

KING. Then he was afraid.

CALOMARDE. He'd already recanted in writing.

KING. Under torture?

CALOMARDE. [*Looking away*]   If he'd been tortured, he was no longer suffering, but he was afraid. The "hero" of Las Cabezas,† the

---

* Several different Masonic orders were established in Spain in the early 1800s. The Masons (or Freemasons) were anathema to Fernando VII because of their liberal aims.

† Las Cabezas: Cabezas de San Juan, the town where Colonel Rafael de Riego Nuñez initiated a liberal uprising in 1820. Riego, a hero in the struggle against the French invaders, was publicly humiliated and then executed for treason on November 7, 1823.

charlatan of the Cortes,* that small-time general, was smelling of fear. As they dragged him by, the crowds were laughing and holding their noses.

KING. [*With a grimace of revulsion*]   Spare me the details.

CALOMARDE.   Why not say, sir, that the liberal vainglory ended with an attack of diarrhea?

KING.   Because they're not all so cowardly.

CALOMARDE.   Is Your Majesty perhaps thinking of the author of that letter?

KING.   Anyone who writes that way today is either a fool or a brave man.

CALOMARDE.   A witless dummy, sir, like all that cowardly band of poets and painters! Look how many of them have escaped to France.

KING.   Not he.

CALOMARDE.   He's hidden himself in his country place on the other side of the river. Like a child who closes his eyes and imagines he's safe, he thinks Your Majesty can't reach him. Nevertheless, from this very balcony you can see his house with your spyglass. [*He hands it to him. The* KING *puts his embroidery aside, stands, adjusts the spyglass and points it toward the audience.*]

KING.   Is it that house near the Segovia Bridge?

CALOMARDE.   The second one, at left.

KING.   I can hardly see it for the trees. . . . He hasn't come to pay me homage since I returned to Madrid.

CALOMARDE.   Or to collect his wages, sir. He doesn't dare.

KING.   What do you suppose he's doing?

CALOMARDE.   Trembling.

KING.   That peasant doesn't tremble so easily. He was always a proud and stubborn man. When I asked him to paint the face of my first wife in his portrait of the royal family, he told me he didn't retouch his canvases.

CALOMARDE.   Outrageous!

KING.   Only an excuse of his. The real reason was that he detested me. Of course, I paid him back in the same coin. He's painted me only a few times, and my wives not at all.

CALOMARDE.   A light punishment, sir. That letter . . .

KING.   We must think it over.

CALOMARDE.   He's not the great painter they say, sir! Artless drawings, harsh colors . . . [*The* KING *lowers his spyglass.*] Royal portraits without dignity or beauty . . . Insidious engravings against the dynasty, against the clergy . . . Now Vicente López is a great painter.

---

* Las Cortes: the Cortes (or Parliament) of Cadiz which proclaimed the Spanish constitution of 1812, curtailing the power of the king.

KING. Such severity, Tadeo! Has he offended you in some way?

CALOMARDE. Much less than he has offended Your Majesty. He did refuse to paint my portrait once.

[*The* KING *glances at him.*]

But my feelings have nothing to do with trivialities. . . . It is the enemy of King and country that I hate.

KING. [*Smiling*] What do you recommend for our hotheaded painter? The same death as Riego's?

CALOMARDE. [*Softly*] It was Your Majesty who thought of that when he read the letter.

KING. [*Resuming his embroidering*] His prestige is great.

CALOMARDE. He deserves the gallows for that piece of paper. [*A moment of silence. He leans over again to appreciate the* KING'S *embroidery.*] What exquisite greens, sir! Embroidery is a form of painting. . . . [*Smiling*] Your Majesty paints better than that senile old fool.

KING. [*After a moment*] To whom was it addressed?

CALOMARDE. Martín Zapater, sir. A friend of his from childhood.

KING. Is he a Mason? A Comunero?*

CALOMARDE. There's no information on him . . . I'm investigating.

[*A dull heartbeat becomes audible. The* KING *looks up quickly from his work. The beating increases in intensity and speeds up until it culminates in three or four heavy thuds, followed by others which are softer and spaced out. The* KING *stands up before the sound stops and steps back toward the left. A silence*]

KING. What was that sound?

CALOMARDE. [*Perplexed*] I don't know, sir.

KING. Go see.

[CALOMARDE *exits right. The* KING *takes the pistol from the table and clutches it.* CALOMARDE *returns.*]

CALOMARDE. They didn't hear anything outside, sir.

KING. There was a noise, wasn't there?

CALOMARDE. [*Stammering*] A faint noise.

KING. Faint? [*He puts the pistol down, sits, and returns to his embroidery pensively.*] Have the guard doubled tonight.

CALOMARDE. Yes, Majesty.

KING. [*He embroiders; then stops.*] I don't want fighting cocks. I want obedient vassals, who tremble. And an ocean of tears for all the insults to my person.

CALOMARDE. [*Quietly*] Very just, sir.

[*The* KING *embroiders.*]

---

* Comunero: a member of the "Confederación de Caballeros Comuneros," a liberal secret society similar to Masonry that flourished in Spain during the brief period of constitutional government (1820-23) prior to the autocratic rule of Fernando VII. Like the Masons, they were considered traitors by the king.

KING. Listen, Calomarde. This is confidential. You will tell the Commander General of the Royal Volunteers to come to see me tomorrow at ten.

CALOMARDE. [*Quietly*] It will be done, sir.

KING. [*After a moment*] And Don José Duaso . . . [*He breaks off.*]

CALOMARDE. . . . Father Duaso.

KING. You will say that I expect him too.

CALOMARDE. At the same hour?

KING. Later. Don't let them see each other. At three in the afternoon.

CALOMARDE. I understand.

KING. Isn't Father Duaso Aragonese?

CALOMARDE. Aragonese, sir, like me. [*Brief pause*] And like Don Francisco de Goya.

[*They exchange glances. The* KING *smiles and applies himself to his embroidery. Slow fade.*]

Scene 2

When the lights come up again, we see downstage an old man who is looking through a spyglass toward the audience. Goya's "Aquelarre" ("Witches' Sabbath") is projected gradually on the background. The hair and sideburns of the short but vigorous and erect old man are now white. He is wearing an old smock covered with paint splotches. When he lowers the spyglass, he reveals surly and unmistakable facial features: those of FRANCISCO DE GOYA. *The aged painter looks through the spyglass again. He sighs, goes to the table, leaves the instrument there and picks up a pair of eyeglasses which he puts on. He turns around and looks at the projected painting for a few seconds. Then he goes over to the chest, takes palette and brushes, climbs on the ladder and gives a few brushstrokes to the "Aquelarre." Suddenly we hear a soft meowing.* GOYA *stops without turning his head and presently continues painting. Another meow. He stops again. The meows are repeated; they come from several cats almost simultaneously.* GOYA *shakes his head and covers an ear with his free hand. Silence. He gets down from the ladder, puts aside his equipment, and walks around the stage looking into the corners. A long meow forces him to look toward the doorway. Silence. The painter tosses his glasses on the table, takes off his smock, and screams out in his shrill deaf-man's voice.*

GOYA. Lco! [*Brief pause*] Leocadia! [*IIe goes to the sofa and picks up a large frock coat.*] Isn't there anyone at home? [*Putting on the coat, he goes to the door.*] Child! Mariquita!

[*He waits anxiously. We hear the laughter of an eight-year-old child. A feeble, far-off, strange laughter which is suddenly cut off. Upset,* GOYA *returns to center stage and puts his hands over his ears. In an outburst of silent fury, he seizes the little bell from the table and*

shakes it repeatedly, without making the slightest sound. DOÑA
LEOCADIA ZORRILLA *enters left, with angry gestures and hurling inau-*
dible words. She is a woman of thirty-five, not unattractive but far
from being beautiful; a haughty Basque with dark hair, firm limbs,
and vivid eyes under her dark brows.]

LEOCADIA.   «What's all the shouting about? What's your hurry? Did a
    scorpion bite you?»

GOYA. [*Sourly*]   What are you saying?
    [LEOCADIA *sighs — which we don't hear either — and rapidly forms let-*
    ters in Bonet's alphabet* with her right hand.]
    No, I haven't been stung by a scorpion! Where's the child?

LEOCADIA. [*Pointing right*]   «In there.»

GOYA.   You lie! I've called her and she doesn't come. Where have you
    sent her?

LEOCADIA. [*Not at all bothered by her lie*]   «For a walk.»

GOYA. [*Angrily*]   With your hand!
    [LEOCADIA *forms signs and shouts inaudibly in anger at the same*
    time.]

LEOCADIA.   «For a walk!»

GOYA.   For a walk in these times? [*He takes her by the wrist.*] Are you
    out of your mind?

LEOCADIA. [*Struggling*]   «Let go!»

GOYA.   You don't act like her mother! But you are, and you're sup-
    posed to look after your children! Your days of partying and
    flaunting yourself are over.

LEOCADIA. [*Speaking incessantly at the same time*]   «Of course I am!
    And I know what to do. And I'll send them where I please!
    Besides, who are you to be giving me lessons! . . . »

GOYA. [*Her gesticulating makes him furious. Shouting*]   I'm fed up with
    your angry looks!
    [LEOCADIA *steps back disdainfully and makes a few signs.*]
    Well and fine! But she shouldn't be in the orchard either if there's
    no one with her.
    [LEOCADIA *signs.*]
    Her brother's a child too!
    [*He strides brusquely to the left.*]
    Where have you put my hat and cane?
    [*She points right. When* GOYA *starts to leave, we hear a meow. He*
    stops, turns around and looks at LEOCADIA. *She questions him with a*
    movement of her head.]

LEOCADIA.   «Where are you going?»

GOYA.   I can't paint today!
    [*He starts to leave and turns around again.*]

---

* The system of sign language used in Spain in Goya's time. It was invented by Juan
  Pablo Bonet (1560-1620?), a Spanish writer and diplomat who dedicated a great part of
  his life to improving the condition of the deaf.

Where are the cats now?

LEOCADIA. [*Puzzled, she uses sign language.*]   «In the kitchen.»

GOYA.   Did you see them in the kitchen?

[*She nods*]

Of course. Where else would they be? Goodbye.

[*He exits.* LEOCADIA *hurries to the door and watches him go. Then she makes a signal, and* DOCTOR ARRIETA, *hat and cane in hand, enters cautiously.* DON EUGENIO GARCIA ARRIETA *is between fifty-five and sixty. He is vigorous but gaunt. His blond hair is turning gray; he hides his incipient baldness by combing his hair forward; he has a large cranium and the sharp features of an ascetic; his eyes have a gentle and melancholy look. He is about to speak but* LEOCADIA *motions him to keep silent. A door slams in the distance.*]

ARRIETA.   You shouldn't have let him go out.

LEOCADIA.   I wanted to speak with you first. [*She goes to the sofa and sits.*] Please sit down, Doctor Arrieta.

ARRIETA. [*Taking a chair*]   Thank you, señora. María de Rosario and little Guillermo, are they well?

LEOCADIA.   Yes, thanks to God. They're not at home now. [*She stirs the brazier.*] We'll have snow for Christmas.

ARRIETA.   What's wrong with Don Francisco?

[*Goya's "Saturn" is projected to the right of the "Witches' Sabbath."*]

LEOCADIA.   Doctor, you cured him four years ago. Cure him for me now.

ARRIETA.   Of what?

LEOCADIA.   It's nothing you can see. No pains, or cough, or fever . . . Only his deafness, but you already know about that. [*She wrings her hands nervously.*] And that's why I asked you to come. Three years ago you made the effort to learn sign language to speak with him. You must talk to him to cure him, and it will be difficult.

ARRIETA.   Tell me everything you can, señora.

[*Goya's "Judith" appears at the left of the "Witches' Sabbath."*]

LEOCADIA.   For the past two years he's almost never gone away from the house; he almost never speaks.

ARRIETA.   Withdrawn, unsociable . . . It's not an illness.

LEOCADIA.   Have you noticed the paintings on the walls?

ARRIETA. [*He studies the projected paintings.*]   These?

LEOCADIA.   And all the ones upstairs. He was an artist who never retouched, but he retouches these endlessly. What do you think of them?

ARRIETA.   They're strange.

LEOCADIA.   They're appalling! [*She stands and walks about.*]

ARRIETA.   I remember similar things in his etchings.

LEOCADIA.   They weren't the same. These are the horrible paintings of an old man.

ARRIETA.   Don Francisco *is* an old man.

LEOCADIA. [*She stops and looks at him.*]   A demented old man.

ARRIETA. [*Getting up slowly*]   Are you suggesting he's lost his mind?
[*She closes her eyes and nods.*]
What evidence do you have? Only the paintings?

LEOCADIA. [*Listening*]   Be quiet! [*A moment of silence*] Did you hear
something?

ARRIETA.   No.

LEOCADIA. [*Taking a few steps left*]   It must have been the cats in the
kitchen. . . . [*Turning back to him*] He hardly ever talks with me,
but he talks with someone . . . who doesn't exist. Or he laughs for
no reason, or lashes out against invisible beings. Look at that.
Doesn't it frighten you?

ARRIETA. [*Facing the "Witches' Sabbath"*]   The devil, the witches . . .
He doesn't believe in witches, señora. These paintings may be
frightening to you, but they're the work of a satirist, not a madman.

LEOCADIA.   Those paintings are about me.

[ARRIETA *stops before "Judith" and looks back at* LEOCADIA.]

ARRIETA.   About you?

[*The "Witches' Sabbath" changes into "Asmodea" ("Fantastic Vision").*]

LEOCADIA. [*Nodding*]   He says I'm the witch who's drying up his
blood. Look at that one!

[ARRIETA *faces the "Asmodea."*]
The woman is leading the man to the Witches' Sabbath, and he's
terrified, with his mouth gagged with an evil stone. I'm the
woman.

[*As she speaks, "Saturn" changes to "The Busybodies."* ARRIETA *studies them.*]
You would have to live with us to understand how . . . insane
he's become.

ARRIETA.   This scene . . . does it refer to you too?

[LEOCADIA *turns around and is silent for a moment when she sees the
painting.*]

LEOCADIA.   I don't know.

[ARRIETA *looks at the painting and observes* LEOCADIA.]

ARRIETA. [*Puzzled*]   What are they doing?

LEOCADIA.   He hasn't said.

ARRIETA.   But you have some idea. [*A silence*] Or don't you?

LEOCADIA.   I think it's . . . an obscene painting.

ARRIETA.   Obscene?

LEOCADIA. [*Embarrassed*]   Don't you see it? Those two girls are making fun of . . . that poor old fool's pleasure.

[*Very surprised,* ARRIETA *looks at the painting again. Then he studies
the "Asmodea" and "Judith."* LEOCADIA *is looking at the floor.* ARRIETA
goes to her side.]

ARRIETA. How old is Goya now?

LEOCADIA. Seventy-six.

ARRIETA. [*Hesitating*] Permit me a very delicate question. [*She looks at him uneasily.*] When did you stop having intimate relations?

LEOCADIA. We've never stopped. Not completely at least.

ARRIETA. [*Sitting down beside her*] Not completely? . . .

LEOCADIA. [*With difficulty*] Francho . . . Excuse me . . . We call him Francho at home. Don Francisco is one of those men who stays young until late in life. When he began to court me, I permitted his advances because I was curious . . . and amused. But when he actually made love to me, I was like a lamb in the jaws of a great wolf. He was sixty-four then.

ARRIETA. And now, twelve years later.

LEOCADIA. He still desires me . . . occasionally. Oh, my God! For months on end he avoids me at night and never speaks to me by day . . . because . . . he's no longer so vigorous. . . .

[ARRIETA *takes a melancholy look at the paintings and appears to be in deep thought.*]

ARRIETA. [*Calmly*] Doña Leocadia . . . [*She is extremely uncomfortable when she looks at him.*] Do you have any reason to suspect that Don Francisco . . . attends to his needs like the old man in the painting?

LEOCADIA. [*Avoiding his eyes*] I don't know.

ARRIETA. How old are you now?

LEOCADIA. Thirty-five. [*A brief pause*] Shhh! Don't you hear something? [*She gets up and goes left to listen.*] It must be the servants.

ARRIETA. I'll examine him. But you need attention too. I find you nervous and distraught. Perhaps a change of scene would help.

LEOCADIA. [*Turning to him, forcefully*] He's the one who needs a change! Let's not talk about me any more, please. Francho's madness is just that! He refuses a change of scene! He's not afraid.

ARRIETA. I don't understand.

LEOCADIA. [*With growing agitation*] Do you know that no one comes to see us, Doctor?

ARRIETA. You live in an out-of-the-way place.

LEOCADIA. That's their excuse! The truth is they know he was on the losing side and that the king hates him.

ARRIETA. You must not say that, señora.

LEOCADIA. You know very well it's true. Every day people are banished, whipped, and executed. . . . Francho is one of the liberals, and in Spain there'll be no mercy for them for years to come. The hunt has begun, and they'll come for him too. And he knows it! [*Transition*] But he remains indifferent. He paints, he shouts at the servants, he goes for walks . . . And when I beg him to take precautions, to escape like so many of his friends, he insists there's no reason to. Isn't that madness?

ARRIETA.   Perhaps he's exhausted.

LEOCADIA.   Not as exhausted as I am! You have to be insane not to be afraid. I have all my wits about me, and I'm afraid. [*She moves close to* ARRIETA.] Give him the fear he needs, Doctor. Force him to leave!

ARRIETA. [*Standing up*]   It can be fatal to make an old person afraid.

LEOCADIA. [*With a strange hope in her voice as she uses all her powers of persuasion.*]   Then don't scare him. Tell him he needs a change . . . that the waters at a French resort would help him.

ARRIETA.   I'll think it over, Doña Leocadia.

[*She gives him a pleading look, sighs, and sits again. Suddenly she loses control and lets out a wracking sob.* ARRIETA *goes to her with compassion.*]

Are you ill?

LEOCADIA.   I can't stand it. [*A door slams offstage. She looks up.*] Now I do hear something.

GOYA'S VOICE.   Didn't the postman come today?

LEOCADIA.   It's Francho.

GOYA.   You never know anything. [*The voice comes nearer.*] Go back to the kitchen!

LEOCADIA. [*Pleading*]   Help us.

[*They look left.* GOYA *enters and stops when he sees them.* LEOCADIA *stands up.*]

GOYA.   Doctor Arrieta! [LEOCADIA *takes his hat and cane and puts them on a chair.*] We've missed you in this house! [*He embraces the* DOCTOR *effusively.*] As a friend, of course! We'd hate to need you as a physician. [ARRIETA *smiles.* LEOCADIA *helps* GOYA *take off his coat.*] Sit down! Leo, bring two glasses of wine. [*The* DOCTOR *shakes his head.*] Really! If you don't drink, I will! Or is it forbidden to me? [ARRIETA *makes a gesture of doubt.*] I assure you I'm as strong as a bull!

ARRIETA. [*Laughing*]   «That's easy to see.» [*He sits.*]

GOYA.   There's nothing like the open spaces for the good life, Don Eugenio. These hills are the essence of health itself. You'll see the color in Mariquita's cheeks. Has she come back, Leo? I looked for her when I went out but I didn't see her. [LEOCADIA *nods quickly.*] Have you seen her, Doctor? [ARRIETA *shakes his head.*] Well, bring her, woman! And the wine! [*With a questioning gesture,* LEOCADIA *speaks with her hands.* GOYA's *voice loses its exuberance.*] I turned back at the bridge.

LEOCADIA. [*With a look of concern*]   «Why?»

GOYA.   They've installed a platoon of the Royal Volunteers, and they're stopping everyone.

LEOCADIA. [*Disturbed, she goes to his side.*]   «There was none there before.»

GOYA.   They must have assigned them today. [*She questions with her hands.*] How do I know how long they're going to stay! I can't stand their criminal faces and stupid laughter. I certainly wasn't going to tell them I'm deaf, even if I didn't understand what they were saying. So I came back. Bring the wine. The doctor is waiting. [*She nods and runs left.*] Wait! [*She stops.*] Has the postman come? [*She shakes her head and exits.* GOYA *sits and stirs the brazier with a poker. "The Busybodies" changes into "Leocadia" and "Asmodea" into "The Holy Office."*] I'll bet she told you I'm sick and that we should run off to France. [ARRIETA *is momentarily speechless. He laughs.*] She dreams of France. It's boring here. [*Becoming aroused*] But why the devil should I go? This is my house, this is my country! I haven't gone back to the palace, and old flat nose doesn't like my paintings. For ten years he's had that mealy-mouthed, sanctimonious Vicente López do his portraits. It's better that way. I, in my house, unremembered, and painting what I feel like painting. But tell me what's happening in Madrid. [ARRIETA *opens his arms in a gesture of dismay.*] No, don't say anything. Accusations, persecutions . . . Spain. It's not easy to paint. But I shall. Have you noticed the walls? [ARRIETA *avoids an answer and asks a question in sign language.*] Afraid? No. [*He thinks about it.*] Sad, perhaps. [*The sound of light heartbeats.* GOYA *perceives them.*] No, not afraid. [LEOCADIA *reappears with a crockery pitcher and two glasses on a tray.* ARRIETA *gets up and accepts one of the glasses with a bow. "Judith" is transformed into the "Two Friars."* GOYA *takes the other glass.*] The wine will cure your troubles, doctor. To your health. [*They touch glasses and drink,* LEOCADIA *deposits the tray on the table. The heartbeats fade quickly when the painter drains his glass.* LEOCADIA *moves downstage and looks out toward the left from an imaginary balcony.*] Excellent, isn't it? Martín Zapater sent me a whole skin of it, so that I'd forgive him for not coming to spend a few days. He's so tied down in Zaragoza. [*He breaks off and resumes in a loud, harsh voice that catches* LEOCADIA *and the* DOCTOR *off guard.*] What are you looking at?

LEOCADIA. [*Turning around and responding weakly*] «The . . . bridge.»

GOYA.   There's nothing you have to see on the bridge.

LEOCADIA. [*Surprised*] «Why not?»

GOYA.   Bring your children so they can see the doctor! [LEOCADIA *mutters to herself and exits left with a gesture of dismay to* ARRIETA *behind the painter's back. The heartbeats have resumed, and* GOYA *nervously presses his ear with a finger. Then he leaves his glass on the tray and goes upstage.*] Come here, Don Eugenio. What do you think? [ARRIETA *follows him upstage, still holding his glass from which he sips while puckering his lips approvingly. They are standing before "The Holy Office."*] Don't they resemble animals? They're looking at us, not realizing how ugly they are. They're looking at me.

ARRIETA.   «At you?»

GOYA. Exactly as they did when they denounced me to the Holy
Inquisition. They looked at me like insects with their insect eyes
because I'd painted a nude woman. They're insects that believe
themselves human. Ants around a fat queen [*He laughs.*] . . . who
is the big-bellied friar. [ARRIETA *questions in sign language.*] They
think it's a beautiful day, but I can see the dark clouds. [ARRIETA
points to a section of the painting.] Yes. The sun is shining in the
background. And there is the mountain, but they don't see it.
[ARRIETA *signs.* GOYA *hesitates.*] It's a mountain I know is there.
[*The sounds of the heartbeats have faded and stopped.* GOYA *jabs his
ear and listens in vain.* ARRIETA *observes him and moves to the left to
ask something about the "Two Friars."*]
ARRIETA. [*Pointing*]   «What are they doing?»
GOYA. The goat with a beard is deaf too. Who knows what the other
one is saying to him? Though perhaps greybeard hears something . . . [*He moves right and turns around.*] Or does he? [ARRIETA
makes a gesture of perplexity. GOYA *looks at him enigmatically and
turns back to the painting.* ARRIETA *points to the painting at right,
which is behind* GOYA's *back, and inquires with brief signs.*] Yes. It's
Leocadia. So aware of her splendor. She's in a cemetery.
ARRIETA. «What?» [*We hear a meow.* GOYA *peers toward the corners of
the room.*]
GOYA. The rock where she's reclining is a tomb. [*Another meow.*GOYA
is silent for a moment and then continues.] That's where she's put
her husband and me. [*He laughs. Several meows coming together
distract him.* ARRIETA *doesn't take his eyes off him.* GOYA *laughs
again.*] The cats are prowling behind the tomb.
[*"Two Friars" changes again into "Judith."*]
ARRIETA. «Cats?»
GOYA. They're always around. [*"The Holy Office" changes to "The Pilgrimage." We hear the beating of the wings of a gigantic bird. The
painter presses one ear and speaks nervously.*] More wine, doctor?
[*He goes to the table.* ARRIETA *shakes his head and cautions him.*] It's
pure juice. It won't hurt you.
ARRIETA. «No thank you.»
GOYA. [*As he pours himself a glass*]   Do you see "The Pilgrimage"? More
insects. They pluck at a lute, scream, and think it's music. They
don't know they're in the tomb. [*He drinks. The beating of the
wings fades away and stops.* GOYA *looks into the empty air.*]
ARRIETA. [*His voice perfectly audible*]   "Divine Reason."
GOYA. Exactly. [*He drinks again but is suddenly startled and looks at
ARRIETA who is contemplating the painting.*] What did you say?
[ARRIETA, *intrigued by his tone, signs.*] Too dark? Is that what you
said? [ARRIETA *nods.*] It's that . . . they see us dark. They are so
luminous . . .
ARRIETA. «Who?»

[GOYA *watches him as he is thinking. He drains his glass and leaves it on the tray.*]

GOYA.   Doctor, I'd like to consult you about something. [*"Leocadia" changes to "The Busybodies." The painter crosses to sit on the sofa.*] Sit here beside me. [ARRIETA *points to the picture and asks about it with signs.* GOYA *takes time to respond, but he finally does, avoiding eye contact with the doctor.*] Those are two inquisitive women. [ARRIETA *sits beside him. A pause.*] I've been deaf for thirty-one years. At first I heard buzzings, wisps of music. Then nothing. [ARRIETA *nods.*] Nevertheless, since the beginning of the year, the sounds have come back. [*Surprised,* ARRIETA *questions with his hands.*] Yes, voices too. [ARRIETA *signs.*] Not when I go to sleep, but wide awake. Tiny voices. I know what you're going to say: my mind is creating fantasies to alleviate my loneliness. But I ask you: isn't it possible I've recovered a trace of my hearing? [ARRIETA *shakes his head.*] The voices are . . . very real. [*Growing uneasy,* ARRIETA *shakes his head sadly and traces signs and more signs. Then he gets up, indicating to* GOYA *that he should not move. He goes to the table and strikes it hard but inaudibly with his fist. He looks at* GOYA *questioningly.*] No, but . . . [ARRIETA *interrupts him with a gesture, picks up the bell, and shakes it with all his might. We hear nothing.*] No! . . . [ARRIETA *goes to* GOYA'S *side and shakes the bell close to his ear.* GOYA *shakes his head somberly.* THE DOCTOR *replaces the bell on the table. "The Pilgrimage" changes to "Asmodea."*] So, according to you, it's all in here. [*He points to his forehead.* ARRIETA *nods. Far-off, a dog bays.*] If I told you I just heard a dog baying, you'd tell me I didn't. [ARRIETA *shakes his head, confirming it.* GOYA *gets up and goes upstage.*] Do you find my paintings repulsive? Don't pretend. Everyone does. . . . Maybe I do myself. [*Moved,* ARRIETA *invites him with a gesture to reject his dark thoughts and points to "Asmodea" with a questioning gesture.*] Asmodea. [THE DOCTOR'S *movements show his surprise.*] Like the crippled devil,* but here it's an angelical she-devil. Below, there are wars, blood, and hatred, as always. It doesn't really matter. They're off to the mountain.

ARRIETA.   «To the mountain?»

GOYA.   Asmodea carries him off, for he still trembles at what he sees below. He'll still see it from the mountaintop, but the beings that live there will console him. It's a very steep mountain. Flying is the only way to ascend it. [*He laughs.* ARRIETA *signs.*] Like the sky, but it isn't the sky. [*He decides to show him something.*] Look at this. [*He picks up the painting that is leaning against the wall, brings it downstage, and props it against the table.*] It's almost the same subject. I painted this recently when I finally understood that

---

* Reference to the novel *El Diablo Cojuelo (The Lame Devil)* by Vélez de Guevara.

they aren't flying by magic as I thought . . . [*Points at "Asmodea"*]
. . . but with mechanical devices.

ARRIETA.   «Who?»

GOYA. [*He looks at him for a moment.*]   These bird-men. Their wings
are artificial. Below, as you see, the people are burning. The flyers couldn't help them. I don't know why they don't. Perhaps
they feel only disgust for us. They must live very happily in
those round houses you see above. [ARRIETA *observes it, disturbed.*] I'll show you an etching where you can see them better.
I'm not certain the wings are like the ones I've drawn. I used my
imagination a little. [*The doctor looks astonished.*] But, of course.
You can't see them well from a distance. [*He has said this with a
smile. It is uncertain whether he is in earnest or playing a joke on the
doctor.*] I won't be long.

[GOYA *exits right.* ARRIETA *looks at "Asmodea" and the strange
smaller painting he has just been shown.* LEOCADIA *looks in cautiously from left.*]

LEOCADIA.   Did you ring the bell?

ARRIETA.   Yes. I was trying to prove to him that he wasn't regaining
his hearing.

LEOCADIA.   What do you think?

ARRIETA.   I still don't know.

LEOCADIA. [*Nervous, she moves closer to him.*]   Surely you do! You can
see it in his eyes. He's insane. [*Annoyed with her,* ARRIETA *shakes
his head without conviction. She goes right to be sure no one is coming and then returns.*] The servants have just told me something
dreadful. [*She crosses to peer out from the imaginary balcony.*]

ARRIETA.   What is it, señora?

LEOCADIA.   Andrés, the coachman, heard it this morning in the mar-
ket. They're going to announce new decrees. . . . They say they
were drawn up by Calomarde and that the king approves them.
My God, what will we do?

ARRIETA.   For heaven's sake, señora, explain what you're talking
about.

LEOCADIA. [*With difficulty*]   One decree . . . will pardon anyone who
has committed an atrocity on the person or property of a liberal
. . . except murderers. [ARRIETA *turns pale.*] They're free to rob,
destroy, and attack with impunity.

ARRIETA.   And the other decree?

LEOCADIA.   The death penalty for all Masons and comuneros, except
those who turn themselves in or denounce the rest.

ARRIETA.   It may only be rumors. . . .

LEOCADIA.   Doesn't it frighten you? Or are you as crazy as he is?

ARRIETA.   I'm not crazy and I am afraid. I fear that the government
itself may have spread these rumors . . . to provoke attacks.

LEOCADIA.   We must escape!

ARRIETA.   Don't speak to Don Francisco of these decrees.

LEOCADIA.   Not tell him?

ARRIETA.   Please, let me think of the best way.

LEOCADIA.   And if his life is in danger?

ARRIETA.   There's no life without health, señora.

LEOCADIA.   There's no health without life!

ARRIETA.   Perhaps we exaggerate the danger. Don Francisco has
always been respected. . . .

[*His words fade away into silence as* GOYA'S VOICE *is heard offstage
and grows louder.*]

GOYA'S VOICE.   You're probably wondering, doctor, if all I said about
flyers was drivel. [*He enters right, looking at the print he has in his
hand.*] Look at this etching. [*He sees them.* ARRIETA *has stopped
talking. Suspicious,* GOYA *wants an explanation from* LEOCADIA.] Do
you want something?

LEOCADIA. [*Shaking her head*]   «Nothing.» [*Points*] «I'm going to take
away the wine.»

[*She crosses, takes the tray, and exits right under the painter's dis-
trusting gaze.*]

GOYA.   That witch has some shady business in store for me today . . .
[ARRIETA *has crossed to him and takes the print. Both move to the
table, and* ARRIETA *puts the print down to look at it.*] Look, doctor.
This is from a collection I call "Dreams," although they're more
than dreams. Do you think it would be possible to fly like that?
[ARRIETA *shakes his head.*] Leonardo conceived a similar device.
[ARRIETA *begins to sign.*] He didn't fly, but perhaps we will some
day. [*He is looking at the doctor mysteriously.* ARRIETA *returns his
stare and shakes his head.* LEOCADIA *reappears from right and
crosses slowly.* ARRIETA'S *involuntary glance alerts* GOYA *to her presence.*] You still haven't brought Mariquita!

LEOCADIA. [*We hear her perfectly.*]   Mariquita . . . has died.

[*She makes a quick exit left.*]

GOYA.   Did she say something? [ARRIETA *nods and signs.*] She's going to
bring her? [ARRIETA *nods. A silence.* GOYA *sighs and sits down,
brooding behind the table. Finally, he comes to a decision and
speaks.*] I'm going to tell you something in confidence, something
incredible. Promise me your silence. [ARRIETA *nods, expectant.*] I
have seen these flying men. [*He points to the print.*]

ARRIETA.   «What?»

GOYA.   In the hills beyond. [ARRIETA *slowly takes a seat, observing him
with apprehension.*] It must have been two years ago. Far off, but
the windows of something that appeared to be a house were
shining on the highest point. And they were flying around, very
white. [ARRIETA *signs.*] They weren't birds. I thought they might
be the French, operating some new machines. But we would
have heard about it before now. [*More signs from* ARRIETA. GOYA

shakes his head and interrupts him.] No! I'm not dreaming of angels! They live on the earth, but I don't know who they are.

ARRIETA. [*Pointing at Goya's eyes and shaking his head*] «Our eyes can deceive us.»

GOYA.   My eyes haven't deceived me. And they've seen our wiser brothers. Maybe they've lived in the mountains for years . . . I'll tell you my greatest desire: that one day . . . they'll come down. To finish off the king and put an end to all the cruelties in the world. Maybe one day they'll descend like a shining army and knock on every door. With blows so thunderous . . . that even I will hear them. [*A silence.* ARRIETA *observes him and then looks away.*] You think I'm a lunatic. [ARRIETA *shakes his head feebly.*] Let's drop the subject. [ARRIETA *gets up and walks about. He looks first at "The Busybodies" and then at the painter and sadly draws his conclusion. He returns to* GOYA's *side and speaks with his hands.*] Of course women still excite me. [*Quick signs from* ARRIETA] Agreed, not as much as before. Painting is more and more important to me and I forget the other. [ARRIETA *signs.*] Troubled? Who isn't? [*More signs*] Now? [ARRIETA *nods.* GOYA *is thinking how to answer as he sits beside* ARRIETA. *He takes up the poker and toys with it.*] Now I'm troubled about a letter. [*Gesture of interrogation from* ARRIETA] I wrote to Martín Zapater days ago and I haven't had a reply. I don't think anything's wrong . . . [*Brief pause*] But I was imprudent. Martín is like a brother to me, and I was so in need of getting things off my chest. [ARRIETA *goes through the motions of writing and asks with a gesture.*] Trivial matters. [*He laughs.*] But I did settle accounts with flat nose. [ARRIETA *shows his concern and signs.*] Gross insults? Yes! Fewer than he deserves. [*His smile fades as he sees the expression on* ARRIETA's *face.*] You're afraid something has gone wrong? [ARRIETA *signs.*] Two weeks. [ARRIETA *gets up and moves around. We hear the slow, dull sound of a heartbeat.*] I'm not so important to them that they'd open my letters. . . . [ARRIETA *stops and signs. The heartbeats suddenly increase in rhythm and strength.*] I know what the Green Book is. What they say it is. [ARRIETA *signs.*] Thank you. You will write to Martín if it's necessary. But within a few days. Let's hope. [ARRIETA *puts his hand on* GOYA's *shoulder and speaks with his other hand.*] To France. [ARRIETA *nods vehemently.*] Do you truly think that . . . I'm in danger? [ARRIETA *nods.* GOYA *hesitates a moment.*] Of death? [ARRIETA *nods after a moment of hesitation.* GOYA *stands and begins to pace nervously.*] I must paint here! Here!

ARRIETA. [*Taking him by the arm*] «You must save yourself!»

GOYA. [*Laughing, as the heartbeats grow louder*]   I am Goya! And they will respect me!

[LEOCADIA *rushes in from left and goes to his side. While he walks about, she speaks, trying in vain to stop him.*]

LEOCADIA. «They'll drag you in a basket like Riego if you stay! And they'll drag me! And the children!» [*But* GOYA *shakes his head and goes on speaking, with growing anger, above the increasing sound of the heartbeat.*]

GOYA. No, no, and no! Are you listening? We stay here. I'll ask nothing of that big-nosed piece of shit, that murderer! I'll stay with my children, with my painting, and taking my walks through those blessed hills. And I'll celebrate Christmas Eve here, with you, and with your children, and with my family and my grandson.

LEOCADIA. «They'll kill us!»

GOYA. Shut up! Neither you nor the king gives orders here! Here I'm in command!

LEOCADIA. [*Screaming inaudibly*] «Crazy man!»

ARRIETA. [*Coming to her aid*] «Señora, calm yourself and don't upset him. It only makes matters worse.» [*The heartbeats are now very loud.* ARRIETA *takes* GOYA *by the arm.*] «Don Francisco, get control of yourself. Come.» [*He leads him to a chair, craftily taking his pulse at the same time.* GOYA *snorts, grimaces, and murmurs some unclear words. The heartbeats gradually fade away.* ARRIETA *studies* GOYA'S *face for a few moments; then he takes his hat and cane and signs.*]

GOYA. Accept my apologies, doctor. [ARRIETA *starts left with a goodbye gesture.* GOYA'S *voice sounds humble.*] Will you come back soon? [ARRIETA *nods, bows, and exits, accompanied by* LEOCADIA. *The heartbeats are muffled, and their rhythm is like that of a tired heart.*] Child! . . . Mariquita! . . . Where are you? . . . [*He gets up as he speaks and looks out at left. From the right we hear* MARIQUITA'S VOICE. *He turns around.*]

MARIQUITA'S VOICE. They're leading me through a dark corridor. I can't see.

OLD MAN'S VOICE. "The boogyman's on his way."

OLD WOMAN'S VOICE. "They've carried her away." [*Long pause*]

MARIQUITA'S VOICE. You'll never see me again. . . .

[GOYA *has been listening with growing anxiety. The heartbeats, already very faint, cease completely. Silence. The painter mops his forehead with his hand and sighs. The projected paintings are slowly erased, and only the one of "Saturn" reappears.* GOYA *takes the spyglass and goes to the balcony to look toward the palace.* LEOCADIA *reappears from left, holding a cup and silently stirring the liquid in it. She looks at him coldly.*]

LEOCADIA. «Drink this.»

GOYA. I don't need a purge.

LEOCADIA. [*Pointing left*] «The doctor ordered it.»

GOYA. [*Shrugging his shoulders*] I won't argue. Let me have it. [*He takes the cup and sits by the table where he leaves the spyglass. As he drinks,* LEOCADIA *faces him making signs.*] Liberal, yes. But they're

not going to hang all the liberals! [*She continues to sign.*] What?
[*She signs.*] Old women's gossip!

LEOCADIA. [*Hands together, beseeching*] «We must leave!»

GOYA. [*Draining the cup and getting up suddenly*] Do you think I don't
see through your game? You're dreaming of France ... and
Frenchmen! [*He seizes her by the arm.*] But you won't put horns on
me! I can still make you moan with pleasure or pain. You choose!
[*He pushes her away violently, with a look of immense suffering.
Fearful but determined,* LEOCADIA *holds her ground.*] Fetch Mariquita. I haven't seen her all day. [LEOCADIA *looks at him coldly.*]
What are you waiting for? [LEOCADIA *signs.*] You've left your children at the house of the architect Pérez?

MARIQUITA'S VOICE. You'll never see me again ... [LEOCADIA *continues.* GOYA *is puzzled.*]

GOYA. Safer than here ... [*Suddenly he understands and takes a step
toward her.*] Are you telling me they stay there? [*She nods yes. He
is overcome with anger.*] Why? [*She continues.*] Yes, they're your
children! But she is my daughter! And she's learning to paint
with me, and she's going to be a great painter! I'm the one who
decides what's best for my daughter! Her father! [LEOCADIA
shakes her head nervously.] No, you say? Well, I'll leave now for
Tiburcio's house and bring them back. [*She puts herself between
him and the door and shakes her head.*] Get out of my way!

LEOCADIA. «Don't bring them back!» [*He tries to leave and she restrains
him tearfully.*]

GOYA. Let go!

LEOCADIA. «Wait!» [*She begs him to be calm and signs.*]

GOYA. The child is not afraid. [LEOCADIA *insists with her eyes and
makes a circular gesture toward the paintings. The "Saturn" begins to
increase in size.*]

LEOCADIA. «The child ... » [*She indicates her height with her hand.*]
«Here ... » [*Her hands point to the air and to the walls.*] «She's
afraid.» [*She mimes the child's fear and crying, pointing to the
upstage painting.*] «When she sleeps ... » [*She mimes the sleeping
and waking up screaming and in tears.*]

GOYA. She has nightmares? [*She nods.*] I would have noticed! [*She
shakes her head vehemently and points to his ears. Then she takes
him by the arm and leads him to the balcony, indicating something to
him.*] The Royal Volunteers?

LEOCADIA. [*Nodding and forming the word*] «Danger!»

GOYA. [*Without conviction*] They won't bother the children. [*She
makes motions to suggest they will, points to the outside, and mimes
the action of striking a child, indicating that the Volunteers have done
it many times.*] Even if it were true, I would have to bring them
here for Christmas. [*She shows her perplexity.*] Then I'd have to go
to my friend Tiburcio's house every day to see my daughter.

[LEOCADIA *shakes her head.*] What do you mean no? [LEOCADIA *points to the balcony again, points to him, and mimes the action of beating.* GOYA *looks out from the balcony cautiously. The muffled heartbeats resume.* LEOCADIA *steps back, surveys him with enigmatic eyes, and exits furtively left. The painter shakes his head, turns upstage and, wrapped in thought, contemplates the growing and threatening image of Saturn. Then he collects himself, runs left, and shouts.*] Damn witch! What are you plotting now? [*Under the dull heartbeats, he returns to the table, picks up the bell and shakes it. The heartbeats cease.* THE PAINTER *stops his motions and the beating resumes. Looking at the enormous head of Saturn, he shakes the bell again, and the heartbeats stop. He holds his arm still and they are heard again. The light fades slowly, and when the heartbeats cease, we hear the bell very faintly, followed by faint heartbeats. Then we hear the bell louder, and when it stops, the heartbeats are almost inaudible. The bell sounds twice. Silence.*]

Scene 3

The light slowly returns. "Leocadia," "The Holy Office," and "The Reading" are projected on the background. The painting of the flyers has disap-peared. LEOCADIA *and* DOÑA GUMERSINDA GOICOECHEA *are sitting stiffly near the brazier.* GUMERSINDA, *who is very dressed up, is about thirty-five. Not bad looking and all smiles, her sharp features and keen eyes lack any trace of gentleness.*

LEOCADIA.   You must pardon the loud ringing. It was the only way he could summon that lout Emiliano.
GUMERSINDA.   Please, I understand. How is your master?
LEOCADIA. [*Looking at her sharply, for she understands the intended insult*]   Francho? Very happy and well, with the energy of a boy.
GUMERSINDA.   For everything, I hope. Does he eat well? How is his cough?
LEOCADIA.   It hasn't been long since you saw him. He's the same.
GUMERSINDA.   It's just that at his age he could take a turn for the worse at any time.
LEOCADIA.   I'm sure he'll be around for a few more years. [*Throwing out a challenge*] I imagine he might even consider marriage.
GUMERSINDA. [*Stunned by her boldness*]   God will he doesn't fall into that delusion. Only a strumpet would go along with such a mockery, to inherit his property and put a pair of horns on his head.
LEOCADIA.   Don't worry. He isn't considering it yet.
GUMERSINDA.   But I still haven't asked you about your dear husband. Is he well?
LEOCADIA.   You know I never see him . . .

GUMERSINDA.   Forgive me! I'm so forgetful . . . Your husband is still
  quite young, thank God, and he must be fit and healthy. He's the
  one with a long life before him. [*She sighs.*] Well, I came to find
  out, Leocadia, if we would celebrate Christmas here as always.
  It's the fifteenth of December, and one must make preparations.
  Will you set up a Nativity Scene this year? Will you let me bring
  the Three Wise Men to Mariquita?
LEOCADIA.   My children won't be here.
GUMERSINDA.   No? How is that?
LEOCADIA. [*Hesitating*]   Doña Gumersinda, I beg you to help me con-
  vince Francho . . . to celebrate Christmas at your house this year.
GUMERSINDA. [*Coldly*]   Why?
LEOCADIA.   Your father-in-law is in danger. Francho should leave
  Spain but he refuses to. If he at least left this house . . . and went
  to yours perhaps . . .
GUMERSINDA.   My father-in-law has done nothing wrong. Why do you
  think he should go into hiding?
LEOCADIA.   Others who did nothing have been persecuted and killed.
GUMERSINDA.   Our house is not a good hiding place. My husband isn't
  exactly in favor either . . . as the son of his father. [*She smiles.*]
  But they're not going to molest either of them.
LEOCADIA. [*Standing, nervous*]   And if something does happen to him . . .
GUMERSINDA.   I can see that you're afraid, but we shouldn't upset my
  father-in-law. We'll put on a good face in his presence. [*She steps
  back and takes a good look at the "Leocadia."*]
LEOCADIA. [*Containing her indignation*]   I'll use the little power I have
  to see that Francho does not spend the holidays here.
GUMERSINDA.   Don't think yourself so influential, my dear. And don't
  call him Francho again. It sounds so ridiculous in your mouth.
  [GOYA *enters from right.*]
GOYA. [*Warmly*]   Gumersinda!
GUMERSINDA.   «Father.» [*They embrace.* GUMERSINDA *gives him a peck
  on the cheek.*]
GOYA.   It's good to see you! Where on earth is my Paco? [GUMERSINDA
  shakes her head with a prissy, regretful look.] What? My heartless
  son hasn't come with you? [*He laughs.*] But you have brought my
  grandson to see me? Are you going to tell me where he is? I'll bet
  he's in the stable admiring the horses. [*He crosses.*] Marianito!
  Marianito! . . . [GUMERSINDA *runs after him, stops him, and shakes
  her head.*] What?
GUMERSINDA.   «Little Mariano couldn't come . . . »
GOYA.   You didn't bring him? [GUMERSINDA *shakes her head, trying to
  convey humble regret.*]
GUMERSINDA.   «Ma-ria-ni-to . . . » [*Placing her hands together in a gesture
  of asking forgiveness.*] «Asks-you-to-for-give-him. And he sends
  you kisses.» [*She throws a kiss and then plants a kiss on his cheek.*]

GOYA.   Enough. [*He returns the kiss mechanically.*] He didn't come.
[*Depressed, he sits down at the table and begins to draw.*]

GUMERSINDA. [*Going over to him and kissing the back of his head*] «Don't
be angry with me . . . one of these days I'll bring him. That's a
promise . . .» [*She kisses her crossed fingers.*]

GOYA. [*Upset because he doesn't understand her*]   Leo! What is she saying? [LEOCADIA *goes to his side and makes rapid signs.* GUMERSINDA
*indicates that it isn't necessary. She takes a pencil and writes on a
sheet of paper, but* LEOCADIA *goes on speaking with her hands.* GOYA
smiles after looking at the paper and at LEOCADIA.] One of you tells
me she'll bring my grandson before Christmas Eve and the other
says she won't bring him. Who can trust a woman!

GUMERSINDA. [*To* LEOCADIA]   «That's what I said!» [*She points to the
paper.*]

LEOCADIA.   «I told him what I understood.» [*She uses sign language and*
GUMERSINDA *writes again nervously.*]

GOYA. [*Grimly*]   And so it's been for thirty-one years. [*He looks at the
paper.*] No, you don't agree. [*To* LEOCADIA] But I can reply to you. I
won't hear to celebrating Christmas outside this house.

[GUMERSINDA *smiles, triumphant. Thwarted,* LEOCADIA *speaks with
her hands again.* GUMERSINDA *caresses the painter; and, touching her
temple with a finger, she indicates that* LEOCADIA *is out of her mind.*]

LEOCADIA.   «You're evil-minded. You have no shame.»

GUMERSINDA.   «Look who's talking about shame.»

LEOCADIA.   «You're malicious.»

GUMERSINDA.   «Watch what you say.»

LEOCADIA.   «It's evil to trick an old man like that.»

GOYA. [*Tired of not understanding, he startles them with a great inaudible
blow with his fist on the table.*]   The devil can take the two of you!
I want you here, seated and quiet. [*He points, and the two women
go to the sofa and sit down.*] And now bicker to your hearts' content. But at Christmas, all here, with me. [LEOCADIA *signs timidly.*]
Your children too! And no more sour faces! You look like monkeys. [*He becomes absorbed in his drawing.* GUMERSINDA *and*
LEOCADIA *exchange harsh words in the silence. The exchange
between the two women soon becomes bitter again; their gestures
show the contempt they feel for each other.*] Didn't the postman
come today either? [*They look at him, and* LEOCADIA *shakes her
head.*] Go on. Go on with your sweet chatter. [*He sketches, and
they resume their argument. A light cackling sound begins, and* GOYA
looks up. The cackling grows louder, and GOYA *looks toward the sofa,
indicating that the cackling appears to come from* LEOCADIA's *lips,
since she is the one who is speaking at the moment. The sounds
increase; it is evident that* LEOCADIA *is furious. With a haughty gesture,* GUMERSINDA *interrupts her and replies with a disagreeable
bray.* GOYA *observes them with a strange expression on his face;*

although he is containing his amusement, there is a trace of terror in his eyes. The cackling sounds and the brays alternate from the mouths of the two women. There is growing surprise in LEOCADIA'S *cackles and victory in* GUMERSINDA'S *brays. Livid,* LEOCADIA *suddenly stands up and emits two angry cackles which amount to a nervous question.* GUMERSINDA *rises and responds with a solemn bray that seems a sonorous assertion. Holding his ears,* GOYA *laughs broadly. They turn to look at him; then at each other. Going over to the old man,* GUMERSINDA *says goodbye with affectionate kisses.*] You're leaving already? [*She nods and emits a tender little bray.* GOYA *doesn't know whether to be frightened or to laugh.*] Well, kiss those two ingrates for me. [GUMERSINDA *nods, genuflects, and directs a cold nod of the head to* LEOCADIA—*which is barely returned—and exits rapidly left. A pause.* LEOCADIA *is looking at* GOYA *angrily. Still affected by the joke his ears have played on him,* GOYA *sketches. We hear a cat's meow.* GOYA *stops his work and looks somberly straight ahead.* LEOCADIA *crosses to him, takes his head in her hands and turns it violently so that he can see her. She begins to speak with her hands.* GOYA *is bothered. A pause.* LEOCADIA *questions with an imperious movement of her head.* GOYA *bursts out:*] Gumersinda has a loose tongue!

LEOCADIA.   «Then it's true?»

GOYA.   [*Throws down his pencil and stands*]   Yes! It's true!

LEOCADIA.   [*Her movements suggest genuine despair.*]   «My God! That's how you repay me! That's your love for Mariquita. My children and I will end up begging in the streets!»

GOYA.   [*Walking away from her*]   What's all the fuss about? . . . Calm down and listen . . . You've got to understand it! [*He takes her by the arm.*] Shut up! [*She screams inaudibly.*] I can't hear you, but shut up! [*She pulls free and sits.*] Pay attention, woman. The king is a monster, and his advisors—jackals he urges on not just to rob but to kill. Protected by the law and the blessings of our prelates! Strip a liberal of his property? He'd better not complain or he'll get the gallows. We're not Spaniards but demons, and they're the angels who are fighting against Hell. I get even. I paint them with the faces of witches and devil worshippers in their rites that they call the Celebration of the Kingdom. But I also get up early, because I'm no fool. Three months ago I went to the notary and ceded this estate to my grandson Marianito. [LEOCADIA *signs excitedly.*] It couldn't be willed to Mariquita!

LEOCADIA.   «She's your daughter!»

GOYA.   She's my daughter, but not in the eyes of the law or the church! Oh, I don't know why I bother to tell you! [LEOCADIA *moves her hands vigorously.*] I haven't given everything away. I'll put aside special bequests for you . . .

LEOCADIA.   [*Stands up and signs as she forms the words with her mouth.*] «They'll take it all. Your son's a greedy opportunist and your daughter-in-law's a witch!»

GOYA. My son is not an opportunist!

LEOCADIA. [*Signing*] «They're waiting for your death like vultures.»

GOYA. They're not vultures! They're not waiting for me to die!

LEOCADIA. [*More signs*] «That's all your good-for-nothing grandson looks forward to!»

GOYA. [*Suddenly wounded, he goes after her.*] Harpy! My grandson is not a good-for-nothing, and he loves me! You're going to respect my Marianito! Do you hear me? [LEOCADIA *is suddenly aware of something at left.*] Do you hear me? [*She motions to him to keep quiet, that something is going on in the house. "Leocadia" and "The Reading" disappear.*] I've had enough of your tricks! You're not going to fool me even if I am deaf. [*She begs him to keep quiet.*] Listen to me, I tell you!

LEOCADIA. [*She whirls around, exasperated, and makes rapid signs.*] «You're impossible! I'm leaving!»

GOYA. Then go! [*He seizes her arm hard.*] Go off with your children and one of those Volunteers you flirt with at the bridge.

LEOCADIA. [*Taken aback*] «What?»

GOYA. That fine lad with the moustache! The sergeant!

LEOCADIA. [*Confused*] «What are you saying?»

GOYA. [*He pushes her violently downstage, but she manages an uneasy glance to the left.*] I saw you from here! You can't go off to France to solicit, can you! Whore! [*He shoves her from him and exits angrily right without noticing* FATHER DUASO, *who has appeared at left a moment before. "The Holy Office" increases in size.*]

LEOCADIA. [*Calling after him*] Francho! . . . Francho! . . .

DUASO. [*Taking off his priest's hat*] You know he can't hear you, señora. [LEOCADIA *turns around in surprise.* DON JOSÉ DUASO Y LATRE *is a forty-eight-year-old priest. He is unusually tall. His dark hair accentuates the pallor of his delicate and pleasant features. His penetrating eyes reveal his intelligence. Full lips suggest a sensual nature that he combats with constant study and activity. He wears a calotte (skullcap) on the back of his head. The cross of Carlos III gleams on his cassock.*] Forgive me for coming unannounced.

LEOCADIA. I hope Your Reverence will forgive my screaming. Don Francisco . . .

DUASO. [*Raising his hand*] I understand, señora.

LEOCADIA. Please have a seat, Reverend Father. [*She indicates the sofa.*]

DUASO. Thank you. It's better here, if you don't mind. Heat doesn't agree with me. [*He removes his cloak.* LEOCADIA *hastens to take it and places it on a chair.*]

LEOCADIA. Permit me, Father.

DUASO. Thank you, my daughter.

LEOCADIA.   Your Reverence will want to speak with Don Francisco . . .

DUASO.   After a chat with you, Doña Leocadia. [*He indicates with a courteous gesture that she should sit on the sofa.*]

LEOCADIA.   As Your Reverence commands. [*She sits and* DUASO *takes the chair behind the table.*]

DUASO.   I've been to this house only once before, but I was a neighbor of yours in the Calle Valverde.

LEOCADIA.   I remember it very well. Your Reverence is Don José Duaso. [*He gives a little bow with a smile.*] Don Francisco will be very pleased. And I also thank you for your visit, Reverend Father.

DUASO.   Why, my daughter?

LEOCADIA.   Your Reverence knows to what extremes passions have been unleashed. I fear for Don Francisco . . .

DUASO.   Has anyone bothered you?

LEOCADIA.   Not yet.

DUASO.   Your concern for him does you honor. If I'm not mistaken, you've served him . . . as housekeeper for some ten years.

LEOCADIA. [*Looking down*]   Yes, Father.

DUASO. [*Coldly*]   Your husband . . . is he still living?

LEOCADIA.   Yes, Father.

DUASO.   It's regrettable that you haven't achieved a reconciliation after so long. Incompatibility between husband and wife is, if you will permit me to say so, a great sin.

LEOCADIA.   I know, Father, but he disowned me.

DUASO.   I'm not unaware of that, my child.

[*A far-off ringing of a bell.* LEOCADIA *looks left for a moment.*]

LEOCADIA.   Someone rang. With your permission, I'll see who it is. [*She crosses left.* DUASO *stands up and nods his agreement but continues talking, obliging her to stop.*]

DUASO.   I seem to recall that your children live with you. . . .

LEOCADIA. [*Turning around*]   So they do, Father.

DUASO.   Are they coming of age?

LEOCADIA.   My Guillermo is fourteen. [DUASO *approves with a smile.*] And María del Rosario, nine. [DUASO *gives her a hard look. Upset, she adds:*] But she'll soon be ten.

DUASO.   Beati pauperes spiritu . . . I shall pray to the Virgin, señora, that those innocent ones will always have good examples and that they'll be raised in the fear of God.

LEOCADIA. [*Embarrassed*]   Thank you, Reverend Father.

[DOCTOR ARRIETA *appears at left and bows.*]

ARRIETA.   I'm sorry if I've disturbed you.

DUASO. [*Smiles*]   On the contrary, Doctor Arrieta. I'm delighted to see you after so many years.

ARRIETA.   Very many, Father Duaso. May I congratulate you on your recent honors and advancement.

DUASO. Advancement?

ARRIETA. Did you know, Doña Leocadia? Father Duaso has been named chaplain to His Majesty. And since May he has been in charge of the censorship of publications.

[LEOCADIA *makes a courteous bow of congratulation.*]

DUASO. [*With a grin, after a moment*] I'm from Aragón, my dear Arrieta. And, consequently, very frank. Don't I detect a certain disapproval in your words?

ARRIETA. [*Wary*] I don't understand.

DUASO. Am I wrong to think that you're not pleased with my appointment in the palace nor with my work in the office of censorship?

ARRIETA. I only concern myself with the health of bodies, Reverend.

LEOCADIA. [*Uneasy*] Please be seated. Would you like a cup of chocolate?

ARRIETA. Not for me, Doña Leocadia . . .

DUASO. Don't bother, señora. And give us the honor of your company. [LEOCADIA *sits.* DUASO *and* ARRIETA *imitate her. A sigh from* DUASO] I'm not trying to interrogate you, Doctor Arrieta. I seek only true friendship. People are too silent in Spain, and that's not good.

ARRIETA. True, Father, but a great silence has been imposed, and the censorship Your Reverence exercises proves it. Anyone who dares to break it will pay dearly. But I never took sides in any struggle except the one for our glorious independence. I'm only a doctor.

DUASO. [*Sighing again*] And you only want to speak about the health of bodies. Should I conclude then, seeing you here, that Don Francisco is not well?

ARRIETA. Perhaps.

DUASO. Perhaps?

ARRIETA. Look at the paintings on the walls.

DUASO. Are they his? At first I thought they might be old frescos . . .

ARRIETA. Because you find them disagreeable, like everyone else.

DUASO. [*Looking at the walls*] They could hardly be considered beautiful. There is so much violence, so much satire in them. Yes, they're his . . . It's a world we've already seen in some of his etchings . . . .

ARRIETA. His etchings were circulated. Now, under the great silence, the painter is consumed, and he cries out from within this tomb so that no one will hear him.

DUASO. Is he afraid?

ARRIETA. Afraid or insane. Perhaps both. And I fear a sad ending . . . Goya is now very old.

LEOCADIA. Father Duaso will not leave us without protection!

DUASO. [*After looking at her, to* ARRIETA] Have you thought of a solution?

ARRIETA. For the moment, to get him out of this hole where he must breathe the foul and noxious air of a swamp.

DUASO.　From this house, you mean?

ARRIETA.　You know I mean this country, Father Duaso. [DUASO *frowns.*]

LEOCADIA.　To France!

DUASO.　France is the true swamp. . . . Isn't it possible to cure a Spaniard in Spain?

ARRIETA.　That is a question Your Reverence must answer for himself. [*A silence. The sound of a flight of giant birds in the air.* GOYA *rushes in from right. They all stand.* LEOCADIA *runs to his side.*]

LEOCADIA.　«What's wrong with you?»

[*The painter looks at her wide-eyed.* DUASO *approaches him.*]

DUASO.　«Don Francisco, let me embrace you.»

GOYA.　[*Looking at them as if they were all strangers*]　It's growing dark. Bring lights, Leocadia. [*She nods and exits left.*] Let them see light in my house; so they'll know it's not abandoned. [DUASO *and* ARRIETA *exchange perplexed looks.* GOYA *attempts to regain his composure.*] That I'm at home, with my friends! And with my dogs! Father Duaso, I thank you for your visit. Have they, perhaps, also entrusted you with the censorship of the arts? [DUASO *denies it vigorously.*] If you've come to judge my paintings, don't hide it.

DUASO.　[*Opening his arms*]　«My son, I come as a friend . . . »　[GOYA *looks at him dubiously, but he ends up embracing him with a sad smile.*]

GOYA.　Fellow countryman! . . . [LEOCADIA *enters with a lighted lamp and places it on the table.*] Excuse my outburst. No, I'm not crazy; just enraged!

LEOCADIA.　«Why?»

GOYA.　They've just painted a cross on my door.

LEOCADIA.　'«What are you saying?»

[*They all move quickly to the balcony to have a look.* GOYA *moves them aside and peers out.*]

GOYA.　They've already gone. [LEOCADIA *is distraught.* ARRIETA *tries to calm her.* DUASO *frowns.*] Have Andrés and Emiliana take a bucket of water and clean the door. [LEOCADIA *exits left.*] Another unclean one: Francisco de Goya. I've heard about those crosses. [*He crosses and turns to face* DUASO *with a perverse smile.*] Your friends, paisano. [DUASO *shakes his head in denial.*] Forgive me, I don't know what I'm saying. We should all sit down. [ARRIETA *takes a seat near the brazier;* DUASO, *behind the table.*] And I beside you, so that I can read what you may wish to tell me. [*He hands* DUASO *a pencil and sits at the end of the table.*] Because it's rained since your last visit . . . [DUASO *is about to write.*] Don't apologize. I'm familiar with your scruples. I'm not a priest, and my housekeeper is a young woman. [DUASO *starts to write.*] And married to boot. [DUASO *lowers his eyes.*] But do tell me how old Goya can be of service to you. [ARRIETA *goes to peer over the balcony.* DUASO *writes.* GOYA *reads.*] The way we talk in Aragón, Father. Straight-forward. Does your visit have a purpose or not? [*To* ARRIETA] Are they washing away the cross, Doctor? [ARRIETA *nods.* DUASO *writes.* GOYA *smiles warmly and presses the priest's hand.*] Thank you. From my heart. I have no need of assistance. [ARRIETA *reacts and sits again.* DUASO *insists he does and writes again.*] I'm not afraid of that rabble. When they come back, I'll fire on them. [DUASO *shakes his head and writes.*] Don't you believe me? [DUASO *affirms with his head and writes.*] I was never a Mason! [DUASO *writes.* LEOCADIA *enters left.*] What did those sons of bitches put on the door?

LEOCADIA.   «A cross.» [*She sketches it in the air.*]

GOYA.   And something more. [*Distressed, she shakes her head.*] I saw them write something too! What was it? [*She hesitates.*] Answer me! [*She signs.* GOYA *lets out a mocking grunt and looks at Duaso.*] What they've written concerns you, Father.

DUASO. [*Surprised*]   «Me?»

GOYA.   They must be theologians. They've written "heretic." [DUASO *frowns.*] Blessed country, heaven's favorite! Even the criminals work for the Inquisition!

[*Suddenly* LEOCADIA *runs and throws herself at* DUASO's *feet. He stands and tries to lift her up.*]

LEOCADIA.   «Please, Father, don't take his words seriously! And save him! Tell him to put aside his pride and accept!»

DUASO. [*At the same time*]   «In the name of God, señora, control your-self. You know I've come to be of help! . . . »

GOYA. [*Almost at the same time, he goes to Leocadia's side and manages to get her to her feet.*]   For thirty years I've been witnessing a play I don't understand! . . . Get up! . . . [*She stands, gasping silently.* DUASO *puts his hand on Goya's shoulder and indicates to him to note what he then writes.* GOYA *remains standing.*] No. I have nothing to ask forgiveness for!

LEOCADIA.   «Father Duaso is right! Humble yourself!»

GOYA.   I shall not humble myself before the king! [LEOCADIA *steps back in consternation.* DUASO *writes and* GOYA *reads.*] What? [*The painter breaks into laughter and begins to walk back and forth.* LEOCADIA *rushes to the table to read.*] Divine right, you say, pai-sano? [DUASO *nods.*] Submission to the royal authority even when it's unjust? Church doctrine? [DUASO *looks at him hard without responding.*] What do you think of that, Arrieta? [*Inhibited,* ARRIETA *points to* DUASO.] Father Duaso, you're no small-time vil-lage priest, but a sensible linguist with a chair waiting for you in the Spanish Academy. You don't believe that. [DUASO *confirms that he does energetically.*] You do? And you are certain that the blood of our most beloved Fernando VII is that of his predecessor King Carlos? [*Tightlipped,* DUASO *writes.*] Well, I do dare to think

evil! [*Nervous,* DUASO *begins to write again.*] Rest assured that our
dear Virgin of Pilar did not believe in the virtue of Queen María
Luisa. [*Angry,* DUASO *throws down the pencil and takes a few steps.*
LEOCADIA *makes signs to him to forgive the painter's irreverence and
looks at Goya with desperation in her eyes.*] Forgive me, I didn't
mean to offend you. [DUASO *looks at him sadly.*]

DUASO. [*His voice is perfectly audible.*]   The French infection . . .

GOYA.   Yes. You would have said that. Anyone knows what you probably said. [*With a gesture,* DUASO *declares he doesn't understand.*
GOYA *approaches him in a friendly manner and takes him by the
arm.*] Paisano, though I might wish to humble myself before the
king, I couldn't. I'd be disobeying him. [DUASO *gives him a look of
amazement.* ARRIETA *stands up.*]

DUASO.   «What?»

GOYA.   In 1814, when we committed the barbarity of bringing back
the "desired one," I did return to the palace. And do you know
what he sprung on me? First, that I deserved the gallows. . . .
And then, with that tight little smile of his, he ordered me never
to appear in his presence until he summoned me himself. [DUASO
looks at him a moment and runs to write, leading GOYA *with him.*
GOYA *then reads.*] That is my misfortune. I can't forget that I'm in
his hands. But, hidden away in this house . . . perhaps I'll be far
from his thoughts. [*Alarmed,* LEOCADIA *signs.*] Don't offend the
priest, woman. A peasant from my land doesn't sell his fellow-
peasant. So I can tell him frankly how much it saddens me to see
him in the service of so bad a cause. [DUASO *writes;* GOYA *goes on
talking.*] When the country was about to revive, they beat and
kicked it back into submissiveness. [DUASO *looks at him sharply.
"The Holy Office" changes into the "Fight With Clubs."* GOYA *reads.*
DUASO *writes something and points to what he has written.*] I could
have said with clubs. [DUASO *shakes his head and writes.* GOYA
reads and steps away gloomily.] Of course I know who Matías
Vinuesa was. The priest from Tamajón. An insane fool determined to stain the country with blood. [DUASO *has been writing
and shows him the paper.* GOYA *reads reluctantly.*] They were days
of danger. They assaulted the jail, and they beat him to death.
[DUASO *shakes his head. A pause.* GOYA *lowers his voice.*] They
killed him with their canes. [*A pause. "The Trapped Dog" appears
at the left of the "Fight." The two men look at each other.* GOYA *goes
upstage and contemplates the "Fight."* DUASO *joins him.* GOYA *speaks
with gravity.*] It's true. We are all participants in crime. [*A pause*] It
remains to be known if there are just causes even though crimes
go with them. What a trap! Eh, paisano? If you answer that crime
erases all justice, then the cause that you serve is not just either.
And if you say that there are just causes, we'll go back to arguing
which of the causes is the just one. [*Pointing to the painting*] God

knows for how many centuries still. [*He turns completely around to face the audience. A pause*] I have painted that barbarism, Father, because I have seen it. And afterwards I painted the lonely dog without a master. . . . You have seen the barbarism, but you stay on at the court, with your master. . . . I am a dog that wants to think and doesn't know how. But, after racking my brain, I reflect on how it was: centuries ago someone took something that was not his. By force. And others responded to that force, and to them still others. . . . And so we've continued. Hammer in hand. [DUASO *moves to the table.* LEOCADIA *implores him silently.* DUASO *writes and* GOYA *continues to speak.*] Don't insist, Father. I won't return to the palace. We'll spend Christmas Eve here, and nothing will happen. With the New Year, we'll decide. First I must finish these paintings! [DUASO *writes and touches his arm.* GOYA *reads and shows sudden pleasure.*] Will you come by the day before Christmas Eve? [DUASO *nods and smiles.*] And why not spend that blessed night with us? Eh, Leocadia? [LEOCADIA *doesn't conceal her disapproval well after realizing that* DUASO *is accepting the idea of the painter staying on at the house.*] There'll be candies and sweets, and the local wine is pure honey! And music to the treetops!

DUASO. [*Shaking his head affably*] «I can't.»

GOYA.   How sorry I am. No doubt you have your obligations . . . [DUASO *nods.*] . . . at the palace. [DUASO *looks down and* ARRIETA *watches him.*] Well, until the day before Christmas Eve, Father. I'll show you out. [THE PRIEST *gives* GOYA *an embrace.*]

DUASO. [*Bowing to* ARRIETA] «God keep you, Doctor.»

ARRIETA.   «May he be with Your Reverence.»
[LEOCADIA *hands* DUASO *his belongings. He thanks her with a paternal parting gesture. He extends his hand, and she kisses it. He exits left accompanied by* GOYA.]

GOYA'S VOICE.   Bundle up, Father. It's turning cold.
[*Sound of glass breaking. A rock wrapped in a paper falls to the floor.* LEOCADIA *screams.* DUASO *reappears hurriedly.*]

DUASO.   What happened?

ARRIETA. [*Showing him the rock*]   Look.
[LEOCADIA *attempts to restrain* DUASO *who tries, angrily, to peer over the balcony.*]

LEOCADIA.   Don't let them see you. They may throw another one.
[GOYA *reappears left.*]

GOYA.   Did you forget something, Father? [*Gradually he understands what has happened.*] A rock?

ARRIETA.   «With a paper.» [*He says this while looking at* DUASO *who approaches and holds out his hand.*]

DUASO.   «Give it to me.»

GOYA. [*Coming between them, grimly*]   No, paisano! The message is for me. [*He snatches the paper, goes to the table, puts on his glasses and reads.*]

LEOCADIA.   «What does it say?»

GOYA.   Some artistic advice. They're painters too. [*They look at him perplexed.*] Listen: What is the difference between a Mason and a Mason's lackey? Paint a gallows with an old frog hanging and put underneath: Although I didn't join, I danced to the tune. [LEOCADIA *has to sit down.* ARRIETA *looks outside.*] Don't show yourself, Doctor. They've probably hidden in the shadows.

LEOCADIA.   «Take him away from here, Father Duaso! . . . » [DUASO *starts to write but a gesture from* GOYA *stops him.*]

GOYA.   I won't leave!

DUASO. [*Touching his forehead*]   «Are you crazy?»

GOYA.   I'm not crazy. And now leave, Father. They won't harm a priest; they're very pious. Nor anyone who goes with him; so you go too, Doctor, with Father Duaso. I'll expect both of you the twenty-third of this month. [DUASO *is about to insist;* GOYA *cuts him off incisively.*] Go with God! [DUASO *sighs, presses his arm with feeling, and crosses left.* ARRIETA *bows to* GOYA *and joins* DUASO. *Her face revealing her fears,* LEOCADIA *precedes them, showing the way. The three exit. A pause. Then we hear the far-off baying of a dog, and the painter turns around brusquely to look at the one he has painted. Slow, dull heartbeats become audible. With teeth clenched,* GOYA *shakes his head; finally, he turns his back on the painting and goes toward the balcony.*] My friends are leaving . . . In the desert again. [*The heartbeats grow stronger.* GOYA *shakes his head again and with visible effort he tries to hear nothing. The heartbeats fade; the "Fight" changes to "Asmodea,"* MARIQUITA'S VOICE *sounds over the very light heartbeats.*]

MARIQUITA'S VOICE.   Others are leaving the house. . . . Now. . . . Don't you hear them?

GOYA. [*He smiles bitterly but he distrusts what he "hears."*]   It can't be Leocadia. [*He goes left and then returns, disgusted with himself.*] I won't listen to you. Go. I know you don't exist. [*The heartbeats cease.* GOYA *looks left, curious in spite of himself.*]

MARIQUITA'S VOICE.   You don't know . . . [GOYA *stops his ears.*] Stop your ears . . . . How can you block out the voice of your Asmodea?

GOYA.   Asmodea?

MARIQUITA'S VOICE. [*In a laughing tone*]   My hand gives a soft caress. I'll lead you to the mountain, mountain, tun, tun, tun. . . .

GOYA. [*Trembling*]   Mariquita!

MARIQUITA'S VOICE.   . . . quita, quita, Mariquita. Mari, Mari . . . Marasmodea . . . dea, dea, dea . . . Martyr. [*Silence.* GOYA *grabs his palette and picks up his brushes. When he is about to climb on the ladder,* LEOCADIA *returns, tearful but without outward signs of emotion.*]

GOYA.   Tomorrow I'm bringing your children here. [*She shakes her head slowly. She signs.* GOYA *is silent a moment and then stands motionless, his eyes flashing. Then he puts down his palette and brushes and runs to the door at left.*] Andrés! Emiliana! [*He exits, and his voice comes from offstage.*] Worthless trash! Leeches! Is that the way you repay me? I order you to stay! . . . [*Brief pause.* GOYA *returns.*] They've gone. [LEOCADIA *nods.*] Like rats.

LEOCADIA. [*Her voice perfectly audible*]   It's because they aren't crazy. [GOYA *gives her a startled look. Then he looks at "Asmodea" and crosses to the table, poking his ear. He turns around.*]

GOYA.   Tomorrow you can go into the city and look for new servants. [LEOCADIA *signs.*] They will come. This is a good house! [*Before she can deny this, she stops short in fear.*] Do you hear something? [*She points toward the balcony. The thumping heartbeats start again.* LEOCADIA *tries to keep* GOYA *back from the balcony. He pulls loose and looks out.*] Leo, put out that light. [*She extinguishes the lamp. The paintings fade away; the room remains lighted only by a faint moonglow.*] There are shapes near the door.

LEOCADIA. [*Stifling a scream and pointing outside as she mimics blows on the door.*]   «They're beating on the door!» [*The heartbeats are now more rapid.*]

GOYA.   Go bar the door! [*He exits left, followed by* LEOCADIA. *As soon as they disappear, the heartbeats stop abruptly and we hear the din of blows, voices, and loud laughter.*]

VOICES.   Heretic! Mason! We'll hang you with your bitch! We'll teach you to respect your country. When your tongue's gone, you'll stop your blasphemy, and your whore can speak for you. .
[*Raucous laughter. Blows on the outside door.* GOYA *returns, red with anger, and goes to the balcony to peer out. The moment he enters, all the outside sounds cease and the heartbeats, stronger and more rapid, resume.* LEOCADIA *reappears shortly from left, wringing her hands. Without noticing her, the old painter feels the impulse of his Aragonese blood and rushes upstage. He grabs the gun, tests to see if it is loaded and goes right.* LEOCADIA *screams, shaking her head as she runs to his side.*]

LEOCADIA.   «No, Francho! Don't do that!»
[GOYA *pushes her away and exits right; she follows him. As soon as they leave, the heartbeats stop, and the uproar outside the house is heard again.*]

VOICE. [*Along with laughter from the others*]   Show yourself, clown, traitor!

LEOCADIA'S VOICE.   Francho, for God's sake!

VOICE.   Open up, whore! [*Blows on the door*]

LEOCADIA.   They'll drag us off, they'll kill us.

VOICE.   Open, traitor! We've brought the clubs to break your bones. . . .

LEOCADIA'S VOICE.   Give me that gun! . . . [*Moaning*] Give it to me! . . .

VOICE.   Are you in bed?

LEOCADIA'S VOICE. [*Sobbing*]   Francho, think of me!
VOICE.   Cover up, the boogyman's coming! . . .
[*Loud laughter, which suddenly ceases when* GOYA *reappears right,
followed by* LEOCADIA. *The heartbeats are heard again, very strong.
Bewildered, the painter seems to have lost his daring. Her face covered with tears,* LEOCADIA *gently takes the gun from his hands and
leaves it on the chest.* GOYA *steps forward and stops dead in front of
the table, with a lost look on his face.* LEOCADIA *crosses and stops in
front of the brazier, trembling. The two face forward as the heartbeats
thunder.*]

Curtain

PART TWO
Scene 1

The lights come up on the downstage area. At left THE KING *sits embroidering as in the first scene.* FATHER DUASO *stands waiting respectfully.* THE
KING *looks at him out of the corner of his eye, smiles, and leaves off his nee-
dlework.*

KING.   Well, Father Duaso?
DUASO.   Sir, Don Francisco de Goya does not seem inclined to return
    to the palace. He only aspires to work in the privacy of his coun-
    try place.
KING.   He's a court painter.
DUASO.   I suppose, sir, that he feels he's in decline. And since he's not
    had a commission from the court in years, I believe he prefers
    not to impose on the palace any paintings that would not be to
    Your Majesty's taste.
KING. [*Laughs*]   You suppose, you believe. There's no doubt of your
    friendship for Goya. . . . What did he say?
DUASO. [*Hesitating*]   I was not able to convince him, sir, that he should
    ask Your Majesty's indulgence.
KING. [*Sarcastically*]   How surprising, Father Duaso. . . . What were
    his words?
DUASO. [*Embarrassed*]   He said . . . not believing he'd done anything
    wrong . . . he found no reason for seeking your pardon.
KING. [*With a sigh*]   Such obstinacy! Liberals never think they've done
    anything wrong. Did you offer to intercede for him?
DUASO.   Yes, Majesty. But he begged me . . . not to make any effort on
    his behalf.
KING. [*After a moment*]   How does he live?
DUASO.   Like an inoffensive old man, sir. He decorates his walls with
    ugly, artless paintings.

KING.   Is he afraid?

DUASO.   Who can say? He's deaf, and it's difficult to converse with him. He seems tranquil.

KING.   Tranquil?

DUASO.   Undaunted, at least. But his physician suspects it could be a sign of senility.

KING.   Who is his physician?

DUASO.   Doctor Arrieta, sir.

KING.   Arrieta. . . . His name doesn't sound familiar. Probably some Mason.

DUASO.   He appears not to have called attention to himself, sir.

KING.   Father Duaso, what can be done? We open our arms lovingly to our children and they reject us.

DUASO.   If Your Majesty permits, I'll go back and plead with Goya to prostrate himself before the throne.

KING.   [Nodding]   You may count on my gratitude, Father.

DUASO.   I promised Goya to visit him on the twenty-third, the day before Christmas Eve. May I assure him that Your Majesty revokes his former order?

KING.   [Curious]   What former order?

DUASO.   Goya has confided in me that, in 1814, Your Majesty told him that he deserved the gallows and ordered him never to appear at the palace until he was summoned.

KING.   [Smiling]   I said that to him in jest! [He sighs.] It was a joke. Why would I think that Goya should be hanged?

DUASO.   [Relieved]   Then may I assure him? . . .

KING.   [Cutting him short and smiling]   No. In spite of everything, he's been an opponent of my absolute rights, and he must beg my pardon without my taking the first step. I've given him a discreet nudge through your visit. I only want that hardhead to learn the submission due to the Church and Crown. Do you understand, Father Duaso?

DUASO.   I understand and I applaud it, sir. I would like, nevertheless . . . [He breaks off.]

KING.   [Affably]   Speak, Father.

DUASO.   Majesty, although Goya has asked me not to intercede in his favor, the feelings I profess for him oblige me to do so.

KING.   But I've told you, Father, that I'm not going to punish Goya. He only has to beg my pardon.

DUASO.   I know, sir. But on the occasion of my first visit I happened to witness an unpleasant incident.

KING.   What kind of incident?

DUASO.   They painted a cross and wrote the word "heretic" on his door. They threw a stone through the window with an insulting message.

KING.   [Frowning]   Who did this?

DUASO.   We didn't see them, sir. It was too dark.

KING. [*Pondering*]   We'll have to restrain such excesses.

DUASO.   The times are propitious, sir, for other excesses. I fear for my
fellow-countryman. If Your Majesty would give me license to be
more explicit with him. . . .

KING.   Stress the risk he runs, Father Duaso! Perhaps it will persuade
him to ask for my favor. Didn't the incident frighten him?

DUASO.   Rather it irritated him. [*A silence*]

KING.   Fear is also a Christian virtue. [*He lifts the embroidery frame and
makes a stitch in the material.*] Did you say you would visit him soon?

DUASO.   The twenty-third, sir. [*A silence.* THE KING *makes another stitch.*]

KING.   Father Duaso, I'm confident you'll get him to accept our protection. [*Stitch*] But don't go before eight o'clock in the evening.

DUASO. [*Surprised*]   Not before eight?

KING. [*Giving him the familiar smile*]   For Goya's sake. Someday I'll
explain why I'm making this request. You may take it as an order.

DUASO. [*Perplexed*]   I shall, sir.

KING. [*Dismissing him with a movement of his hand*]   Thank you for
your assistance, Father Duaso. [*He becomes absorbed in his
embroidery.* DUASO *kneels, stands up, and steps back. Blackout.*]

Scene 2

*A chorus of faint guffaws. "The Busybodies," "Witches' Sabbath," and "Judith"
appear on the upstage wall.* GOYA, *huddled on the ladder, can be seen in silhouette. Then the lights come up. Wrapped in an old robe to protect himself
from the cold,* GOYA *is working on the figure of the seated woman on the right
side of "Witches' Sabbath." From time to time he shivers and blows on his fingers. The brazier table, minus the brazier, shows its mouth. Light, multiple,
insistent, the chorus of mysterious laughs peoples the old man's loneliness. He
stops to listen, shakes his head, and continues painting.*

GOYA.   Fantasies. [*Two mocking feminine voices stand out from the merry
chorus.*] I won't listen! [*He concentrates on his work. The screeching
of owls is added to the laughter. Irritated,* GOYA *stops.*] I'll will the
sounds to stop, and they'll go away. [*He paints, making vague negative motions with his head. The screeching and laughter die down. A
louder guffaw provokes a silent rebuff from the painter. The noises
fade and cease.* GOYA *makes sure of the silence and sighs. He blows
on his fingers, takes up a brush, and goes back to work.*]

MARIQUITA'S VOICE.   No. [GOYA *stops abruptly and listens.*] You can't
silence the voices. [GOYA *gives his head a twist. A pause*] Am I the
one you're painting? [GOYA *looks with surprise at the figure on
which he is working.*] Leocadia says it's she, but it's I. A child who
doesn't fear the witches. The greatest witch of all. [*She laughs.*]

GOYA. [*Bowing his head*]   It's the deafness.

MARIQUITA'S VOICE.   Don't believe it.

GOYA.   The deafness.

MARIQUITA'S VOICE.   I warn you of things happening that you don't see
. . . the departure of the servants.

GOYA.   I can guess those things! [*A pause*]

MARIQUITA'S VOICE.   What were you looking for before all over the
house? In her desk, under her pillow?

GOYA.   I won't listen. [*He prepares to paint again.*]

MARIQUITA'S VOICE.   They no longer throw rocks. They no longer
paint crosses. [GOYA *stops to listen but says nothing. The owls
screech again, and the two mocking feminine voices laugh in the
midst of the din.* GOYA *puts down his palette and tries to stop his
ears.*] She's late. [*He steps down from the ladder, blowing on his fingers, and surveys the road from the balcony. The voice whispers.*]
She's always late, for days now . . . [*Tenuous chorus of laughter*]
Yesterday you were bent on going to the hills . . . [*A silence*] To
look for me.

GOYA.   I'm not crazy. I know where my Mariquita is. . . .

MARIQUITA'S VOICE.   I'm there. But the thousand-year-old child . . . is
in the hills. [*The painter returns to the table and sits gloomily.*]
When you came back yesterday you noticed something. Evidence of a visitor. A smell perhaps. [*A silence*] Look for the button. [GOYA *is startled. The voice laughs.*] You haven't looked in the
jewel case . . .

GOYA.   It might have fallen off his jacket.

MARIQUITA'S VOICE.   A sergeant of the Royal Volunteers lost a button?
He was hanging around here this morning, and you noticed the
missing button. . . .

GOYA.   It probably fell off. . . .

MARIQUITA'S VOICE.   He could have given it to her as a present.

GOYA.   My mind's playing tricks on me. But one thing I know. Even
though I'm speaking to you, you don't exist. Why should I suffer?
I won't look for the button.

[*Chorus of tenuous laughter. A woman's voice stands out.*]

WOMAN'S VOICE.   Don't look for it, dying man. What's left for you on
this earth? Not even us.

SECOND WOMAN'S VOICE.   Don't look for the button. Look for the
memory of us.

WOMAN'S VOICE.   You are alone.

SECOND WOMAN'S VOICE.   Follow the example of that poor imbecile in
your painting. [*The* TWO VOICES *laugh.*]

WOMAN'S VOICE. [*Amid laughs*]   Admit that you want to . . . [*With his
eyes closed and face contracted,* GOYA *nods "yes" over and over.*]

SECOND WOMAN'S VOICE.   Give yourself pleasure, since she has abandoned you.

WOMAN'S VOICE.   We won't laugh. [GOYA *gets up, glances wildly at "The Busybodies" and crosses right. When he is about to exit, he hears* MARIQUITA'S VOICE.]

MARIQUITA'S VOICE.   You're not old yet, Francho. Will you look for the button or will you lock the door . . . to remember? [GOYA *hesitates.*] If it were in the jewel case, would you believe me?

VOICES OF THE TWO WOMEN.   You are alone.

[GOYA *exits. A long pause during which the central painting changes to "The Fates." From offstage left, panting sounds from* LEOCADIA *who is climbing the stairs with effort. Reaching the landing, she stops to get her breath and enters. Her hair uncombed, she shows the effects of the hard duties required of her since the departure of the servants. She is almost ugly. She is wearing a cloth shawl over her shoulders. She is carrying the lighted brazier and has a broom under her arm. She is a bit surprised not to see Goya. She lets the broom drop to the floor and places the brazier on its table. After arranging it, she takes a look over the balcony. She sighs, steps back, and picks up the broom with a weak groan that betrays her aches and pains. Trembling with cold, she peers through the door at right. Hearing nothing, she begins to sweep the floor. In a few seconds, "The Busybodies" happens to catch her eye; she stops sweeping, uneasy. Then she looks right again. She returns to her work but it is obvious that she is upset by what she thinks the painter may be doing.* GOYA *returns moments later. He is walking straight, with his hands in the pockets of his dressing gown. There is a gleam in his eyes, and he appears rejuvenated. For a few moments they stand looking at each other.*]

GOYA. [*Harshly*]   You were late getting back. [*Wearily, she begins to sign. He interrupts her with a curt gesture.*] I know! You were buying firewood, feeding the horses . . . [LEOCADIA *resumes her work.* GOYA *advances, looking at her with anger.*] I don't want your bleeding-martyr looks! New servants will come! [*She shakes her head.*] Gumersinda will bring them! [*She stops sweeping and makes a scornful face. He goes to the balcony and rubs his hands together as he searches for words. She notices his tension and is disturbed.*] Hasn't the postman come? [*He turns around to look at her. She makes a negative gesture with her arms.* GOYA *continues in a mild voice.*] And yesterday afternoon . . . no one came? [*After a moment, she shakes her head.* GOYA *steps toward her quickly and then stops. Alarmed by the look on his face, she steps back. He looks away, sits down on the sofa, and warms his hands over the brazier. Glancing at him furtively, she resumes her work.* GOYA'S *voice gives her a jolt.*] Come here. [*She obeys.* GOYA *has spoken without looking at her and he continues with his eyes fixed on the brazier.*] Are you still afraid? [*She nods. He looks up at her.*] Eh? [*She nods again.*] I'd say you weren't. You don't speak of leaving any more . . . [LEOCADIA *shakes her head wearily, expressing the futility of further discus-*

sion, and starts to leave.] Wait! Why have you lost your fear? [*She doesn't manage an answer.*] Isn't it a singular change? The intrepid Amazon, the coquette who dreams of France, works like a beast and has no time to be afraid. But she doesn't complain . . . [*Brief pause.* LEOCADIA *sits beside him.*] And there are no more crosses on the door, and no more rocks through the windows. But I haven't made a deal with anyone. [*Very softly*] Have you? [LEOCADIA *looks down. Her breathing has altered noticeably.*] No answer? [*She slips her hand over his on the sofa.*] Is this your answer? [LEOCADIA *lifts* GOYA's *hand to her face and places a long kiss on his palm.*] What are you up to? [*She places his hand against her cheek and signs with her free hand.* GOYA *smiles sarcastically.*] Have you said you love me? [*She nods, caressing and kissing his hand.*] Then answer my question. [*She makes a gesture of desperation and signs.*] And what have I done all these years but shelter you?

LEOCADIA. [*Embracing him*]   «Continue sheltering me . . . you must understand.» [*Abruptly her kisses become ardent. She kisses him on the mouth. She slips into his lap. She grabs Goya's hand and moves it over her body, pressing close to him. Pushing her away with all his strength,* GOYA *stands up. She holds out her arms pleadingly and then lets them fall inert at her side.*] «Save me.»

GOYA.   Whore. [*In tears, she shakes her head.* GOYA *reaches into his pocket and takes out a metal button which he holds up.* LEOCADIA *stifles a scream.* GOYA *makes an affirmative gesture and places the button on the table.*] It's better there. Out of its hiding place. The missing button from a pimp's jacket that you put away like some jewel. [*She shakes her head almost imperceptively. At the same time* LEOCADIA'S VOICE *is heard in the air.* GOYA *is momentarily taken aback.*]

LEOCADIA'S VOICE.   Take me!

GOYA.   A fine fellow, wasn't he! Handsome, tall . . . everything you lacked, and suddenly you had it. A stud to service you and assure the safety of this house. As payment, your body. But you gave it willingly. [*She denies it. We hear her voice again in the air.*]

LEOCADIA'S VOICE.   Do whatever you want. . . .

GOYA.   Don't deny it. Don't try your love farce on me! I won't forgive you for that. You were offering yourself to a disgusting old man while you were thinking of him. [*She shakes her head convulsively, but at the same time her voice sounds in the air:*]

LEOCADIA'S VOICE.   You *are* a disgusting old man. . . .

GOYA. [*Inflamed by the tricks his mind is playing on him, of which she is unaware.*]   You can't get him out of your mind since you rolled about with him yesterday in this very room! [*Denying it with her gestures, she pleads with him on her knees. But her voice comes through the air.*]

LEOCADIA'S VOICE.   You're seventy-six years old! [GOYA *turns red and rushes toward her with his hands like claws.*]

GOYA.   Filthy Bitch! [*He seizes her by the neck. She manages to get away from him and stand up, moving back from him. His features are contracted; he fights back the tears; very softly he murmurs:*] Seventy-six. [*From the opposite side of the brazier* LEOCADIA *begins timid signs that he refuses to watch. She comes a few steps closer.*] Leave me alone. [*He looks at her with hatred and sadness.*] Go! [*She shakes her head and begins her pathetic pantomime. She points to the outside, to the lover who is attributed to her, and to herself; she joins her two index fingers and denies with her head. Then she kisses her fingers as a cross and raises her right hand in a gesture of swearing.*] Spare me your lies. [*She kisses her crossed fingers again and denies vehemently. She runs to the table, picks up the metal button and shows it to him.* GOYA *looks at her fixedly. She points to the floor—the house—and shakes her head. Then she points toward the outside.* GOYA'S *voice has a terrible resonance.*] You did not find it in the dust of the road. He gave it to you! [*She affirms what he has said energetically.*] Then? [LEOCADIA *sighs, resolved to continue, and she repeats, pointing to the floor, her denial; then pointing to the outside, she sketches the shape of a bridge in the air.*]

LEOCADIA.   «The bridge.»

GOYA.   He gave it to you on the bridge? [*She nods.*] He was walking with you. [*She nods.* GOYA *takes the button from her hand and holds it up.*] And you accepted his gift! [*Embarrassed, she traces a few signs. Pause.* GOYA *puts the button on the table.*] From fear? [*She nods. He grabs her suddenly.*] And why didn't you throw it in the river?

LEOCADIA.   «You're hurting me!»

GOYA. [*Releasing her violently*]   More lies!

LEOCADIA. [*Shaking her head and pointing outside*]   «He . . .» [*She points to herself.*] «Me . . .» [*Her hand describes the syllables that come from her mouth.*] «Said . . .» [*Her finger points to the outside and traces a trajectory to the house.*] «He'll come . . .» [*Points to the floor*] «Here . . .» [*Vague gesture*] «One day . . .» [*She points to the table and mimes the action of picking something up.*] . . . to get the button.

GOYA.   He'll come one day so that you can return it to him? [*She nods.*] You lie.

LEOCADIA.   «I swear it's true.» [GOYA *is uncertain. Exhausted, she starts to sit near the brazier.* GOYA'S *VOICE sounds in the air.*]

GOYA'S VOICE.   "Who would believe it."
   [*Brief pause. We hear a soft meowing.* GOYA *reacts. After a moment of silence,* LEOCADIA'S *VOICE is heard in the air. It comes in sonorous gusts that almost fade into inaudibility at times.*]

LEOCADIA'S VOICE.   Don't you believe your Judith? Your Judas? . . . I'll put an end to you. Judith will take her knife, while the cats wail and the bat flutters in the air and drinks your blood and Judas kisses you and Judith kisses you and sinks the blade into you and screams that you tried to strangle her and she had to defend herself. Beware of Judith, beware of the king; the king is the scaffold and Judith is hell. . . . [GOYA *takes her by the hair and turns her head so that he can look into her eyes.*]

GOYA.   How to know? [*She looks at him, her teeth clenched. Her voice vibrates in the air and echoes back.*]

LEOCADIA'S VOICE.   A fiery shroud envelopes you and turns to ice. I'll ride by laughing on the croup of a horse as you lie in your icy wrappings. . . . [LEOCADIA *hears something as the words echo; she points left.*]

LEOCADIA.   «Someone's knocking . . . » [*She touches the painter's arm to draw him from his abstraction.*] «They're knocking.» [GOYA *slowly comes out of his delirium.*]

GOYA.   Someone's knocking at the door? [*She nods. He motions her to wait and crosses to look from the balcony.* LEOCADIA *stands up, expectant.*] Doctor Arrieta. [LEOCADIA *exits left.* GOYA *remains at the balcony and withdraws into himself again.*]

MARIQUITA'S VOICE. [*Very lightly*]   Buttons are not given as presents in the street but in the bedroom. [GOYA *closes his eyes.*] Search for me. You're not too old for me. Fathers aren't old to their children, and Asmodea is a thousand years old. I'll take you by the hand, my little child, and you'll never come back.

GOYA. [*He mutters somberly.*]   I won't come back. [*He turns around slowly.* LEOCADIA *and* ARRIETA *enter left.*] Don Eugenio, come in and have a seat. It's a comfort to know that friends remember you. [ARRIETA *makes an affable gesture and signs with his hands as he crosses to the brazier.* GOYA *is looking at* LEOCADIA.] Yes . . . yesterday I was walking in the hills. [ARRIETA *signs as he sits down.*] There's no reason to worry. They've left us in peace! [ARRIETA *indicates his doubt; he appears tired.*] Leo, bring some wine. Even if the doctor doesn't approve. [ARRIETA *does not protest, and* GOYA *observes him closely.* LEOCADIA *exits right. The painter sits near the warmth of the brazier and holds his hands over it.*] Are you ill? You don't look well. [ARRIETA *shakes his head weakly.*] Is something wrong? [ARRIETA *responds with a vague gesture and begins to sign.*] Thank you, I'm fine. [*More signs*] Melancholy. Personal things. [ARRIETA *signs.*] Also concern for Zapater. I still haven't heard from him. [*Brief pause. The doctor points to him and to his ear and makes circular motions in the air.* GOYA *is slow to respond.*] A tiny voice . . . from time to time. I pay it no mind. [*A few signs*] In the hills? What about it? [ARRIETA *points to his own eye and describes the movements of the flyers with his hand.* LEOCADIA *enters with a tray, a jug of wine, and two glasses already filled. The doctor stands up, and* LEOCADIA *serves the wine.*]

ARRIETA.   «Thank you, señora.»

LEOCADIA. [*As she crosses to put the tray on the table*] «I'll leave you
with him, doctor. I still must prepare dinner. Will you excuse
me?»

ARRIETA.   «By all means, señora.»

[GOYA *watches them talking with the irremediable suspicion of the
deaf. As she walks by,* LEOCADIA *picks up the broom and shows it to*
ARRIETA.]

LEOCADIA. «I didn't finish sweeping. We can't get servants.» [ARRIETA
bows and LEOCADIA *exits left. He sits again. Silence.*]

GOYA. [*He looks at* ARRIETA *askance and decides to speak.*]   I haven't
seen the Bird-Men again, if that's what you were asking. [*Assent
from* ARRIETA] And you, Don Eugenio, what have you seen? [*A sad
shrug of the shoulders from the doctor.*] Chains of prisoners, insults
from the mob, corpses along the roads. [ARRIETA *looks down.*]
Men are beasts . . . . And something else I can't find words to
explain. Something I've noted since I lost my hearing and entered
the other world . . . . [ARRIETA *is interested but silent.*] Yes. People
laugh, move, speak to me . . . . I see them dead. And then I wonder if I'm not the one who's dead. I used to love life. Picnics on
the grass, games, songs, girls. Deafness came and I understood
that life is death. A manikin dressed as a duchess laughs and
sways in silence. She's not human. In my arms she speaks words
I don't know and I tell her sweet nothings that I hear only inside
my brain. In the war I saw the wounded scream. It was the
same. Puppets. Bombs exploded and I only imagined a great
laughter . . . . That's why I love people so much; because I could
never give myself completely to them nor they to me. I love
them because it's impossible for me to love them. I've forgotten
my children's voices. I've never heard Leocadia or Mariquita. I'll
die imagining them. How can I ever know who they are? [*Lowering his voice*] How can I know who you are? . . . Ghosts. Am I
really speaking with someone? I know. Arrieta's ghost is going to
tell me I'm deaf. But all that estrangement . . . must mean something more. [ARRIETA *nods.*] Yes? Is it something more? [ARRIETA
nods vigorously.] What? [ARRIETA *signs.* GOYA *reflects a moment.*]
We're all deaf? [ARRIETA *nods.*] I don't understand you. [ARRIETA *is
about to explain further and* GOYA *stops him.*] Yes. Yes, I do understand. Pity us all! [*There are tears in* GOYA'S *eyes.* ARRIETA *places his
hand on* GOYA'S.] Why do we go on living? [ARRIETA *indicates the
walls with a circular gesture.*] To paint like that? These walls are
oozing fear. [ARRIETA *looks surprised.*] Yes, fear! Art cannot be
good if it is born from fear. [ARRIETA *nods his agreement and signs.*]
Against fear? . . . [ARRIETA *nods.*] And who triumphs in those
paintings—courage or fear? [*Indecision from* ARRIETA] I delighted
in painting beautiful forms, and these are filled with maggots. I
drank in all the colors of the world, and on these walls darkness

is draining away the color. I loved reason and I paint witches . . . Yes, in "Asmodea" there is a hope, but so fragile . . . . [*He stands and walks about.* ARRIETA *bows his head.* GOYA *points upstage.*] Look at "The Fates." And the devil-worshipper laughing between them. Well, someone is laughing. It's all too horrible for no one to have a good laugh. I'm the puppet one of them is holding. They'll cut the thread, and the devil's priest will laugh at the rag of flesh whose name was Goya. But I foresaw it! There it is! [ARRIETA *signs.*] Why should I leave Spain? I'll not crawl for a villain like him. I'll paint my fear. [*He grabs the glass he had left on the brazier table and drains it.*] Shall we get drunk, Don Eugenio? [ARRIETA *shakes his head sadly. Impulsively,* GOYA *presses his shoulder.*] Forgive me, I've made you sad.

ARRIETA. [*Shaking his head and signing*] «I have my troubles too.»

GOYA.   Drown them in wine! [*He is about to take the doctor's glass but* ARRIETA *stops him, his expression altered.* GOYA *goes to the table and pours himself a glass of wine, observing his friend out of the corner of his eye.*] You've seemed troubled ever since you arrived. [ARRIETA *looks at him and then turns his eyes away.* GOYA *takes a sip of wine.*] You're keeping something from me. [ARRIETA *signs.* GOYA, *who watches him attentively, suddenly drains his glass and places it angrily on the table.*] You too? [*He goes toward the doctor.* ARRIETA *nods with a hopeless look in his eyes.*] When did they put the cross on your door? [ARRIETA *signs.*] Why have you come? You should hide. [*Signs*] I'm like an oak! [*Signs*] But you're a doctor. [*He goes up behind him and places his hands on* ARRIETA'S *shoulders.*] And my friend. [*Brief pause*] A good doctor. A good painter. Crosses on their doors. Poor Spain. [ARRIETA *stands and walks about in gloom.*] Is there no powerful person among your patients to turn to? [ARRIETA *points to his head, indicating that he is giving it thought.*] If you don't find something better, come to this house. [ARRIETA *smiles, points to him, and traces a cross in the air.*] The cross on my door crucifies me, not you! You'd be in less danger living here. You could celebrate Christmas Eve with us. And you could stay on. [*Timidly*] We'd both be less alone. . . . [ARRIETA *motions to him to be quiet and points left.*] Did the bell ring? [ARRIETA *nods.* GOYA *runs to the balcony.*] The postman! He's finally come! [*We begin to hear the heartbeats, which continue during the scene.* ARRIETA *turns toward the door. Moments later,* LEOCADIA *appears in the doorway with a letter in her hand.* GOYA *goes to meet her.*] Give it to me. [*She hands him the letter. He reads the address.*] Martín Zapater's handwriting. [*"The Fates" slowly changes into "Witches' Sabbath." With the sealed letter in his hand,* GOYA *ponders.*] If I didn't open it . . . [LEOCADIA *and the doctor exchange looks of surprise.*] It would be as if I'd never received it.

LEOCADIA. [*After a moment, with a gesture*]   «Shall I open it for you?»

GOYA.   I could tear it up without reading it. Not from fear but to com-
bat fear. [*He laughs.* ARRIETA *takes a step toward him, uneasy.*] I'm a
fool. I'm trapped and I must play the game to the end. [*He goes to
the table, puts on his glasses, and reads the letter. Then he looks up.
He seems to be deep in thought.*] Don Eugenio, go back to Madrid
and seek friends. My offer stands. [*He leaves his glasses on the
table, puts the letter in his pocket and slowly walks upstage. As he
passes by* LEOCADIA, *she stops him.*]

LEOCADIA.   «What does it say?»

GOYA.   The letter? Dear Martín is worried. He hasn't heard from me
in more than a month. [*He moves on and takes up his palette and
brushes.* LEOCADIA *does not conceal her terror.*] My letter was intercepted. If there is a Green Book, I must be in it. The despot is
thinking of me.

[LEOCADIA *bursts into inaudible moans and slumps down on a chair.*
ARRIETA *runs to her side to calm her. For a moment,* GOYA *watches
her dramatic reaction from his island of deafness and then starts to
paint. The light fades to total darkness; the heartbeats diminish until
there is total silence.*]

Scene 3

The lights come up on the downstage area. At right, FATHER DUASO *and*
ARRIETA *sit looking at each other. The rest of the stage is dark.*

DUASO.   Tomorrow is Christmas Eve. I promised Goya to visit him
today. I'll go after eight. Will you accompany me, Doctor Arrieta?

ARRIETA. [*With a slight bow*]   Perhaps it would be better if we talked
afterwards, if you have other obligations.

DUASO. [*Smiling*]   My time is my own.

ARRIETA. [*Somewhat perplexed*]   Then . . . we could talk on the way, if
we leave now. It's quite a distance, and it will already be dark at
eight.

DUASO. [*After a moment*]   We can chat better here. [ARRIETA *raises his
eyebrows; he doesn't understand.*] Is something wrong with our
friend?

ARRIETA.   Father Duaso, I know that I can trust you. . . .

DUASO.   You may be sure of that.

ARRIETA.   Goya must go into hiding.

DUASO.   What's happened?

ARRIETA.   A letter he wrote to Martín Zapater has been intercepted.
And he criticized the king in it. [DUASO *sits up in surprise.*]

DUASO.   How do you know it was intercepted?

ARRIETA.   Zapater has not received it.

DUASO.   When was it sent?

ARRIETA.   Twenty-two days ago.

DUASO. [*Startled*]   Twenty-two days? [*He calculates on his fingers.*] You're not mistaken?

ARRIETA.   No.

DUASO. [*After a moment of thought*]   Goya must beg the king's pardon without delay. I'll go with him myself.

ARRIETA.   Father Duaso, no one has ever known the king to forgive an offense. I beg you to persuade Goya to go into hiding this very day. . . .

DUASO.   Where could he go?

ARRIETA. [*Hesitating*]   I doubt that his son and daughter-in-law would want to take him in.

DUASO.   What about his friends?

ARRIETA.   Don Francisco has only two friends left.

DUASO.   You and I?

ARRIETA.   That's right. And I can't offer him asylum because, as you perhaps know, they've painted a cross on my door too.

DUASO. [*Coldly*]   I didn't know. Do you think me capable of taking part in those depraved actions?

ARRIETA.   I only meant that you might know of it, as you know of other incidents.

DUASO.   Then you too are in danger?

ARRIETA. [*Shrugging*]   Who isn't?

DUASO.   And you've come to seek help for . . . Goya?

ARRIETA.   You are a friend and fellow countryman of his—not mine.

DUASO. [*He smiles.*]   We'll save Goya. I'll protect you. And I trust it will convince you that we aren't as monstrous as the liberals claim.

ARRIETA.   Certainly you aren't. I only pray to heaven that you don't become a victim yourself.

DUASO.   I don't understand you.

ARRIETA. [*Gravely*]   I'm well acquainted with the excesses of fanaticism. We also suffered under the liberal triennium. Today they call the losers Masons; tomorrow they'll say the same of people like you.

DUASO. [*Haughtily*]   Who are "they"?

ARRIETA.   The most fanatical. They'll turn against you and perhaps against the king himself.

DUASO.   What are you saying, my son!

ARRIETA.   I foresee it. The king will set up bullfighting schools and close the universities. But perhaps it will be in vain . . . . There is a tremendous tumor growing in our country and we all want to be surgeons. Blood has run and it will run again, but the tumor will remain. I wonder whether physicians will come someday to cure us or whether the bloodletters will go on cutting us up.

DUASO. [*Sighing*]   Man is sinful, and neither you nor I can remedy that. So, let us be humble and save Goya.

ARRIETA.   You will save him. But my mind won't be at ease.

DUASO.   Why not?

ARRIETA.   Saving Goya may destroy him. Under the threat of the man
he has insulted he walks a line between terror and insanity. And
in that strange struggle of his soul, should I, an ordinary man,
quicken the terror of a titan so that he will cease to be what he is?

DUASO.   For his health's sake, we must.

ARRIETA.   And for his life's sake. Because I am a doctor! And, besides,
he's no longer a great painter . . . only an old man who puts
smudges on the walls.

DUASO.   Then . . .

ARRIETA.   That's what I want to believe but I'm not sure! What if those
nightmares he paints on the walls are great works? And what if
his strength is in his madness? Would I want a giant to become a
pygmy because I am a pygmy?

DUASO.   You'll carry out your duty as I do mine.

ARRIETA. [Looking at him intensely]   If I were you, Father Duaso, I
wouldn't be so calm either.

DUASO.   What do you mean?

ARRIETA.   I chose to live in shame and therefore I chose silence. I'm
going to break that silence, because your honesty is obvious to
me . . . and because I'm already marked.

DUASO. [Without emotion]   Think before you speak, my son.

ARRIETA.   Let's suppose, Father Duaso . . . it's only a supposition . . .
that His Majesty hesitated to cause a scandal by executing Don
Francisco. He's a renowned artist, he wasn't involved in politics.

DUASO.   It would demonstrate that the king is not incapable of benev-
olence.

ARRIETA.   Or of showing caution. And let us suppose he stopped short
of a sanction with possible repercussions but wanted to take
revenge on the painter. [ARRIETA ignores a reaction of displeasure
from DUASO over his choice of words.] If the proud Goya begged the
king's pardon tearfully and retracted like poor Riego, His Majesty
would be satisfied for the moment.

DUASO.   Doctor Arrieta, I cannot permit you . . .

ARRIETA. [Cutting him short]   Then I won't go on. [Pause]

DUASO.   Forgive me. Continue.

ARRIETA.   Thank you. Since Goya won't set foot in the palace, it would
not be difficult for the king to send someone to suggest it to him.
[DUASO's expression changes.] Understand me, Father, a man desir-
ous of helping a friend . . . who, without being aware of it, is col-
laborating in the royal plan: that the recalcitrant Aragonese
becomes the trembling wreck of a man.

DUASO.   You contradict yourself.

ARRIETA.   No! If Goya accedes, it will prove that he is afraid; if he
doesn't, he'll be taught to fear.

DUASO.   You're misinterpreting the situation!

ARRIETA.   Did you know of the existence of Goya's letter?

DUASO.   With God as my witness, no!

ARRIETA.   I believe you. Am I equally wrong to think that the king has spoken to you about Goya?

DUASO.   [*Wavering*]   I'm not going to answer any more questions.

ARRIETA.   Allow me a few words more. A rumor has reached me that confirms the goodness of your heart, Father Duaso.

DUASO.   What rumor?

ARRIETA.   That you are already hiding in this house some of your fellow-countrymen who are in danger.

DUASO.   They say that?

ARRIETA.   It is the sad gazette of the conquered, whispered among trusted people . . . . I don't want to know if it's true; if Goya comes to your house, it will be. But you are a priest faithful to the throne. It's unbelievable that Father Duaso would shelter anyone, today or tomorrow, without counting beforehand on the royal tolerance. Or am I wrong?

DUASO.   [*After a moment*]   I beg you, spare me your questions.

ARRIETA.   I won't ask again. But I'll tell you my worst suspicion. You promised to visit our friend today. I'll not ask you why it must be after eight and under no circumstances before. [DUASO *looks at him with increasing anxiety.*] But I suspect we will be committing an irreparable error . . . if we don't hasten our visit to Goya and not wait for the stroke of eight. [DUASO *takes out his watch and looks at it nervously.*] But if you *must* not go before that hour . . . [*Watch still in hand,* DUASO *stands and looks at* ARRIETA; *terror comes over his face.* ARRIETA *stands too.*] Father Duaso, if you have been a pawn in some game, don't forget that there can be other pawns. [*Very affected and still trying to find a flaw, he reacts abruptly like someone who realizes he has fallen into a trap.*]

DUASO.   No one is going to play with me that way. If we hurry, we can reach his house at seven-thirty. Let's take my coach. [*He puts his watch away and, serene again, walks left.* ARRIETA *accompanies him and the light follows them.* DUASO *stops before he exits.*] Those paintings on the walls . . . are they really bad?

ARRIETA.   I don't believe they're good.

DUASO.   Why not?

ARRIETA.   He himself gave the answer in one of his etchings . . . "The Sleep of Reason produces monsters."

DUASO.   Always?

ARRIETA.   Perhaps not always . . . if reason does not sleep entirely.

DUASO. [*Sighs*]   Abyssus abyssum invocat . . . [*He exits followed by* ARRIETA. *Fadeout.*]

Scene 4

The stage lights come up slowly. The chairs that ARRIETA *and* DUASO *occupied have disappeared. In lamplight, resting on his arms at the far left of the table—and in the same position as in the famous etching—* GOYA *dozes. A cold lunar light enters through the balcony. Upstage, the "Old Men Eating Gruel" looms enormous. For several moments nothing happens. Then we hear two heavy blows on the door. The sleeping man stirs. With the blows, pale eerie lights invade the room. A third blow sounds, and the strange lights suddenly increase. The light from the lamp becomes a faint greenish glow. Half-illuminated by the light as it grows brighter, an unusual shape becomes visible at left. It is a* CARNIVAL FIGURE *with the mask of a decrepit old man whose ears are great bat wings. Seated on the brazier table with a thick closed book on his knees, he looks impassively at* GOYA. *There is the sound of huge wings in the air. Under the masked stare, the painter overcomes his drowsiness with effort and turns to look with surprise at the strange presence.*

GOYA.   Who are you? [THE FIGURE *does not answer. He opens the book and strikes it sharply a few times. Invoked by the action, another* CARNIVAL FIGURE *appears at right. It flaunts a cat head, and two enormous tits project under its rags. It is carrying an odd wire muzzle with a huge padlock into which a heavy key is inserted. The painter turns his head. At the same time the muffled sounds of small bells and flute-like laughs come from offstage and are repeated from time to time.* GOYA *puts his hands over his ears.*] Am I hearing?
[THE CAT FIGURE *goes up to* GOYA *and stops.* GOYA *looks at both apparitions.* THE BAT MAN *strikes the book lightly and the jangle of the bells grows louder.* GOYA *looks toward the door. Two other* CARNIVAL FIGURES *in pig masks rush in, shrieking stridently as they brandish heavy clubs. Rusty bells hang from their belts.*]
PIG FIGURES.   You don't know me! You don't know who I am! [*Repeating their chant and laughing, they go up to* GOYA, *lift him up by his armpits, and carry him to centerstage.*]
GOYA. [*Struggling*]   Don't touch me!
BAT-MAN.   "No man knows another." [*Another loud blow on the door.* THE MASKED FIGURES *become silent.*]
GOYA.   I only want to live my life.
[THE BAT-MAN *orders silence with a prolonged hiss and points to the table.* GOYA *watches. From behind the table another* MASKED FIGURE *emerges and sits delicately in the armchair.* THE FIGURE *is wearing a black cloak with a hood from which the large horns of a bull protrude. The face is a crude skull.*]
HORNED FIGURE. [*Raising its hand*]   In the name of the priest from Tamajón. [*Laughing,* THE PIG FIGURES *raise their clubs and position them over Goya's head.*]

BAT-MAN.   No. [*He strikes the book.*] See if he has a tail.

GOYA.   A tail? [*He tries to get free.*]

BAT-MAN. [*Reading from the book*]   Jews and Masons have tails. Our
   Lord Jesus Christ inflicted this infernal stigma on them as a
   warning to Christian souls. Proceed.

   [THE PIG FIGURES *turn* GOYA *around.*]

GOYA.   Don't you dare!

[*They lift his coattail and inspect.*]

BAT-MAN.   Does he have a tail?

FIRST PIG FIGURE.   A very long one.

SECOND PIG FIGURE.   Thick and hairy.

FIRST PIG FIGURE.   Very green.

GOYA.   You damn pigs!

SECOND PIG FIGURE.   And it moves.

GOYA.   I'll squash you, bandits. I'll rip you open like worms! . . .
   [THE HORNED FIGURE *makes a sign, and as* GOYA *is speaking* THE PIG
   FIGURES *give him half a turn.* THE CAT FIGURE *goes up and places the
   wire muzzle over Goya's face, fastening the lock with a noisy turn of
   the key. Although his lips continue to utter threats and insults behind
   the grill, the painter's voice is extinguished.*]

BAT-MAN.   Does the accused have something to say?

FIRST PIG.   Nothing. [GOYA *protests and moves his lips without making a
   sound.*]

SECOND PIG.   The accused confesses to possessing a tail.

BOTH PIGS.   He's a Mason and a Jew.

HORNED FIGURE.   His Majesty deigns to embroider a flower.

CAT FIGURE.   Long live the absolutely absolute king!

PIGS. [*As they whirl* GOYA *around, they chant.*]   Swallow it, dog! Dirty
   Freemason! You wanted to end the Inquisition! [*Then they oblige*
   GOYA *to prostrate himself on his knees and raise their clubs.* THE
   HORNED FIGURE *stands and extends its hands solemnly.*]

HORNED FIGURE.   Not yet.

BAT-MAN.   Release him. [THE TWO PIG FIGURES *release the painter and
   step back toward the doors on either side.* GOYA *watches them,
   expectant.*]

CAT FIGURE.   Meow!

BAT-MAN.   His Majesty deigns to embroider another flower. [THE
   HORNED FIGURE *approaches* GOYA *who collects himself and moves
   back toward an exit.* THE PIG FIGURE *that awaits him there raises a
   club and shakes its bells.* GOYA *attempts to cross to the other side,
   and* THE HORNED FIGURE *charges him like a bull.* GOYA *avoids the
   thrust and runs toward the other door. There the other* PIG FIGURE
   awaits him with club and bells. As he steps back, THE HORNED FIG-
   URE *charges again and grazes him. For a moment, the two look at
   each other, motionless.* THE HORNED FIGURE *charges again, and* GOYA
   barely evades him; he charges again and this time he knocks the

painter down. THE CAT FIGURE, *which has meowed at each charge, now lets out a strident howl, and the delighted* PIG FIGURES *jangle their bells.*] Enough. [THE HORNED FIGURE *lifts its head and stands rigid.*] You. [THE PIG FIGURES *begin to approach* GOYA *with clubs half-raised.*]

CAT FIGURE.   Death to the rebels!

BAT-MAN.   [*Reading from his book and talking through his nose in a bored manner*]   Declared a Jew, Mason, liberal, insubordinate, impertinent, incorrigible engraver, painter, masturbator . . .

CAT FIGURE.   "What a golden beak!" [THE PIG FIGURES *are near* GOYA *who is on the floor with his back to them.*]

BAT-MAN.   We deliver you to the secular arm.

CAT FIGURE.   Long live the spotless king and death to the nation!

PIG FIGURES.   [*They lift their clubs slowly and chant a deep accompaniment.*]   Swallow it, dog . . . etc.

[LEOCADIA *appears at the left dressed as the Judith of the painting and with a great knife in her hand.*]

LEOCADIA.   Quiet, all of you! [*They all look at her.* GOYA *lifts his head and sits up with visible fear.*] I shall be the secular arm. [GOYA *kneels. She goes to his side and, seizing him by his hair, she obliges him to bare his neck. When she extends the blade to cut off his head, there are fierce blows on the door.* LEOCADIA *straightens up, fearful. The painter's eyes gleam.*] They've come! [LEOCADIA *exits running at right.* THE BAT-MAN *slams his book shut and stands. The light fades quickly.*]

BAT-MAN.   They? [GOYA *beams with joy as he nods his head. The blows are repeated more urgently.* THE PIG FIGURES *hurriedly lift the painter and replace him in the chair where he was dozing.*] Who are they? [*A beating of giant wings in the air.* THE CAT FIGURE *hastens to open the lock and free Goya from the muzzle. The light returns eerily.*]

GOYA.   The flyers are knocking on all the doors of Madrid! [*A rain of blows on the door*]

ALL.   [*Except* GOYA *and* THE HORNED FIGURE]   No! [*They flee screaming and meowing through both doors.* THE HORNED FIGURE *lifts the painter's chin with unexpected gentleness. The only light comes from the moon and the lamp.*]

HORNED FIGURE.   I'll return. [*He slowly pushes Goya's head until the painter is once again dozing on his folded arms.* THE FIGURE *slips out stealthily and disappears right. Moments later a tremendous banging is heard. "Saturn," "Witches' Sabbath," and "Judith" appear on the upstage wall.* GOYA *rouses himself and looks up. The blows cease at that very moment.* GOYA *stands up, his eyes filled with a wild hope.*]

GOYA.   They're knocking so loud that even I can hear them! [*He runs to the balcony but is unable to distinguish anything. In her normal attire,* LEOCADIA *rushes in from right, horrified. She goes to Goya's side and tugs nervously at his arm.* GOYA *turns and she can only point to the door. Her throat is paralyzed. Rapid heartbeats begin suddenly and continue during the scene.* LEOCADIA *flees right, pulling free from the old man as he tries to hold her back.*] What's going on? [GOYA *is crossing left to look when* FIVE ROYAL VOLUNTEERS *appear in the doorway. Their only weapons are sabers. The chinstraps of their helmets frame their lascivious smiles. The first of the group is a good-looking, strutting* SERGEANT *with a full moustache. A button is missing from his uniform jacket. The two who follow him have their sabers unsheathed. One of the last pair is carrying a cloth bundle.* GOYA *runs to the chest to get his gun, but one of the soldiers with a saber is quicker and puts his hand on the gun while the other soldier subdues the painter.* THE SERGEANT *crosses and leans on the back of the sofa; he signals to the soldier carrying the bundle who tosses it on the sofa and then exits rapidly left with his companion.*] Thugs! [*One of the soldiers subduing Goya gives him a slap.*] You'll get what's coming to you! [*In the silence filled with heartbeats* THE SOLDIERS *laugh broadly without making a sound.* THE TWO SOLDIERS *drag Goya stumbling downstage.* THE SERGEANT *takes a gag from his pocket.*] Vermin! Let go! [THE SERGEANT *chokes off his words with the gag, knotting it roughly on Goya's neck. The painter growls and struggles in vain.* THE SERGEANT *leans back against the table, makes a sign, and* THE TWO ASSASSINS *throw the old man to the floor. When he gets to his knees and tries to stand, he receives a blow with the flat side of a saber.* GOYA *emits a ferocious grunt; he tries to get away but a second saber blow destroys his resistance. Then the two sabers fall repeatedly in quick rhythm on his body until he doubles over in pain.*]

MALE VOICE. [*In the air*] "For that you were born."

[*The* SECOND PAIR OF VOLUNTEERS *return from right bringing* LEOCADIA. GOYA *is no longer crying out against the gag and bears the blows in silence.* LEOCADIA, *disheveled and with her breasts exposed, is subjected to taunts and rough caresses. They force her to look and she screams. One of the men tries to kiss her, and the* SERGEANT *reacts.*]

SERGEANT.   «Keep your hands off that woman, I told you!»

[GOYA *is helpless and has fallen to the floor like a limp rag.* THE VOLUNTEERS *sheath their sabers, laughing and uttering insults. One of them goes to the sofa and unties the bundle, while the other one pulls Goya to his knees and holds up his head so that he can see.* THE FIRST VOLUNTER *now approaches with a "sambenito"—the penitent's gown of the Inquisition—which he holds up in front of Goya. Instead of the customary flames painted between the crosses, there are black silhouettes of clubs. They all laugh silently and the air is filled with the shrieks of bats and owls.* LEOCADIA *moans and makes inaudible pleas.* THE SERGEANT *and a* VOLUNTEER *support Goya while another* VOLUNTEER *puts the gown over the painter's head. Then they lift him under his arms and drag him to the chair where he had been dozing and seat him.* LEOCADIA *screams and struggles. The heartbeats and shrieks grow louder.*]

MALE VOICE. [*In the air*]   "Don't scream, silly fool."

FEMALE VOICE. [*In the air*]   "It's better to sit back and enjoy."

[GOYA *looks at* LEOCADIA. THE VOLUNTEER *goes to the sofa and returns with a cone-shaped cap, while two others tie the old man's hands and feet.*]

MALE VOICE. [*In the air*]   "All this and more!"

[*While the others stand laughing and mocking,* THE VOLUNTEER *who brought the penitent's cap takes from inside it a black wooden cross and puts it in the painter's bound hands. Then he puts the cap on his head, transforming Goya into one of the penitents he engraved and painted so many times.*]

FIRST VOLUNTEER.   «We'll crack your ugly skull.»

SECOND VOLUNTEER.   «With clubs!»

[*Smiling,* THE SERGEANT *crosses toward the sofa under the leering eyes of the* VOLUNTEER *who is holding* LEOCADIA. *The other three sway back and forth chanting in front of* GOYA.]

VOLUNTEERS.   «Swallow it, dog! Dirty Freemason! You wanted to end the Inquisition!» [*They shout in his face and then dance around in a chorus and repeat their soundless chant.* THE VOLUNTEER *who was holding Leocadia shoves her to the floor at Goya's feet. She grasps the chair, looking at the old man through her tears.* THE SERGEANT *signals from the sofa and the dancers join the other* VOLUNTEER, *still chanting snatches of the "Swallow it, dog . . . " The animal sounds die away gradually.*]

SERGEANT. [*Going over to the four* VOLUNTEERS *and speaking to them privately.*]   «Take what you want. The house is yours.»

FIRST VOLUNTEER. [*Smiling*]   «I'll try the bedrooms!»

SECOND VOLUNTEER. [*Eagerly*]   «Let's look for the food!»

[VOLUNTEERS *1 and 2 exit right, almost on tiptoe; on passing in front of the "Saturn," one of them makes a face of mock terror.* VOLUNTEERS *3 and 4 exit left with knowing winks. The animal sounds cease completely at this moment.* GOYA *looks at* THE SERGEANT *and at* LEOCADIA. *She continues watching the frightened painter. The heartbeats become stronger and faster. With his eyes fixed on* LEOCADIA, THE SERGEANT *calmly removes his helmet and tosses it on the sofa. Then he begins to unfasten his baldric. Suddenly* LEOCADIA *notices that there are no sounds in the room and looks up in fright. She does not dare to look behind her, for she senses that the sergeant is there. The heartbeats speed up. Goya's eyes are fixed on Leocadia. Then she turns around slowly and sees the smiling sergeant. He lets his baldric fall to the floor.* LEOCADIA *stifles a scream and runs upstage. But* THE SERGEANT *grabs her brutally, kisses her fiercely on the mouth, and drags her to the sofa. She struggles, the sofa is overturned, and the thrashing couple disappear behind it. At the same instant a tempest of sounds is unleashed. Shrieks, brays, crowing, and terrifying howls are added to the continuing heartbeats. The pandemonium goes on a few seconds and then calms down a bit, becoming long waves of laughter punctuated by diverse voices.*]

FEMALE VOICE. [*Ironic*] "Two of a kind."

MALE VOICE. [*Indignant*] "It's forbidden to watch." [GOYA *averts his eyes and gazes into the emptiness.*]

FEMALE VOICE. "Take advantage of the moment."

FEMALE VOICES. [*Over the laughter*] "And they are like animals." "And they are like animals."

MALE VOICE. "There's no hope now."

FEMALE VOICES. "And they are like animals."

MALE VOICE. "Why?" [*The shrieks and laughter stop.* GOYA *looks behind the overturned sofa. The heartbeats stop too.* MARIQUITA'S VOICE *is heard in the deep silence.*]

MARIQUITA'S VOICE. They're hurting me. [*The old man listens trembling.*] What's happening to me, Don Francho? They've broken my hand. My arm is melting. . . . I can't feel my legs, they're a puddle on the floor.

GOYA'S VOICE. "Truth died."

MARIQUITA'S VOICE. There's something slimy on my cheek. . . . I can't see. . . . Help me!

GOYA'S VOICE. "Divine Reason, don't spare a one of them."

MARIQUITA'S VOICE. [*Broken*] I can't . . . speak. My tongue . . . my mouth . . . is pus. [*Silence. With immense sorrow,* GOYA *looks again at the hidden pair. There is an avalanche of howls, and the heartbeats resume, strong and rapid.*]

GOYA'S VOICE. [*Very sonorous*] "There's no one to help us."

[*The uproar reaches its peak; then it slowly dies down: the cries cease, the heartbeats lose their rhythm and stop. Goya's head falls over as if he had fainted. Silence reigns again. The Sergeant's boots, which had been sticking out from behind the sofa, disappear. He stands up, his clothes in disarray. While he buttons up, he looks at Goya, who is motionless. He recovers his baldric and puts it on; he reaches for his helmet and places it on his head. He goes a few steps closer to the painter and looks at him for a moment with an ironic expression on his face. Then he turns around and grins at the woman lying on the floor. Fingering his empty buttonhole, he crosses in front of* GOYA, *goes to the table and searches. Smiling, he picks up the metal button. He holds it up so that* GOYA *can see and then puts it away arrogantly. His expression becomes serious; he checks the time on the table clock and walks upstage with a military gait, clapping his hands and shouting inaudibly.*]

SERGEANT. «Pascual, Basilio! Get a move on you! It's time to go!» [*He claps again.*] «Hurry!» [*Moments later two of the* VOLUNTEERS *appear. One of them is carrying a small wooden box in one hand. He is taking bites from a large cake he has in his other hand.* THE SECOND VOLUNTEER *is holding a ham and is eating something.* THE SERGEANT *opens the box and approves with a quick gesture. He goes back to Goya's side. The painter can hardly open his glassy eyes.* THE SER-GEANT *lifts Goya's head and indicates with his free hand for him to wait as he says:*] «We'll be back!» [*Then he exits left, followed by the two* VOLUNTEERS *who nudge each other and point at Leocadia's body.*]

[*A long pause, during which "Saturn" and "Judith" slowly fade.* LEOCADIA *pulls herself up and slowly stands, revealing her loose clothing and battered face. Supporting herself against the sofa, she looks at the figure dressed in the penitent's gown and cap.* GOYA *stares at her without blinking. The "Witches' Sabbath" grows in size. In tears,* LEOCADIA *takes a few uncertain steps, but there is something in Goya's eyes that stops her. But she goes to him, kneels down, and unties his feet. Then she stands, takes the cross from his hands, and unties the cords that hold his arms. Reacting to the pain in his shoulders,* GOYA *lifts his arms and unties the gag, spitting the rag from his mouth. When he stands, he is like a huge grotesque puppet. With an angry swipe of his hand, he knocks the cap from his head. He keeps on looking at* LEOCADIA. *Suddenly he runs upstage, although the beating he has received makes him limp and groan.* LEOCADIA *runs to his assistance, but he stops and refuses her aid.*]

GOYA.   You brought them here. [*She shakes her head weakly.*] For your own shameful pleasure. [*She denies it again. He grabs the gun, cocks it, and puts a trembling hand on the trigger.*]

LEOCADIA. [*Frightened*]   «Francho!» [*She steps back in terror and stumbles over the overturned sofa. Filled with pain and anger,* GOYA *moves slowly downstage.*]

GOYA.   Don't move! And beg God to forgive you. [*He keeps the gun raised from downstage.*] Are you praying? [*With her back still to him, she nods. He thrusts the gun in her face.*]

LEOCADIA. [*Her voice, sorrowful and serene, is perfectly audible.*]   Shoot me. [*Without lowering the gun,* GOYA *reacts and listens to the voice he thinks he has heard. For the moment he perceives nothing. Her voice rises and falls like gusts of wind.*] I'll go on giving myself to others if you don't kill me. I'm guilty, but I don't know who bears the greater guilt. [GOYA *slowly lowers the gun and continues to stare at Leocadia's neck.*] My poor Francho, I've loved you without knowing you. You lived behind a wall, and still I stayed at your side . . . watching over you, enduring a fear that was not yours. The lonely nights . . . the cold bed. From my bedroom I could hear you moan in your sleep, knowing that you would come to me no more . . . and preferring it that way, for you were only a tired old man. Alone, trying to save my children and this house and you and me from your awful obstinacy . . . [*She begins to turn around slowly as her voice continues clearly. She gives* GOYA *an anguished look and bows her head.*] I should have gone along with

the sergeant, given him promises. . . . We were at his mercy . . .
And I don't know if I called him with my desire. . . . Shoot me. [*A
pause*] What else do you want? Your suspicions torment you. . . .
[GOYA *listens with a stunned expression.* A VOICE *is heard in the air,
and he looks up.*]

MALE VOICE.   "There is no one to help us."

LEOCADIA.   I won't lie to you . . . . He was brutal and he hurt me. Yet I
was like a bitch in heat. I was eager . . . under your very eyes. . .
I was thinking with horror . . . and pleasure . . . of our first times
together. I used to think of other men when I gave myself to you;
now I'll think of you when I give myself to other men. [*With a
moan*] Untie my life. Open the only door that's left. [*A silence. He
props the gun against the table.*]

GOYA. [*To himself*]   I'll never know what you've said. [*He steps forward.*] But perhaps I've understood you at last. [*He stops centerstage and smiles sadly.*] And you've understood me. How funny! A
puppet show! Come in, ladies and gentlemen. Laugh at the jeal-
ousy of the old Methuselah and the tricks of the cunning young
soldier. . . . The old fool threatens his young mistress because he
doesn't dare to defy the others. That's the way it was! When they
came in, I didn't reach the gun in time because I didn't want to.
Because I didn't dare. Pure comedy! [LEOCADIA *breaks into sobs,
runs to his side, and throws her arms around him.*]

LEOCADIA.   «Francho!» [*A pause*]

MALE VOICE.   "There's no one who can break our bond."

[GOYA *crumples under his sorrow.*]

LEOCADIA.   «My poor Francho, they've destroyed you!»

GOYA.   Help me. [*Leaning on her, he walks to a chair and sits, stifling his
moans of pain.*]

LEOCADIA.   «Francho, go to bed. I'll take care of you.» [*She tries to
remove the penitent's gown, but he objects.*]

GOYA.   I'm not hurt. They hit me with the flat of their swords. [*She
signs rapidly.*] No, no. There's nothing left to do but rot away as I
paint the decay around me. [*She puts her hand on his shoulder and
looks at him, frightened by the wild deranged look in his eyes. He
murmurs incoherently.* LEOCADIA *hears something from left.*] "It's the
same everywhere, . . . this is how it happened . . . it always happens."

[*Wary and scared,* GUMERSINDA *appears from left carrying a sack of
provisions.*]

GUMERSINDA.   «What happened?»

LEOCADIA.   «The Royal Volunteers.» [GUMERSINDA'S *hand goes to her
mouth.*]

GOYA.   Who is it? [GUMERSINDA *leaves the sack on a chair and crosses,
not believing what she sees. After making sure that the figure in the
penitent's gown is her father-in-law, she reacts with an excessive dis-*

play of indignation.] Is it you, Gumersinda? Did you bring the Christmas wreaths? There will be no celebration now. . . .

GUMERSINDA.   «Help me get this horrible thing off him!» [*She tries to remove the gown and he resists.*]

GOYA.   Leave it be. They don't want me to take it off, and I must obey. [*It is unclear whether he is actually deranged or is making a joke.*] I'll ask Vicente López to give me drawing lessons . . . And you, Gumersinda . . . [*She has moved back a few steps in her amazement. She is convinced he has gone mad and screams.*] Stop screaming! Come here. [*She obeys, managing to control herself.*] I want to ask you to take me to my son and grandson. If I stay here, they'll beat me to death with their clubs. [GUMERSINDA *shakes her head repeatedly and starts screaming again.*]

GUMERSINDA.   «You can't go there!»

GOYA. [*Lifting himself up with effort*]   Are you denying me asylum?

GUMERSINDA. [*She spreads her arms wide and then joins her hands in supplication*]   «They'll beat us all! You can't come to our house! You must understand! No! No!» [*She screams hysterically.*]

GOYA. [*As she screams*]   It's my son's house, and I deeded it to you as I've deeded this place to you! [*His voice has gained strength; he is incensed.*] I'm asking you to save me! And not scream at me! [*Before the unleashed negatives of his daughter-in-law*] Shut up! [*He slaps her.* GUMERSINDA *swallows hard, and her inaudible screams stop on the spot. Then she frets silently and backs away.* GOYA *gains control of himself and smiles sadly.*] Once again I've turned my anger on the wrong person. The comedy all over again. Am I no better than those scoundrels? [*Pause.*] What have they turned me into, Leocadia? [*To himself*] What have I done to myself? [LEOCADIA *touches his arm, looking left. Alarmed,* GUMERSINDA *turns to look too.* FATHER DUASO *and* DOCTOR ARRIETA *rush in and with one glance understand what has happened.*]

ARRIETA.   «Too late!»

DUASO.   «Assist me, doctor.» [*He starts to remove the penitent's gown from Goya.*]

GOYA.   No! No!

DUASO. [*Energetically*]   «Yes!» [*Between them they remove the gown, which* DUASO *throws on the floor with scorn.* GOYA *rubs his sore shoulder.*]

ARRIETA. [*To* LEOCADIA]   «Did they beat him?» [*She nods.* ARRIETA *puts his hand on the painter's forehead and signs rapidly.*]

GOYA.   I can still stand . . . even though I'm old. [*With deep melancholy*] Yes. I'm just a feeble old man. An old man at the edge of the grave. [ARRIETA *shakes his head in disagreement.*] A country at the edge of the grave, whose reason sleeps . . . [*The others are perplexed.*] I don't know what I'm saying. Father Duaso, I've lived too long.

MALE VOICE. [*Very softly*] "If it dawns, we will go away."

GOYA. [*Who has heard it*] Look at what they made me wear! They'll come back with their clubs. [*He takes hold of Duaso's cassock. The priest takes him by the hand, leads him to the table, and then writes.*] You command and I obey. I'll go to your house. [GUMERSINDA *runs to Duaso's side and kisses his hand as she mouths a confusion of words.* DUASO *solemnly cuts short her effusion and writes again.*] I give you my permission. When you think it prudent, beg His Majesty, in my name, to forgive me . . . [DUASO *lowers his troubled eyes.* GOYA *and* ARRIETA *exchange melancholy looks.*] And to grant his permission for me to go to France to take the waters in Plombières. [*Weighed down by the detested mission he is now concluding,* DUASO *nods sadly.* ARRIETA *withdraws somberly to one side.*]

FEMALE VOICE. [*Very softly*] "If it dawns, we will go."

GOYA. Leocadia, we'll have to be apart for some time. Will you pack my paintings, my portfolios, and my plates for me . . . . Please carry my things to Father Duaso's house. Then go to the house of Tiburcio Pérez with your children. Tell him that old Goya wishes him a happy Christmas and begs a corner of his home for you. [LEOCADIA *nods.*] Father Duaso, if I'm a long time in coming back to this woman, I ask you to watch over her. Don't let them harm her . . . because of me. [LEOCADIA *steps away deeply moved.* DUASO *and* ARRIETA *observe her with concern.* DUASO *nods.*]

MALE VOICE. I know that a man is finishing a piece of embroidery now . . .

GOYA. [*Absorbed*] And he says . . . it has turned out perfectly for me . . . . [ARRIETA *steps forward.* GOYA *looks at him.*] What did I say?

MALE VOICE. Who causes us to be afraid?

GOYA. The one who is dead from fear himself. A great fear in my stomach. They have conquered me. But he was already conquered.

DUASO. [*Taking him gently by the arm*] «Shall we go?»

GOYA. Yes, yes. Whenever you say. [*They start left.*]

MALE AND FEMALE VOICES. "If it dawns, we will go." [*Other whispers join the voices; tiny voices of both sexes that repeat, like the swelling and ebbing of the waves.*]

VOICES. "If it dawns, we will go!" "If it dawns, we will go!"

GOYA. Will the flyers come? [*The chorus of voices is augmented.*] And if they come, won't they treat us like dogs? [*A little laugh*] The dogs of Asmodea! [ARRIETA *takes him by the other arm.*]

ARRIETA. «Come, Don Francisco.»

[*They take a few steps.* GOYA *stops, breaks away from his friends and goes to Leocadia. The voices are multiplied.* GOYA *brings his face close to hers. They exchange looks for a moment; hers frightened and expectant, his desperately searching.*]

GOYA. I'll never know.

[DUASO *takes him gently by the arm again.* GOYA *whirls around and gives his paintings a farewell look. Contemplating them, a strange smile calms his face. Then he leans on his friends and walks left.* GUMERSINDA *joins the group, humbly mouthing words of comfort.* LEOCADIA *stands centerstage watching the old painter leave with a sorrowful and mysterious expression.*]

VOICES.   "If it dawns, we will go!"

[*Repeating and repeating the phrase, the confusion of* VOICES *advances like a hurricane on the entire theatre, as the stage lights fade and a huge projection of the "Witches' Sabbath" shines through the deafening din.*]

Curtain

Goya's "Black Paintings"

[In order of first occurrence in the stage directions of *The Sleep of Reason*]

Spanish titles   English translation in play

Part One, Scene 2

1. "Aquelarre"   "Witches' Sabbath"
2. "Saturno"   "Saturn"
3. "Judith"   "Judith"
4. "Asmodea"   "Asmodea" ["Fantastic Vision"]
5. "Las fisgonas"   "The Busybodies"
6. "La Leocadia" ["Una manola"]   "Leocadia"
7. "El santo oficio"   "The Holy Office"
8. "Dos frailes"   "Two Friars"
9. "La romería"   "The Pilgrimage"

Part One, Scene 3

10. "La lectura"   "The Reading"
11. "Riña a garratazos"   "Fight with Clubs"
12. "El perro"   "The Trapped Dog"

Part Two, Scene 2

13. "Las Parcas"   "The Fates"

Part Two, Scene 4

14. "Viejos comiendo sopas"   "Old Men Eating Gruel"

The FOUNDATION

Fable in Two Parts

Characters (in order of appearance)

THOMAS

THE MAN

BERTA

TULIO

MAX

ASEL

LINUS

THE SUPERINTENDENT

THE AIDE

FIRST WAITER

SECOND WAITER

VOICES

In a country whose name is unknown

Note: The stage setting and the physical changes that occur on it are described in the stage directions with an eye to the greatest technical simplicity. Directors can elaborate as their means permit and according to their own inventiveness.

PART ONE
Scene 1

The room could be a part of almost any modern residential complex. It is not spacious or luxurious. The building has been designed for the maximum utilization of space. The walls are gray and bare; no baseboards or cornices. Simple but tasteful furnishings: those of a functional living space where comfort is of prime importance. But the relative crowding of the details that distinguish it curiously increases the sensation of being closed in. However, the ceiling is totally out of view of the audience. The floor, of a neutral color and without tiles or fissures of any kind, appears to be of polished cement. The corner between the right and the upstage walls is not visible: the folds of a long curtain hanging at an angle from above hide it, creating a kind of alcove. Open metal shelves which serve as a cupboard are fastened to the right wall near this curtain, and their appearance contrasts with that of the other furnishings. Fine glassware, china, silver trays, white tablecloths and napkins are arranged on the two shelves. Underneath, there is the white porcelain door of a small refrigerator that is built into the wall; further downstage on the same wall, a simple metal rack from which hang six small duffel bags, each different from the others. Under them and against the wall is a folding bed which forms an upright piece of furniture. In the upstage wall, near the alcove curtain, the only door, which is narrow, low, and paneled. It cannot be seen now because it is open offstage from the right of the frame. The door is set deep into the walls to suggest their great thickness. Over the door there is a light fixture and, higher up, the round grill of a loudspeaker. Next to the door and extending the width of the upstage wall to the extreme left, an enormous glass window of great height, with a sill that is only a little lower than the lintel of the door. Its frame is also set deep into the wall; two simple vertical stringers without bolts support the glass. Under the window and with the head against the left wall is a simple, light bed of modern design. Aligned under it are three bundles covered by burlap or canvas whose use is not apparent for the moment. Fastened to the wall over the bed, a small conical metal light shade. Almost all of the remaining space on the left wall is taken up by a built-in wall unit of fine wood, with spaces and shelves of varying dimensions. On a lower shelf, a television set; another section contains several buttons or knobs. Numerous beautiful and expensively bound books and fine porcelain figurines stand out on some of the shelves. Under the wall unit and near the bed, the top of a small table extends from the wall. It is apparently of metal too: a plain surface on which books, magazines, and a white telephone are placed. Downstage left there is a small rectangular table of light wood polished to a semigloss. On it are newspapers and an illustrated magazine or two; around it, five inviting armchairs of shining metal and gleaming leather. At left, hanging from a long rod that disappears from view above, a huge lighting fixture with a multicolored shade. The door opens out onto what seems to be a narrow exterior gallery, with a metal railing that extends in both directions to create the impression of leading into emptiness. Behind the large window, in the distance, the extensive view of a marvelous landscape: clear sky, majestic mountains, the gleaming silver of a lake, remote buildings that resemble strange cathedrals, the delicate green of meadows and copses, the clean lines of attractive buildings somewhat nearer. The same panorama extends beyond the gallery railing and into the distance. With its contradictory mixture of modernity and overcrowding, the room suggests an efficiency apartment urgently and provisionally put into the service of some important activity that is in progress. Bright spring light floods the landscape; an iridescent brightness, slightly unreal, sifts into the room.

Soft music in the background: The pastorale from Rossini's overture to William Tell, *a fragment which, in spite of its brevity, is repeated without interruption until the action cuts it off. A motionless* MAN *is lying face to the wall on the bed, under flowered sheets and an expensive coverlet. With a shiny new broom,* THOMAS *is sweeping bits of trash toward the door. He is a young man about twenty-five, who is wearing dark pants, a gray shirt, and soft shoes. On his chest there is a small black rectangle where the inscription C-72 stands out in white. He moves the broom lazily and whistles softly some of the music he is hearing; then he stops, accompanying himself with a light movement of his head.*

THOMAS. Rossini . . . [*He turns toward the bed.*] Do you like it? [*There is no reply. He makes a couple of sweeping motions.*] You and I haven't talked much since we came to the Foundation. I don't even know if you like music. [*He stops again.*] It has a soothing effect on sick people. But if it bothers you . . . [*No reply*] It's a melody as serene as the morning air when the sun comes up. It's good to hear it on a day like this. [*He faces the window.*] I wish you could see how clear it is. [*He goes back to his sweeping; he pushes the trash through the door and leaves it outside at left. Then he leans on the railing to look at the landscape. The sun bathes his face. He comes back into the room and pushes the alcove curtain aside slightly to put the broom behind it.*] Would you like to see the view? The air's warm. If you want to, I'll help you get up. How about it? [*No reply. He goes closer to the bed and lowers his voice.*] Are you asleep? [*The sick man does not move.* THOMAS *moves away on tiptoe. We hear the* MAN'S VOICE, *tired and weak.*]

MAN. Talk all you want. But don't ask me any questions . . . I'm tired.

THOMAS. [*He goes to the table and picks up a magazine.*] Of course. You don't eat enough. [*He laughs and sits down.*] Asel has told you that it's bad for you not to take any solid food, and Asel's a doctor. [*He puts the magazine down.*] But I never see you drink anything either. [*Pointing toward the curtain*] Or go to the bathroom. [*He gets up and goes closer.*] Do you get up while we're sleeping? [*He leans over him.*] Huh?

[BERTA *has appeared through the left gallery corridor and enters in time to hear Thomas's last words. She looks at him smiling. She is a girl of gentle and serious expression, with a shiny mane of hair. The white shorts she is wearing reveal her exquisite legs; on her immaculate open-neck shirt, a blue rectangle with the inscription A-72. She is holding something tiny and white in her hands.*]

BERTA.   He won't answer you. He's fallen asleep.

THOMAS. [*Turning around*]   Berta! [*He crosses to embrace her.*]

BERTA. [*Evading him, smiling*]   Careful! [*She comes downstage.*]

THOMAS. [*Behind her*]   Don't try to escape!

BERTA. [*Showing what she has in her hands*]   You'll crush it.

THOMAS.   A white mouse?

BERTA.   From the laboratory. We've become friends. [*She shows it to him.*] He's very tame. He hardly moves.

THOMAS.   They've probably inoculated him with something.

BERTA.   No. We haven't begun work yet. How about you?

THOMAS. [*Putting his arm around her shoulders*]   We haven't either.

BERTA. [*Holding up the mouse*]   He's looking at you. He likes you.

THOMAS.   You're imagining things.

BERTA.   Don't you see the affection?

THOMAS.   Where?

BERTA.   In those little drops of wine he has for eyes. Kiss it. [THOMAS *kisses her neck.*] IIim!

THOMAS.   No thanks!

BERTA.   Try to ignore him, Tommy. He's my boyfriend.

THOMAS. [*Releasing her*]   You've given him my name? [BERTA *nods.* THOMAS *goes toward the table, thinking.*]

BERTA. [*To the mouse*]   Thomas Long Tail, the gentleman is angry. He's selfish.

THOMAS. [*With a half-smile*]   Jealous is a better word.

BERTA. [*Walking toward him*]   Don't you feel sorry for him? I wish you would save him from his fate. You could keep him in the bathroom. . . . He could be your mascot. [*He shakes his head.*] You won't?

THOMAS.   Put him back in his cage, Berta. They need him.

BERTA. [*After a moment*]   I hate the Foundation.

THOMAS.   Thanks to its generosity you're able to go on with your studies, and I'm writing my novel. . . . [*He moves closer.* BERTA *pets the rodent without looking at* THOMAS.] The Foundation is admirable, and you know it.

BERTA.   It sacrifices mice.

THOMAS.   And dogs, and monkeys. . . . Heroes of science. A sweet martyrdom: they don't know that it's happening to them. And they're treated well to the very end. What better destiny? If I were a mouse, I'd accept it.

BERTA. [*She looks at him enigmatically.*] No. [*Brief pause*] You are a mouse, and you don't accept it.

THOMAS. Sometimes I don't understand you.

BERTA. Yes you do.

THOMAS. [*Walking about*] But what's with these belated scruples! It's your work!

BERTA. I'd like to save my little friend.

THOMAS. All mice are the same! [*He puts his arms around her waist.*]

BERTA. This one's name is Thomas . . . like yours. [*She pulls away and turns to face him.*] And I'll save him! [THOMAS *looks at her perplexed.*] Goodbye. [*She goes toward the door.*]

THOMAS. Wait! [*He takes her by the arm.*] My friends will be back soon. And they want to meet you. [*He leads her to a chair. She sits down, petting the mouse.*] They don't quite believe that you've come to the Foundation too.

BERTA. Why not?

THOMAS. They say it's too much of a coincidence. [*He sits on the table beside her.*] They have a blind spot when it comes to chance happenings. [*He points to the number on her shirt.*] Yesterday I told them about that. [*She smiles.*] Is it so hard to believe that my girl is at the Foundation too? – I said – Well, besides that, they've given her the same number as mine: seventy-two.

BERTA. They didn't believe that either?

THOMAS. Even less! They all laughed . . . except Asel. He's the puzzling one.

BERTA. [*Without looking at him*] Did you know him before?

THOMAS. No . . . no. Why do you ask?

BERTA. No reason.

THOMAS. He didn't laugh. He said: That would be more than a coincidence; it would be a miracle. You'll meet them now. They'll see your number for themselves, and they'll be convinced that everything that happens to you and me is miraculous. Right?

BERTA. Right. [*He bends over and gives her a prolonged kiss. She laughs.*] Tommy is going to get away. [*She gets up and grasps the mouse firmly.*] Be still, Long Tail. Don't be jealous. [*She holds him up.*] Look, he's telling me something.

THOMAS. I don't hear anything.

BERTA. It's another miracle. [*She puts the mouse close to her ear.*] He says it's time for lunch. He's probably only jealous, but he's right. I can't stay any longer.

THOMAS. [*Standing up*] Just a minute more! They'll be back soon. . . . [*He takes her by the arm.*] How did you know that I didn't go out for a walk today?

BERTA. Isn't it your turn to clean the room?

THOMAS. How do you know that? We haven't talked since day before yesterday.

BERTA. [*She looks at him intensely.*]   You must have told me.

THOMAS. [*Intrigued*]   No.

BERTA. [*Turning away and looking up*]   I smell a bad odor.

THOMAS.   It's coming from the bathroom. The toilet doesn't flush properly. I've notified the orderly. Even a research center like this has some deficiencies. . . . They were in such a hurry to get it built and opened that there are still no eating facilities, no dining rooms . . .

BERTA.   And the overcrowding.

THOMAS.   Of course. Until they complete the new wings. Do the women have better service?

BERTA.   It's the same. No services at all. And that's why I have to go now. Shall we go, Long Tail? [*She starts to exit.*]

THOMAS. [*Restraining her timidly*]   They'll be here any minute. . . . They're interesting people. You'll like them. Even Tulio. He's a bit vulgar and hates music. . . . But he's an exceptional photographer who's close to an important optical discovery. A real brain, although a bit unbalanced. And Max, another brain. An eminent mathematician. But very nice and accommodating. Linus is an engineer . . . he's experimenting with a new technique for pre-stressing building materials. He doesn't talk a lot but he's a great person.

BERTA.   And Asel?

THOMAS.   Asel. He's the finest of them all.

BERTA. [*Referring to the man in the bed*]   What about him?

THOMAS. [*After a moment*]   You probably won't believe it, but I still don't know what field he's in. [*He goes closer to the bed.*] Since he's sick, we don't bother him with questions.

BERTA.   Do you think he's listening to us?

THOMAS.   He sleeps very soundly. [*He motions to her to come over.*] Look. [*Brief pause*]

BERTA.   It's late, dearest. I do have to go now.

THOMAS. [*He embraces her; his voice becomes husky.*]   Come back tonight.

BERTA. [*Surprised*]   Here?

THOMAS.   They're very understanding. If we go into the bathroom, they won't say anything.

BERTA. [*To the mouse*]   He's crazy, Tommy.

THOMAS.   Crazy about you. Will you come?

BERTA. [*After a moment*]   I hate the Foundation.

THOMAS. [*Kissing her*]   But not me. . . . Come back tonight.

BERTA.   Stop. . . . [*She pulls away from him.*] Stop. [*She goes toward the door.*]

THOMAS.   Will you come?

BERTA. [*From the door, holding up the mouse*]   I have to protect my other boyfriend . . . [*Indicating the curtain*] And it smells bad in the bathroom.

THOMAS.   We'll go somewhere else!

BERTA. [*With a little laugh*]   Where? [*He doesn't know what to answer.*] Goodbye! [*She disappears left.* THOMAS *runs out to the gallery and calls to her.*]

THOMAS.   I know you'll come! [BERTA'S *silvery laugh comes from further off.* THOMAS *watches her leave. Then he looks at the landscape and breathes the fragrant air. He comes back into the room and glances toward the sick man with a smile.*] Dear God, what a morning! As clear and pure as Rossini's. Sleep, sleep. [*He crosses.*] I'll turn down the music a little.

MAN.   I'm awake.

THOMAS. [*Hesitating*]   We thought you were asleep. . . . I guess we bothered you.

MAN.   I dozed a little . . . [*Groggy*] No bother. [THOMAS *continues to the wall unit, turns a knob, and the music becomes softer.*] There's an unpleasant odor.

THOMAS. [*Turning to him, disturbed*]   It's from the bathroom. They'll fix it soon. . . . Do you prefer the music this way? [*There is no reply.* THOMAS *crosses to the table noiselessly and picks up a magazine. When he is about to sit down, four men appear from the right gallery corridor. They look to the left for a moment. As soon as he sees them,* THOMAS *runs to the wall unit to turn off the music. The first to come onstage is* TULIO — *gaunt and in his forties, with sharp, severe features. Like the others, he is wearing a gray shirt; on his black rectangle is the inscription C-81. All are wearing dark pants which differ somewhat.*] How was your walk?

TULIO. [*Gruffly*]   Fine.

[*The others enter immediately.* MAX, *about thirty-five and attractive, C-96 on his shirt, crosses to sit at the table and leafs through the magazine that* THOMAS *has left.*]

MAX.   It was splendid! We even played leapfrog. Can you imagine, grown men playing leapfrog? And Tulio turned out to be an expert! [TULIO *throws him a scowl.*] In falling down, of course. But an expert! [*He laughs and* THOMAS *laughs with him. Meanwhile,* LINUS *crosses and sits at the extreme left of the table. Very vigorous and tightlipped, he appears to be about thirty. C-46 on his shirt.*]

TULIO. [*Sourly*]   I'm going to get a drink of water. [*He goes toward the curtain. Almost immediately* ASEL *has gone over to the bed and observed the man in it. Then he reclines against the foot of the bed and watches* THOMAS. ASEL *is the oldest: about fifty, maybe more. Gray hair, reflective expression. On his rectangle, C-73.*]

THOMAS.   They're only teasing you, Tulio. Can I get you a beer?

TULIO. [*Curtly*]   I prefer water.

ASEL.   And you, Thomas, what have you been doing?

THOMAS.   Killing time. I listened to Rossini, I read. . . . When do we begin our projects?

MAX.   You can start whenever you wish. A writer doesn't need an office or a laboratory. [TULIO *reappears, wiping his mouth with his sleeve.*]

THOMAS.   I've already been taking notes. But I also need isolation.

ASEL.   So you had a quiet morning to yourself. No visitors?

THOMAS. [*Smiling*]   One. [*The others look at him; there is tension in their faces. With a snort of disgust,* TULIO *goes over to one of the bags hanging at right, opens it slightly without taking it down, and takes out a handkerchief, which he puts in his pocket.* LINUS *gets up, glances at* THOMAS, *and goes over to lean against the edge of the door.*]

ASEL.   Who?

THOMAS. [*With a look of amusement*]   Can't you guess?

ASEL. [*Suddenly sitting up*]   Be quiet. Someone's coming. [*He goes over near the door.* MAX *gets up and stations himself beside him.* TULIO *turns to face the door.* THE SUPERINTENDENT *and his young* AIDE *appear, all smiles, from the right gallery. Both are dressed impeccably in black jacket, tailored trousers, and silk tie, in the style of head waiters.* THE SUPERINTENDENT *is a middle-aged man of distinguished bearing.* THOMAS *goes to meet him.*]

THOMAS.   Good morning, sir!

SUPERINTENDENT. [*Turning on his smile*]   Good day, gentlemen. Is everything satisfactory?

THOMAS.   Yes, sir. A few trifles. . . . When will the dining room open?

SUPERINTENDENT. [*With a quiet laugh*]   Very soon. The Foundation hopes you'll forgive these temporary deficiencies. If I may . . . [*He comes in and observes the* MAN *in bed.*] He hasn't gotten up today either?

ASEL.   He's still weak. But it's not serious.

SUPERINTENDENT.   Fine. [*He sniffs the air discreetly without saying anything and gives the room the once-over.*] I'm glad you gentlemen are comfortable. [*He returns to the door.*]

THOMAS.   Thank you very much.

SUPERINTENDENT. [*From the gallery, he flashes a subtle smile.*]   I'm always at your disposal, gentlemen. [*He exits left.* THE AIDE *bows, all smiles, and disappears in turn.*]

THOMAS.   They're very thoughtful. [*With a scornful grunt,* TULIO *crosses and picks up a small, tattered book from the table, which he leans against to leaf through the book.* LINUS *peers out the door.* ASEL *sits again at the end of the bed.*]

LINUS.   The slop will be here soon.

MAX. [*Crossing to sit at the table*]   That's no way to talk about our catered dinners.

THOMAS.   The food's delicious.

LINUS.   I'm sorry, Thomas. It's the way I talk.

THOMAS.   You don't have to apologize. Who wants a beer? [*Without looking up from his book,* TULIO *lets out another of his contemptuous grunts.* THOMAS *looks at him.* MAX *makes a motion to him not to pay any attention to* TULIO.]

MAX.   I prefer whisky. I'll pour my own. [*Still reading,* TULIO *laughs sarcastically.* ASEL *reprimands him with a movement of his head.*] And a tranquilizer for him.

THOMAS. [*With a laugh*]   He certainly needs it.

TULIO. [*Without looking up from the book*]   I was laughing at something . . . that's written here.

[THOMAS *goes to the refrigerator and opens it. We get a glimpse of bottles and containers.* LINUS *absentmindedly hums an absurd and discordant tune: improvised tones that become grating at times.* THOMAS, *who is deciding what to take from the refrigerator, looks at him uneasily.*]

THOMAS.   If you wish, I'll turn on the music. [LINUS *looks at him, says nothing, and shrugs.*] Would you like a beer? [LINUS *looks at* ASEL, *who gives him a faint nod of assent.*]

LINUS.   Fine.

ASEL. [*Looking at* TULIO]   Another for me.

[TULIO *gives him a look of contempt.* THOMAS *takes an opener from the shelf and opens a bottle of beer.* MAX *takes down two tall glasses and holds them out to* THOMAS, *who fills them.* MAX *goes over to* LINUS *and hands him one.*]

MAX.   Here.

LINUS.   Thanks. [*But he doesn't take it.* THOMAS *is opening another bottle. He takes another glass from the shelf and serves himself.*]

MAX. [*To* LINUS]   Here, man . . . [THOMAS *looks at them.*]

LINUS. [*Reluctantly*]   Give it to me. [*He takes the glass.* MAX *goes over to* ASEL.]

ASEL.   Who visited you this morning, Thomas? You haven't told us. [LINUS, *about to take a swallow, stops.* TULIO *closes his book and looks at them.* MAX *pauses.*]

THOMAS. [*Laughing*]   I don't know if I should tell you. [*He starts to drink, pauses, and holds his glass toward* TULIO.] I'm sorry, Tulio. Would you like one? [TULIO *looks at him angrily.*]

MAX.   Shall I put in some strychnine to make it taste better? [*He and* THOMAS *laugh.* TULIO *slams the book on the table.*]

THOMAS.   Really now, don't get so excited! [*He takes a swallow.*]

MAX.   Your beer, Asel. [*He hands him the glass.*]

ASEL. [*Taking it*]   Thank you.

[LINUS *crosses to the table with his eyes lowered and quietly leaves the drink which he has not touched. He sits down and begins to tap on the arm of his chair with his fingers.*]

THOMAS.   And your whisky, Max?

[MAX *goes to the shelf and takes down a glass that already contains a few jiggers of whisky.*]

MAX.   Here it is. Will you put some ice in it for me?
  [THOMAS *looks at him with surprise and takes a metal container from
  the refrigerator.*]
THOMAS.   When did you pour the whisky?
MAX. [*With a quick glance at the others*]   A moment ago. Didn't you see
  me?
THOMAS.   No. [*He takes out a few ice cubes with tongs and puts them in
  the glass.* MAX *stirs his drink.* THOMAS *puts everything away and
  closes the refrigerator.*]
ASEL. [*Softly*]   Thomas, tell us who came.
  [LINUS *interrupts his strumming and waits for the answer.* TULIO
  crosses his arms and looks at THOMAS. MAX *drinks, keeping his eyes
  on him.*]
THOMAS.   Well . . . it was that lovely little creature whose presence at
  the Foundation you persist in denying. [*They exchange glances.*]
ASEL.   Your girlfriend?
THOMAS. [*Boastful*]   And with the number seventy-two on her blouse!
  You just missed bumping into the miracle, Asel! It hasn't been
  five minutes since she left. [TULIO *sits down with a snort.*] They
  don't believe me, Max. They think I like to invent things. [*He
  paces and drinks.*] Let them ask the sick man. He was awake
  when she came.
TULIO. [*Irate*]   Oh, shut up!
ASEL.   Tulio!
TULIO.   I can't stand any more of this. [*He gets up and crosses to look
  out from the doorway.*]
ASEL.   What is it you can't stand? [TULIO *gives him an angry look.*] Try to
  control yourself. Your nerves have been on edge. . . .
THOMAS. [*Smiling at* TULIO, *he goes toward him.*]   If it bothers Tulio, I
  won't mention her again.
TULIO.   Talk about anything you wish.
THOMAS. [*Reflecting*]   We've been rather isolated here. . . . That may
  be the reason.
ASEL.   The reason for what?
THOMAS.   Asel, you get news of your wife and children. You had a let-
  ter yesterday.
ASEL.   That's right.
THOMAS.   Max's mother visits him, and Linus also gets letters, from
  his parents. . . . Are you married, Tulio? [*Silence.*]
ASEL.   He doesn't have anyone.
THOMAS.   I hope you'll forgive me. I'll tell Berta . . .
TULIO. [*He paces; excitedly.*]   Not to come here? Thank you, thank
  you! Let them all come! I wish the whole world would come! [*To
  the others*] The reason my nerves are on edge is not what Thomas
  supposes, and you all know that quite well!
ASEL.   Don't shout, Tulio.

TULIO.   Isn't shouting permitted either?

THOMAS.   What are you talking about?

[LINUS *strums on the table again.*]

ASEL.   Please, let's keep control of ourselves. Thomas, ask Berta, for all of us, to pay us a visit at the earliest opportunity.

TULIO.   That's a mistake!

ASEL. [*Slowly*]   What are you saying? . . .

MAX. [*Smiling*]   It's not a mistake, and you should offer Thomas an apology.

THOMAS.   That's not necessary.

MAX.   But it is. To you and to us. [*He laughs.*] Why don't you make one of your marvelous photographs of us? The good friends at the Foundation having a friendly drink together. How does that sound?

TULIO. [*In a low voice*]   You're all off your rocker.

MAX.   If you give me the camera, I'll take it, with you in the middle. On condition that you watch the birdie and smile. It will be a historic smile! [*They all laugh except* TULIO; *even the absorbed* LINUS *laughs in spite of himself.*]

TULIO. [*With a distorted smile*]   Agreed. Provided that Berta stands beside me for the picture.

[THOMAS'S *annoyance shows through.*]

ASEL.   That's a crude thing to say, Tulio.

[TULIO *shrugs. The telephone begins to ring softly. No one acknowledges it.*]

THOMAS. [*Coldly*]   You can take a picture of Berta, if you wish. But not now since she's not here.

TULIO.   Right you are. She's not here.

[*Angered,* THOMAS *takes a step toward him; he regains control and manages to smile.*]

THOMAS.   Tulio, I give up on you! [*He finishes off his beer.*] Isn't anyone going to answer the phone? [*The others exchange glances.*] It's been ringing for quite a while now. It could be your wife, Asel. Or maybe your mother, Max. . . .

MAX.   I'll get it.

TULIO. [*Through his teeth*]   And so you will.

[MAX *picks up the phone; all except* LINUS *watch.*]

MAX.   Hello. . . . No, no. This is not Thomas. . . . [*He winks at* THOMAS, *who smiles.*] This is Max. . . . How nice of you! We'd all like to meet you too. . . . [*With a long face,* TULIO *crosses and disappears behind the alcove curtain.* THOMAS *gives him a look of triumph.*] Well, almost all of us. . . . [THOMAS *is beside him, nervous.*] Thanks very much. I'll put Thomas on. He's standing here biting his nails. . . .

THOMAS.   Don't be silly.

[ASEL *goes to the table and sits down as he observes* THOMAS.]

MAX. [*Laughing*]   He's already eaten his little finger. Be careful with him. He's capable of chewing up the phone!

THOMAS.   Give it here, you fool! [*He snatches the telephone from him. MAX goes over to the curtain and, as if he were seeing TULIO through it, points to THOMAS with a gesture that asks: "What do you have to say now?" Afterwards he goes to the bed, observes the sick man an instant, and then leans against the foot of the bed.*] Berta, you got back so quickly! . . . In your car? I thought you had walked. . . . [*Putting his hand over the mouthpiece.*] It runs, but I've promised her something better after we're married. [*He removes his hand.*] Since we saw each other? Oh, I can still see you! . . . Of course I can! . . . [*He turns toward the window.*] From here I can see you in your lodge. Listen, is Thomas still alive?

ASEL.   Thomas?

THOMAS. [*Covering the mouthpiece*]   A mouse from the laboratory. She gave him my name. [*Removing his hand*] Tell him we'll see about that! I'll hang him up by his tail. They hate that most of all. . . . On the contrary! You called at a perfect time. Certain people who were denying your existence have had to bite the dust. Tonight they'll offer you their apologies. . . . No, no! I don't want to hear it! You're coming tonight. . . . So that my friends can see how beautiful you are! [*The roar of a toilet being flushed behind the curtain interrupts him.*] No, I can't hear you very well right now. . . . [*Bothered by the prolonged noise, he covers his free ear. TULIO reappears fastening his trousers.*] Listen! . . . You come tonight! . . . [*Upset, he hangs up the phone.*] She's hung up on me. Or the connection was broken. I don't know which. . . . I expect she'll come. Tonight or tomorrow at the latest.

TULIO.   Or day after tomorrow.

THOMAS. [*Dryly*]   Thanks for the kind thoughts. At least you can't say she's not here.

TULIO. [*He crosses to sit at the table.*]   I didn't speak to her on the phone.

THOMAS.   But Max did! And he talked with her! And if it weren't for that damn noise you made, probably on purpose! . . . You could have decided to relieve yourself at some other moment, I believe. . . .

ASEL.   Not again! Please . . .

TULIO.   Don't worry. I'll keep my mouth shut.

THOMAS.   So will I. [*He paces. LINUS resumes his strange humming. THOMAS stops in front of the window and contemplates the countryside.*]

LINUS.   How long is it till lunch?

ASEL.   Ten minutes or so. [*He takes out a short pipe, old and scorched, and sucks on it intently.*]

LINUS.   That long?

MAX. No. Less than five minutes. [*Pause*]

LINUS. [*To* ASEL, *in a low voice, pointing to the sick man.*]   Is it your turn to get his ration?

[THOMAS *turns around slowly, listening to them with a vague uneasiness.*]

ASEL. [*Sighing*]   Well . . . yes. I'm sorry.

[THOMAS *starts to say something but holds back when he hears* LINUS. MAX *leafs through a magazine.*]

LINUS.   If we at least had something to smoke in the meantime. . . .
[ASEL *takes the pipe from his mouth and smells it with pleasure.* TULIO *takes out his handkerchief and passes it over his lips.*] You don't have any left, do you, Max? [MAX *shakes his head.*]

ASEL.   Patience. It's another flaw in this admirable Foundation. I don't think the cooperative store will be opening for a few days yet.

THOMAS. [*Stepping forward happily*]   I can solve the problem for you right now!

LINUS. [*Hopeful*]   You've got some cigarettes left?

THOMAS.   Of course I have! I don't smoke very often. [*He goes to the duffel bags at right.*] And drink your beer, man! You haven't even tasted it! [LINUS *picks up his glass and takes a sip, keeping an eye on* THOMAS. TULIO *buries himself in his book.* MAX *takes another sip of whisky.* ASEL *watches* THOMAS, *who takes a pack of cigarettes from one of the bags and holds it up to view. Nevertheless, something disappoints* LINUS *keenly, for he bows his head.*] Have a smoke!
[THOMAS *opens the pack and offers it around.*]

ASEL.   Take your cigarette, Linus. [LINUS *takes a cigarette from the pack with clumsy fingers and holds it in his hand.*]

THOMAS. [*To* ASEL]   None for you?

ASEL. [*Putting his pipe in his mouth.*]   You know that I'm trying to give up the habit.

MAX.   I'm a hopeless addict. Let me have one. [*He accepts a cigarette and takes a box of matches from his pocket.*]

THOMAS. [*Timidly*]   Tulio . . . [*Without looking up,* TULIO *refuses with a movement of his finger.*] But you smoke . . . [*Angry,* TULIO *shakes his head.* THOMAS *looks at the others and makes a gesture of dismay.*]

ASEL. [*Gently*]   You also refused his beer. Don't slight him a second time. He thinks a lot of you.

TULIO. [*He strikes the table with his fist, and with a grimace of impotence, he strikes it again and again.*]   Enough sermons! Fine. I offer my apologies! [*Flushed with anger*] And I'll prove to him that I also think a lot of him! I'll prove it to all of you! [*Calmer*] Forgive me, I have a quick temper. [THOMAS *offers him the pack of cigarettes.*] No. I said I don't want to, and I don't. [*He gets up and crosses. He turns back toward* THOMAS.] Thank you. [*He stations himself in front of the door and looks out.* MAX *lights his cigarette and offers a light to* LINUS, *who hesitates.* MAX *insists;* LINUS *puts the cigarette in*

his mouth and lights it. But after two or three draws, he lets it burn
away on an ashtray. THOMAS *takes out a cigarette and puts the pack*
away.]

THOMAS.   Will you give me a light? [MAX *lights the cigarette for him.*]
Thank you. Shall I turn on the television?

MAX.   It's all too insipid at this time of day.

THOMAS.   With all the silliness going on I forgot to set the table. I'll do
it in a flash.

MAX.   And how! If literature fails you, you can become a waiter in a
resort hotel. They earn more than novelists. . . .

THOMAS. [*Laughing*]   I'll give it some thought. [*He has gone to the table*
and gathered up all the newspapers and magazines, which he leaves
on the small table. TULIO *turns and looks at him with sad eyes.*]

TULIO. [*Humbly*]   Can I help you?

ASEL.   Bravo, Tulio! [TULIO *manages an embarrassed smile.*].

THOMAS. [*Touched*]   If you wish. I could use some help. Collect the
glasses, please. Have you all finished?

MAX. [*Hurrying to drain his glass*]   Finished.

[TULIO *approaches the table with uncertainty.* THOMAS *picks up the*
ashtray where LINUS'S *cigarette is still sending up its column of*
smoke.]

THOMAS.   Don't you like this brand, Linus? [*He snubs out the butt.*]

LINUS.   What? Yes. I like any brand.

THOMAS. [*He leaves the ashtray on the small table.*]   You let it burn
away in the ashtray.

LINUS. [*Disconcerted, he looks at the others.*]   I wasn't thinking.

THOMAS.   Ask me for another whenever you wish. [*He has hardly put*
down the ashtray when he stops in amazement at the incredible per-
formance of TULIO *who, after miming the collecting and arranging of*
the glasses, starts toward the shelves with his imaginary load. He has
not even touched the glasses which are visible on the table. The others
do not seem to find anything irregular in his actions. MAX *stands up,*
taking a final draw from his cigarette and leaving the butt in the ash-
tray. He then goes to the bed and takes a discreet look at the man in
it. LINUS *strums absentmindedly on the table with both hands. Smil-*
ing and savoring his empty pipe, ASEL *watches* TULIO. THOMAS *con-*
trols his anger.] You shouldn't offer to help just to make fun of me.
[*They all look at him in surprise. Unnerved,* TULIO *stops and turns*
around. ASEL, *paying close attention, walks toward them.*]

TULIO.   Were you speaking to me?

THOMAS. [*Coldly*]   Who else? [*He goes to the table.*]

TULIO.   And why . . . are you saying that?

THOMAS.   What are you doing?

TULIO.   Carrying the glasses . . . to the cabinet.

THOMAS.   What glasses?

TULIO. [*Hardly daring to lift his hand*]   These.

THOMAS. I don't know what to think about you. [*He collects the glasses on the table with distinct clinking sounds.*]

TULIO. But . . . I . . .

MAX. [*Quickly*] It was a joke, Thomas.

THOMAS. In very bad taste! [*He crosses with the glasses to the shelves.*]

ASEL. No doubt, but don't let it upset you. . . .

THOMAS. [*Taking a print tablecloth from the shelf.*] He offered to help just to make fun of me!

TULIO. No!

THOMAS. [*Going to the table and laying the cloth*] I'll ask the superintendent to move him to another room.

MAX. [*Helping him spread the tablecloth*] Don't you understand? You have to excuse him. . . .

TULIO. [*To* ASEL] I wanted to please him!

THOMAS. And he still insists! [*He goes to the shelves to get napkins.*] I don't want to hear another word! The matter is closed. [*With an angry look at* TULIO] Forever.

ASEL. No, Thomas . . .

THOMAS. Are you going to take his side?

MAX. Give me the napkins. [*He takes the napkins and starts placing them.*]

ASEL. It wasn't a joke, Thomas. [THOMAS *goes to look for knives and forks.*]

TULIO. [*With a grunt of sarcasm, he points to* MAX.] Well, now! It seems that I'm the only one who doesn't know how to help.

MAX. [*To* THOMAS] I'll set the wine glasses. [*He goes to the shelves and takes down some wine glasses which he carries to the table.*]

TULIO. [*With contempt*] Wine glasses!

ASEL. [*Going to* THOMAS] You've got to understand. He didn't know what he was doing.

MAX. I'll get the wine.

TULIO. Asel, if you're going to explain it that way, I prefer to do it myself!

ASEL. Don't be so easily offended. [*To* THOMAS] And you, come here. [MAX *carries a bottle of wine to the table.* THOMAS *leaves the knives and forks on the table.*]

THOMAS. I have set the table. [*He gets the plates.*]

ASEL. [*Following him*] Listen to me, please. [*He takes* THOMAS *by the arm.*]

THOMAS. Leave me alone.

ASEL. [*Leading him downstage*] Come.

TULIO. [*Following them*] I tell you not that way! I've had enough.

ASEL. [*Sharply*] Just be quiet!

[*Brief pause*]

TULIO. [*With a deep sigh.*] Do it your way! I'll go on being patient. [*He withdraws to the table and sits at the left end of it, folding his arms.*]

ASEL. [*In a low voice*] Thomas, you know that Tulio . . .

THOMAS.   I don't know anything.

ASEL.   You know that he's . . . an unusual person.

[*Brief pause*]

You have to be patient too. And understanding.

THOMAS.   All right, all right! If you say so. [*He goes to the table and puts down the plates; then he returns to get more.* MAX *helps him place them.*] Thanks.

[TULIO *is angered by* MAX'S *participation and the abruptness with which* THOMAS *has set a plate in front of him. He pushes himself up from the table and, with eyes averted, pounds on it with his hands.*]

MAX.   [*Trying to relieve the tension*]   What kind of car do you intend to buy when you get married, Thomas?

[ASEL *sits.*]

THOMAS.   I don't know. . . . What do you recommend? [*To* LINUS] Or you, engineer. You must know a lot about such things. What make do you recommend?

LINUS.   I don't really know much about cars. I'm an engineer.

THOMAS.   That's why I asked! What make do you drive?

LINUS. [*Laughing softly*]   It's . . . the best.

THOMAS. [*Setting the final plate and laughing*]   I don't doubt it! [*He surveys the table and rubs his hands together.*] It's all ready. [*He stands near the bed and looks through the window.*] What a beautiful day!

[*They look at one another behind his back.*]

LINUS.   And what a long one! It's been five hours now since breakfast. [*He puts his head down on the table between his folded arms and resumes his curious humming.*]

TULIO.   Damn it, that smell keeps getting worse!

THOMAS. [*To* ASEL]   Oh! . . . that's been taken care of too.

[*They all look at him.*]

MAX.   Taken care of?

THOMAS.   I reported it this morning.

[LINUS *toys with the plate in front of him.* TULIO *clenches his fists.*]

ASEL. [*Getting up slowly*]   To whom?

THOMAS.   To the superintendent. He came by earlier.

[LINUS *gets up and, without putting down his plate, goes to the door and peers out cautiously. Then he turns around to listen, turning the plate nervously in his hands.*]

ASEL. [*At the same time*]   You said that there was only one visitor.

THOMAS.   Berta. But the superintendent came earlier. You'd hardly left.

MAX.   Aren't you confusing this with another day?

THOMAS.   Why should I confuse it? He noticed the smell, and I explained to him what the problem was. He promised to call the plumber at once.

[TULIO *turns his back and props himself against the table.*]

ASEL.   Did he have anything else to say?

[*Without turning around,* TULIO *stiffens.*]

THOMAS.   The usual courtesies. Are we satisfied . . . all that.

ASEL. [*Smiling*]   You must have something else to say to him, novelist. You like to talk.

THOMAS. [*Laughing*]   I told him about Berta, and about how nice you all are. . . . [*Looking at* TULIO]

ASEL. [*After a moment*]   Did he also talk with the sick man?

THOMAS.   I . . . don't believe so. He was sleeping, just as he is now.

MAN. [*Without moving*]   I'm not asleep. I hear what you're saying.

THOMAS. [*To* ASEL]   Well, he was asleep then. [*The others look at him strangely.*] Why are you looking at me that way? Don't you believe me now either? Ask him when he comes with lunch.

ASEL.   It's not necessary, Thomas.

MAX.   No one doubts your word.

THOMAS. [*Pacing*]   They're taking their time today. . . . I'm beginning to have an appetite too. [*He is facing* LINUS.] It must be the fresh air. We'll all be fat when we leave here. [*He laughs.*] It'll look good on you. . . . You're muscular but a bit skinny.

[*Meanwhile,* ASEL *goes over to* TULIO *and, in a way that* THOMAS *will not notice, says something in an amiable manner and shakes his head in resignation.* TULIO *nods in agreement.*]

ASEL.   You don't have so much weight on you either, Thomas.

THOMAS. [*Turning to face him*]   I don't need it!

ASEL.   Come here, please. [*He steps forward.* THOMAS *comes closer.*] You're pale.

THOMAS.   I was always pale.

ASEL. [*He examines the mucous membrane of one of his eyelids.*]   You're still quite anemic.

THOMAS.   That's not possible!

ASEL. [*Smiling*]   Am I a doctor or am I not?

THOMAS.   You are, but . . .

ASEL.   I've already told you that you need extra nourishment. Let's do something. Apart from all the incursions you wish to make to the refrigerator, today you eat the sick man's ration.

LINUS. [*Annoyed*]   Why?

ASEL   If it's my turn today, I can give it to whomever I wish, can't I?

TULIO.   To whoever needs it. And you need it, Asel.

ASEL.   No. I cede it to Thomas.

THOMAS.   You've done that before. . . . And I can't eat everything I fancy! What about the others?

ASEL.   Your appetite is greater. [*He looks at him hard.*] You said so yourself. It's the fresh air. . . . Admit that you're dying to stuff yourself for just one day. And that you never do.

THOMAS.   It's true. I don't understand it.

ASEL.   Today you'll eat your fill.

THOMAS.   Asel, I shouldn't accept it.

ASEL.   Don't say any more about it. [*He puts his hand on* THOMAS'S
    shoulder.] A prescription from your doctor!
THOMAS. [*Looking down*]   Thank you. [*Silence.*]
TULIO.   If I don't say something, I'll explode.
ASEL.   If it's not something foolish. [*He sits and plays with his pipe.*]
TULIO.   You are the most admirable man I've ever known.
ASEL. [*Smiling*]   That's foolish. [*Brief pause*] Yesterday you also gave
    Thomas part of your food. . . .
TULIO.   Because you asked me to.
ASEL.   Nonsense. You did it of your own free will.
TULIO.   You may believe that. [*Silence*]
MAN.   I'm hungry too. Why have you got me on a diet?
    [*No one acknowledges these words.* THOMAS, *very perplexed, casts a
    glance at the sick man.*]
THOMAS.   I, too, am going to explode if I don't say something, Asel.
ASEL.   Well, say it.
THOMAS.   I don't understand what you're doing . . . as a doctor.
ASEL.   Because you aren't a doctor.
THOMAS.   Shouldn't the sick man eat something?
    [*The others exchange glances without* THOMAS *noticing.*]
ASEL.   Absolute restriction of food.
MAN.   Why?
THOMAS.   Why?
ASEL.   It would take a long time to explain.
THOMAS.   He doesn't even drink.
ASEL.   He drinks. Every night I give him the liquid that he needs.
THOMAS. [*Confused*]   And during the day . . . nothing?
ASEL.   Nothing.
THOMAS.   He'll die of thirst.
ASEL.   No.
THOMAS. [*Timidly*]   Are you going to examine him today?
ASEL.   There's no need. His condition is stabilized.
THOMAS. [*Suspicious*]   I suppose you know what you're doing.
ASEL.   Rest assured.
THOMAS.   But tell me, Asel . . . [*He presses his shoulder.*] If we have
    more food than we need, why do we take his ration every day
    and eat it by turns? [ASEL *falters.*]
MAX.   And why not?
LINUS.   You admitted that you were hungry.
THOMAS. [*Pacing*]   Yes. We all are . . . And I can't figure it out!
MAX.   It's the air.
    [*Silence.* THOMAS *looks at them one by one and gets an innocent look in
    return. Then he goes to the bed and leans over the man in it.*]
THOMAS.   Are you all right? Do you want something? [*There is no reply.*
    THOMAS *straightens up and turns to* ASEL.] You don't suppose some-
    thing's happened to him . . . do you, Asel?

ASEL. No.

THOMAS. [*Taking a few hesitant steps, he turns to look at the land-scape.*] It's beautiful living here. We'd always dreamed of a world like the one we finally have.

[*Silence*]

MAX. Don't mention the toilet to the superintendent again. He might get annoyed.

TULIO. [*Dryly*] It's certain the superintendent won't forget.

THOMAS. Don't worry. [*He goes to the wall unit.*] A little music?

ASEL. Whatever you wish.

[THOMAS *starts to press a button.*]

MAX. Wait. I think lunch is here. [*He goes toward the door with a plate in his hand.*]

LINUS. Yes. They're bringing it.

[TULIO *takes a plate and crosses in turn, lining up behind* LINUS *and* MAX. THOMAS *goes to the table.*]

ASEL. [*With indifference, he puts away his pipe, takes a plate, and stands up.*] You take the sick man's plate.

THOMAS. I was going to. [*He picks up two plates and goes toward the door.* ASEL *places himself behind* TULIO. *Guided by two waiters attired in tails, a chrome, double-leveled serving cart appears along the right gallery corridor. The upper level is heaped with platters of delicious foods and the lower one with succulent desserts.* THE SUPER-INTENDENT *appears, all smiles, between the cart and the railing.*]

SUPERINTENDENT. Good day, gentlemen.

ALL. Good day. [*The* FIRST WAITER *hands* LINUS *a small basket of golden rolls, which* LINUS *quickly passes to* MAX *and he to* TULIO, *who passes it to* ASEL. ASEL *steps out of line for a moment and places the basket on the table.*]

SUPERINTENDENT. [*At the same time*] Today's menu is excellent and varied. [*The waiters smile.*] You have a good selection. [*To* THOMAS, *who is approaching with the two plates*] Is one for the sick man?

THOMAS. Yes. What do you suggest? [*A giggle from the* FIRST WAITER]

SUPERINTENDENT. Can he eat everything?

THOMAS. Everything.

SUPERINTENDENT. [*With a faint little laugh*] Then allow me to recommend these delicious appetizers, the pâté de foie gras, and sirloin with mushrooms.

[*The waiters stifle their giggles of amusement.* THOMAS *holds out a plate and one of them starts filling it.*]

And for dessert . . . I suggest the apple tart. It's delicious.

THOMAS. Perfect. I'll have the same.

SUPERINTENDENT. Thank you. [*The* SECOND WAITER *asks* THOMAS *for the other plate and starts to serve him.*] Does that little odor bother you much? [THOMAS *looks at his companions and hesitates.*] Forgive

me for asking at such an inappropriate moment . . . [*A short burst
of laughter escapes from one of the waiters. The* SUPERINTENDENT
gives him a quick look but smiles too.]

TULIO. [*From the line*]   We hardly notice it.

SUPERINTENDENT. [*Very serious*]   Nevertheless, it will be fixed as
quickly as possible. . . . Have no doubts about that.

[*The curtain falls for a few brief moments or fadeout.*]

Scene 2

*The same iridescent brightness in the room; the upstage landscape,
unchanged and radiant. The door is still open. Although nothing seems different, three changes can be noted if we look closely. Of the five elegant
chairs, the two situated at the right of the table have disappeared, and two
of the three bundles that were under the bed have replaced them. It can now
be seen that each of them consists of an old mattress, thin and narrow,
whose rolled-up spiral is exposed through the edges of their sack covering.
The third change affects the bedclothes: the sheets and coverlet have been
replaced by a drab cover, and the pillow no longer has a case.*

The MAN *remains in the same position. Seated on the floor downstage right,*
TULIO *is reading his tattered book; he puts his handkerchief to his nose
from time to time.* LINUS, *absorbed in thought, is seated in profile on one of
the rolls at the right of the table. Facing forward and seated near the left
end of the table,* THOMAS *comments on a large book of art reproductions to*
ASEL *and* MAX, *who are standing on either side of him. A few moments of
silence.*

THOMAS.   I never get tired of looking at them.

MAX.   Is it a small painting?

THOMAS.   It's probably no more than three feet wide.

MAX.   That's incredible.

[TULIO *grunts contemptuously without looking up.*]

THOMAS.   Notice the gold lamp. Such details! And see how clearly the
map stands out in the background.

TULIO. [*Without interrupting his reading*]   The map in the background,
with its old creases . . .

[*The others exchange glances.*]

THOMAS.   Exactly. Like a piece of oilcloth that's cracked. [*He points to
the page.*] Do you see? It must be very difficult to paint those
effects. But Terborch was a master.

TULIO.   Terborch was a master, but that painting isn't by Terborch.

ASEL.   Tulio, why don't you come over and look at it with us? Why do
you need to sit on the floor?

TULIO. [*Curtly*]   For variety.

THOMAS. [*Bending over the book to read*]   It says Gerard Terborch here.

TULIO.   A painter is seated with his back to the viewer, sketching a
girl crowned with laurel and holding a trumpet. Is that the one?

THOMAS.   The same!

TULIO. [*With a sigh*]   I'm sorry, but I can't help getting into the discus-
sion. That painting is by Vermeer.

THOMAS.   It says here! . . .

TULIO.   I don't care what it says!

THOMAS. [*Bending over the reading closely*]   It says . . . [*Straightening up,
puzzled*] Vermeer. How could I have read Terborch?

ASEL. [*Laughing*]   These Dutch painters are all alike. The window, the
curtain, the glass of wine, the map . . .

MAX.   You simply confused them.

THOMAS. [*Incredulous*]   The names? Besides, I knew that the painting
was by Vermeer. . . . [*He bends over the book again.*] It says so
here. Thank you, Tulio.

[TULIO *gives him a scornful look and says nothing.*]

Do you want to come see? Obviously you like the painting.

TULIO.   I don't feel like getting up.

THOMAS. [*Warmly*]   Not even to look at art books? You have around
you the most beautiful works created by man, and you never
look at them.

ASEL.   Everyone has the right to be himself.

THOMAS.   But it's absurd for him to spend hours with his nose in that
beaten-up old book! A manual on cabinetmaking! Who would
think it? [*He points to the bookshelves.*] He could be enjoying a
great novel. . . . Do you want me to pick one for you?

[TULIO *looks at him coldly.*]

MAX.   Let's look at some more pictures.

THOMAS. [*Perplexed by* TULIO'S *silence*]   Yes . . . yes. [*He looks at the
book.*] Vermeer . . . [*His enthusiasm is rekindled.*] For certain,
there's something curious in this painting. The lamp is almost
identical to the one in an earlier work. [*He searches through the
book.*] A small painting by Van Eyck . . . The portrait of a couple.

TULIO. [*Between his teeth*]   Arnolfini.

MAX.   It's not Italian, Tulio. It's Flemish.

TULIO.   *Arnolfini and his Wife!* It's in the National Gallery in London. But
I'll keep my mouth shut. [*He appears to bury himself in his book.*]

THOMAS.   Yes. That's the one. Here it is. Look! [*He compares the two
pages.*] One would say that it was the same lamp.

MAX.   And if it were the same?

THOMAS.   No. Vermeer copies Van Eyck . . . or it's a mysterious coincidence. It's very improbable that he knew this painting.

TULIO.   All that imagination! Those two lamps are like you and me.

THOMAS.   They're almost the same. Look at them.

TULIO.   I don't need to. In Vermeer's, the lamp has slender arms, a
    spherical body; in the Flemish work, wide arms with fretwork, a
    cylindrical body. . . .

THOMAS.   Slight differences . . .

TULIO.   And a large metal eagle crowns Vermeer's. Or am I wrong?
    [*Silence*]

THOMAS.   I think . . . you're right.

TULIO.   So, there goes your mysterious coincidence.

ASEL.   Your memory is remarkable, Tulio. [TULIO *shrugs.*]

THOMAS.   I'll grant you that. It's natural: a photographer as good as
    you had to know a lot about painting. What's the word for that
    technique you want to perfect?

TULIO. [*He lays down his book but doesn't look at them.*]   Holography. [*He
    sighs.*] Yes. . . . Images that walk among us . . . three-dimensional.
    And yet they're only projections in the air: holograms.

MAX.   Haven't they discovered how to do that already?

TULIO.   It can be improved. It's an immense field. [*Brief pause*] I . . .
    was doing some research in it, yes. With another person. I
    wanted . . . [*He hides his face in his hands.*] My God! I wanted.

ASEL. [*Going to his side*]   You will, Tulio. . . . Don't lose hope.

THOMAS.   That's why you've come to the Foundation. . . . You'll see
    when you get down to work. We'll do all the great things we've
    dreamed of here! Max will solve the problem of N Functions,
    Linus will perfect his technique for prestressing, Asel will sys-
    tematize the science of acupuncture . . .

ASEL.   I've never spoken to you about acupuncture.

THOMAS.   That is your research; someone told me. The microcurrents
    of the skin and their relation to illnesses . . .

ASEL. [*Smiling*]   If you say so. . . .

THOMAS.   And Tulio will fill the world with images undreamed of, and
    I . . . will write my novel. Come over to the table, Tulio. You
    comment on the paintings. [*He turns the pages of the book.*] Look,
    Botticelli . . . El Greco . . . Rembrandt . . . Velázquez . . . Goya
    . . . [*Silence*]

ASEL.   You continue. [*He sits at the table.*]

THOMAS. [*Distressed*]   Something is wrong.

MAX.   Go on!

THOMAS.   Watteau . . . Turner . . . [*He stops.*] Turner! It's like a dia-
    mond of light. [*He turns toward the window.*] Almost as splendid
    as that view. Another rainbow of clouds, of rocks, of fresh water,
    of radiant palaces . . . [*He has been searching nervously for some-
    thing in his pockets. Brief silence.*] Where did I leave my cigarettes?
    I put the pack in my pocket. And it's not there.

    [TULIO *uncovers his face. They all look at* THOMAS.]

ASEL.   Are you sure you put them there?

THOMAS.   What? . . .

MAX. [*Laughing*]   Do you suppose it was a holographic pack?

THOMAS.   Don't joke.

MAX.   You probably put them down someplace and forgot.

THOMAS.   I haven't taken them out of my pocket! We couldn't have smoked them all.

ASEL. [*Looking into his eyes*]   Then think.

THOMAS. [*Smiling in spite of himself*]   Is this a guessing game?

ASEL.   Maybe.

THOMAS.   You've hidden them.

ASEL.   I swear to you that no one has touched your cigarettes.

THOMAS. [*Doubtful*]   It can't be . . .

ASEL. [*Pointedly*]   And nevertheless, it is.

MAX.   Don't worry. They'll turn up.

THOMAS. [*Still suspicious*]   I hope so . . . [*He turns the pages of the book again.*] Manet . . . Van Gogh . . . I hope so . . . [*He lapses into silence.* ASEL *observes him closely.*] I don't know this painter. Do you like him?

ASEL.   Do you?

THOMAS.   Solid line but weak color . . .

[TULIO *is attentive to what he is saying.*]

Must be a nineteenth-century animalist.

MAX.   An animalist?

THOMAS.   You can see for yourself. Mice in a cage. A sordid theme. [*As he speaks these words,* BERTA *appears inconspicuously in the doorway. She is smiling.*] There's something repellent in those creatures. [*Unnoticed,* BERTA *takes a few steps into the room.* THOMAS *is still bent over the book.*] Tom Murray. I don't know who he is.

[*Absorbed in himself,* LINUS *is making his warbling sounds.*]

ASEL.   Do you know his work, Tulio?

TULIO.   No.

[THOMAS *sits up slowly. Without turning around, he seems to realize intuitively that* BERTA *is standing behind him.*]

ASEL.   And what are those poor mice doing?

[BERTA *frowns and steps back in silence.*]

THOMAS. [*Entranced*]   What are they doing?

ASEL.   They're doing something or waiting for something. Right? [BERTA *observes them from the doorway with a grave expression and then disappears left.* THOMAS *stands up and suddenly turns around. He goes to the door and looks out in both directions. He turns around, deep in thought.*] What's wrong with you?

THOMAS.   Nothing. [*A pause, in which the only sound is* LINUS's *humming. Suddenly this stops.* THOMAS *looks at his companions with misgiving; then at the motionless man on the bed. Alarm and doubt show in his eyes.*]

LINUS.   How long until dinner?

ASEL. About four hours.

LINUS. [*He takes a deep breath, covering his mouth and nose. He gets up and goes downstage, taking in air eagerly.*] It's hard to breathe here now.

ASEL. It'll all be over soon.

LINUS. And will it be better?

ASEL. We'll see.

THOMAS. [*Uncertain*] They'll fix the commode right away. . . . [*To LINUS*] If you can't breathe at that window, come to the door. You can smell the countryside from here.

LINUS. Then smell to your heart's content!

THOMAS. [*Murmuring*] Sometimes it's hard to please you. [*He starts to return to the table but stops when he notices LINUS's bedroll.*]

ASEL. [*Getting up and going to LINUS*] A little calm for a while yet, Linus. You know it's necessary. [THOMAS *listens to him and looks at the bedroll again. He goes on to the table and stops beside the book. He looks inquisitively at* MAX.]

MAX. You haven't told us yet what those mice represent.

THOMAS. [*Curtly*] No more paintings for today. I can see that I'm boring you.

ASEL. No, not at all!

[THOMAS *closes the book and returns it to the shelf.*]

MAX. On the contrary! . . .

THOMAS. [*With finality*] Yes. [*He examines the book spines and decides to take another one.* MAX *clicks his tongue and shakes his head.*] What?

MAX. [*Smiling*] If the devotion has ended, the obligation will begin.

THOMAS. What are you talking about?

MAX. Guess the riddle. Who's the shirker in charge of cleaning today?

THOMAS. [*With a look of annoyance*] I'm sorry. I'll take out the trash now. [*He crosses and stops near one of the small armchairs and caresses its back; then near the two mattress rolls which he studies furtively.* ASEL *observes him with keen interest.* THOMAS *leans over and touches the covering of the one at right.*]

ASEL. What are you looking at?

THOMAS. [*Straightening up quickly*] Nothing. [*He goes upstage and disappears for some seconds behind the alcove curtain; he reappears looking with amazement at the broom he has in his hand. It is not the one he used during the morning but an old, dirty broom with a very short handle. He looks at his companions and hesitates.*]

ASEL. Is something wrong?

THOMAS. No . . . but I'd like to know . . . [*Lowering his voice*] I don't understand.

ASEL. What is it you don't understand?

THOMAS. [*He laughs suddenly.*] What's the point of all these jokes?

MAX. [*Good-humoredly*] What jokes?

THOMAS.   Don't pretend. I'm not a fool. You're changing things, or hiding them.

ASEL.   What things? Where?

THOMAS. [*Seriously*]   Are you going to deny it?

ASEL.   I, at least, am not playing jokes. [*They look at each other
intently.*]

THOMAS. [*Morose*]   Let's drop it. [*He considers the broom in his hand
again. He bends over and sweeps out a small pile of trash, which he
leaves in the gallery at left of the door. When he straightens up, he
looks out toward the right.*] They're making their pickups now. I
almost forgot. [*He enters at the same time that the two waiters arrive
by the right corridor. They are carrying a dark box with handles. They
are no longer wearing their dress coats but long aprons over gray
shirts and old trousers. They place the box at left of the door, and the
SECOND WAITER, the only one visible now, takes a small broom and a
dustpan from it. He lifts the box by a handle—it is assumed that the
FIRST WAITER has lifted the other side—and exits left.* THOMAS *starts
to look out but steps back: the door is being closed slowly by the smiling* SUPERINTENDENT *who bows obsequiously and quietly completes
his action. The surface of the door is of light, finely varnished wood;
on its left side there is a bronze knob and, in the center, a peephole.*
THOMAS *reacts with a start.*] Why has he closed the door without
asking permission?

MAX.   He smiled at you. He fixes everything with smiles.

[*Suspicious,* THOMAS *puts the broom behind the curtain.*]

THOMAS.   But why did he close it?

LINUS. [*Annoyed*]   They do it every evening.

THOMAS.   Every evening?

TULIO. [*Getting up and going to the table to put down his book*]   If it bothers you so much, open it.

ASEL.   Don't tell him that.

TULIO.   Why not? [*To* THOMAS] Open it, and call it to his attention so
that he won't do it again.

ASEL.   Are you crazy, Tulio?

TULIO.   You're the one who's crazy! Where is all this getting us?

MAX.   We're going to have to send you to the infirmary, Tulio.

LINUS.   No, not Tulio! [*He points to* THOMAS, *who watches them anxiously.*] Him!

ASEL.   You just keep your mouth shut.

LINUS.   I'm always keeping my mouth shut! But it's time to stop. Let
him go to the infirmary, and us . . . wherever.

ASEL.   What if they talk with him?

TULIO. [*Sitting on the edge of the table*]   Open the door, Thomas!

ASEL. [*Shaking his head vehemently*]   Please!

TULIO.   Open it, boy! [ASEL *stands aside in dismay.*] What difference
does it make to you, Asel. Ending this is part of your plan.

ASEL.   If you could just keep quiet . . .

MAX. [*Laughs*]   Ah! So there's a plan? I trust you'll keep me informed. . . .

ASEL.   Don't pay any attention to him. But if you could all be a little more understanding . . . without any more talk. Try to keep calm, think . . . and then, please, let's proceed.

[MAX *looks at him inquisitively.* LINUS *sighs and sits in an armchair.* TULIO *hangs his head. Silence.*]

THOMAS. [*Full of mistrust*]   What . . . are you talking about?

TULIO. [*To himself*]   This is what they call co-existence . . . and it's maddening.

THOMAS. [*With his hand on the door knob*]   Shall I open it, Asel?

[ASEL *hesitates.*]

TULIO.   It's not going to hurt anything. . . . Tell him to open it. Open it, novelist.

THOMAS. [*He thinks about it. Trembling.*]   I don't dare. . . . What are you doing to me?

TULIO.   Nothing. Nothing harmful to you. [*Standing up*] It's not important, Thomas. Really. Let's try to amuse ourselves. . . . What game can we play?

MAX. [*With a giggle*]   Taking pictures.

ASEL.   Now?

TULIO.   Why not? It's a good idea. Shall I take them, Thomas? When they're developed, you can give them to your parents.

ASEL. [*Severely*]   No more of that, Tulio.

THOMAS. [*Cheerfully*]   Yes, Asel! Tulio wants to prove his friendship, and I appreciate that. I'll give the pictures to Berta. I can't, of course, to my parents. I no longer have any. Get your camera ready, Tulio. [*He steps forward.*] The rest of you, form a group around the table. Come on. [*They begin to place themselves.*] Is there enough light?

TULIO.   Certainly.

THOMAS. [*Crossing*]   I'll turn on the chandelier. It's very strong.

LINUS. [*With sarcasm, to himself*]   The chandelier.

[THOMAS *presses the switch of the large fixture but it doesn't light. He tries again without results.*]

ASEL. [*In a low voice*]   I wouldn't do it, Tulio.

TULIO. [*In a low voice*]   Let me give him the satisfaction.

THOMAS.   It doesn't turn on.

TULIO.   It's all the same. We don't need it.

MAX.   The current's probably off.

THOMAS.   Do you think so? I'll try the television. [*He pushes a button.*] Or the stereo speakers! Do you want to hear some music?

ASEL.   If you're in the mood for it . . .

[THOMAS *presses another button and waits a few seconds.*]

THOMAS.   That's odd. It doesn't work either.

ASEL. [*To the others*]   Which is . . . very interesting!

THOMAS.   And the television won't turn on. . . . I'll leave all the switches

on so we'll know how long it lasts. [*To* TULIO] Is your camera ready?
[*He laughs.*] That will work.

TULIO. In a jiffy. [*He goes to the shelf and takes down an ordinary aluminum
tumbler, while* THOMAS *finds himself a place with the group.*]

THOMAS. [*Sitting*] I'll get here.

MAX. Attention! Smile, everyone. Watch the birdie!

TULIO. One moment. [*He simulates preparing his camera.*] Ready! [*He
turns toward them and pretends to focus on them with the tumbler.* ASEL
does not conceal his uneasiness.] Look this way! [*He strikes the tumbler
with his fingernail.*] Another?

THOMAS. [*Standing up angrily*] No. And I don't want that one either.

TULIO. But it's already made!

THOMAS. I appeal to you! Because now he's played a joke on all of you,
not just me!

ASEL. [*In a low voice*] I was expecting it.

TULIO. I wanted . . .

THOMAS. To make a fool of me again.

TULIO. Asel, I wanted to please him!

[ASEL *sighs.*]

THOMAS. [*Rushing at* TULIO *and snatching the tumbler from his hand.*]
With this? [*Holding it up*] You tell me whether it's madness or a cal-
culated trick! I'm beginning to think the latter!

TULIO. I never do the right thing.

[ASEL *takes out his old pipe and caresses it.*]

THOMAS. [*To* TULIO] Who did you think you were, you dunce?

ASEL. What do you have in your hand, Thomas?

THOMAS. A metal tumbler!

ASEL. [*To all of them*] Take a good look. The reactions are becoming
encouraging.

THOMAS. I don't understand your jargon! [*He grabs* TULIO *by the shirt.*]
And you, you miserable clown, crazy piece of shit, get out of here.
Go live in another room!

TULIO. [*Jerking free*] Go yourself and leave us in peace!

THOMAS. I'm going to! . . . [*He tries to attack him, but the others intercede
and subdue them.*]

ASEL. No, Thomas!

LINUS. [*To* THOMAS] Leave him alone! You're the one at fault!

THOMAS. Shut up, engineer! [*They struggle.* THOMAS *throws himself at*
TULIO *again and is repelled. The others subdue him again.*]

ASEL. [*Forcefully*] Let me speak! All of you listen! Please! . . . I beg you,
Thomas . . . [*They calm down little by little.*]

LINUS. [*He goes to sit down.*] Let him go. Let's end this once and for all.

ASEL. It'll end soon for all of us. And it's ending for him too. Don't you
realize? Just bear with me for a while longer, please.

LINUS. For what? If it's all ending for him too, leave him in peace. He'll
be better off.

ASEL.   No! I assure you it's not the best way.
  [*Morose,* TULIO *crosses, grabs his old book, and sits down as far away from the others as he can.*]
    Thomas, explain to me, if you can, where that tumbler came from.
MAX.   From the shelf.
ASEL.   Will you let him talk?
MAX. [*Sarcastically*]   At your orders, chief.
THOMAS.   Tulio took it from the shelf.
ASEL.   And it was there?
  [THOMAS *doesn't reply.*]
    Had you seen it there before?
THOMAS.   That's what I've been asking myself . . . [*He goes to the shelves, takes down a crystal glass, and compares the two.*] Because here there are only wine goblets and crystal, like this one.
LINUS.   Bad.
ASEL. [*With a smile*]   No. Not completely bad. Where do you suppose that tumbler came from, Thomas?
THOMAS.   This tumbler . . . and other things.
ASEL.   Can't you say?
THOMAS.   You and the others will have to say.
ASEL.   Return the glass and the tumbler to their places, please.
  [THOMAS *does so with a brusque motion and turns around to face him.*]
THOMAS.   You explain it!
ASEL.   Stay beside the shelves. If his camera is still there, Tulio will take your picture.
TULIO.   What are you saying?
ASEL. [*Firmly*]   If your camera is there, you will take the picture! [*To* THOMAS] But is it there?
THOMAS.   It always has been. . . .
ASEL.   Then bring it.
THOMAS. [*He searches in vain on the shelves. He turns around.*]   It's not there!
ASEL.   How curious! As far as I know, no one has hidden it.
THOMAS.   But it has disappeared too.
ASEL.   And in its place, an unexpected metal tumbler.
  [*Silence.* THOMAS *looks at them and thinks hard.*]
THOMAS.   Max, this morning you didn't pour your drink.
MAX.   I assure you I . . .
THOMAS.   I assure you that you took it from here already served. The broom that we had has been transformed. Suddenly neither the television nor the speakers work . . .
MAX.   The current is off.
THOMAS.   Two of the chairs have disappeared.
ASEL. [*Very interested*]   Oh, really?

THOMAS. Yes. And in their place, two bedrolls. And now, a filthy tumbler in place of a camera.

MAX. [*With his little laugh*] What did I tell you! They must be holograms.

ASEL. Forget about your holograms! [*To* THOMAS] There are no devices here, no laser beam projectors. [*To the others*] There's only . . . a little more to eat. I hardly dared to believe that there would be any result, but it's happening. With a rapidity that amazes me, and delights me.

THOMAS. No, please! I've had enough puzzles. The way you're talking proves that you know something I don't. And all these strange things that are happening are a surprise to me but not to you! I insist on an explanation.

TULIO. Why not speak, Asel?

ASEL. I've told you many times. It would be dangerous.

LINUS. For whom?

ASEL. For him, although he doesn't matter to you. But also for us.

LINUS. [*After a moment*] You aren't a doctor.

THOMAS. [*Astounded*] Did he say you aren't . . . ?

ASEL [*To* LINUS] Careful what you say.

LINUS. You're not a doctor. And you don't know what's advisable and what isn't.

ASEL. I know, unfortunately, quite a few things more about life than you.

THOMAS. Is it true, Asel? Aren't you a doctor?

ASEL. What do you think?

THOMAS. I'd like to believe that you are . . . [*He lowers his voice.*] But . . . if you aren't . . . what are we doing to that poor man? [*He points to the man in the bed and his expression suddenly changes when he sees the bedclothes.*] No! Why? What have you done with the sheets and the spread?

TULIO. Nobody's done anything.

THOMAS. There's only a blanket left, and a filthy pillow.

ASEL. [*To the others*] The most difficult moments are coming now! Not a word too much or a word too little. If you help me, I expect that we'll deal with the case successfully.

[MAX *looks at the other two and nods his approval.* TULIO *and* LINUS *look away.*]

THOMAS. I don't understand what's going on!

ASEL. Are you sure? [*Silence.* THOMAS *doesn't know what to answer.* ASEL *goes to him and puts his arm around his shoulder.*] Come with me. [*He leads him toward the bed.*]

THOMAS. Are you going to examine him?

ASEL. There's no need. [*Very confused,* THOMAS *touches the blanket lightly.*] Leave him in peace. [*He points over the bed with his index finger.*] And tell me what you see there.

[THOMAS *looks without comprehending.*]

THOMAS.   Beyond the window?

ASEL. [*After exchanging a glance with the others*]   Beyond the window.

THOMAS.   The landscape.

ASEL. [*He places his pipe in his mouth and sits down.*]   Like a Turner. That's what you said.

THOMAS.   But . . . more beautiful. Because it's real. [*He turns to face the landscape.*] Real! [*To* ASEL] Isn't that so?

ASEL.   Go on.

THOMAS.   Words get in the way. Seeing it is enough. It's our finest evidence.

MAN. [*Motionless*]   They've taken my covers. I'm cold.

THOMAS. [*Perturbed*]   Dazzling evidence. Now the world is like a garden. Men have finally brought it about, with suffering and tears.
    . . .

ASEL. [*Very softly*]   They still exist . . .

THOMAS.   What?

ASEL.   They still exist . . . the suffering and tears . . . don't they? And in abundance.

THOMAS. [*Hesitating*]   Still, yes. But . . .

MAN.   I'm hungry.

THOMAS. [*To* ASEL]   . . . but you know it too: what we see is the future we used to dream of . . .

MAN.   Give me some water!

THOMAS. [*Pointing to the landscape*]   And now it's ours!

MAN. [*Raising his voice*]   Why don't you give me something to eat and drink?

THOMAS.   The Foundation builds and improves. . . . I can see its people from here . . . laughing in the morning sunlight.

MAN. [*Louder*]   Tell Asel to give me something to eat!

THOMAS. [*Nervous*]   Do you hear it, Asel?

ASEL.   People laughing in the sunlight?

THOMAS.   Yes.

ASEL.   Are you certain? Don't you notice sadness in some of the faces?

THOMAS.   They're so far away. . . .

MAN.   Why do you eat my ration?

THOMAS.   Answer, Asel! If you don't the nightmare of the anthropoids has not ended yet!

ASEL.   Answer whom? That man?

MAN. [*Strongly*]   This is the nightmare of the anthropoids!

THOMAS. [*Very nervous, he points to the landscape.*]   No! Men are beginning to be human! Don't prevent it, Asel! And answer!

MAN. [*Shouting*]   Animals! Hypocrites!

THOMAS.   Asel, give him something to eat!

ASEL.   He doesn't need it. You spoke of the morning sunlight. Do you know what time it is?

MAN.   You're devouring me, you're killing me!

THOMAS.   Asel, for pity's sake!

ASEL.   At least you know it's evening and not morning. From which direction is the sun shining on that landscape?

THOMAS.   From the east. . . .

ASEL.   And this morning?

THOMAS.   [*Puzzled*]   From . . . the same.

ASEL.   Doesn't it seem strange that you don't notice the slightest difference? Or do you?

MAN.   Sing and dance for joy . . . I have good news for you . . . I'm dying.

THOMAS.   [*Pointing to the man*]   Asel, he's dying!

MAN. [*Shouting*]   Murderers!

THOMAS.   Murderers! We're helping to kill him! [*He rushes at* ASEL, *who stands up. The others, tense, step closer.*]

MAN.   I can't endure any more.

THOMAS.   [*He puts his fists against his head and lets out a scream.*]   Murderers!

LINUS.   Don't shout!

ASEL.   [*Restraining him*]   Calm down, Thomas. It's only a crisis and it will pass!

MAN.   Water!

THOMAS.   Give him water!

MAN.   I'm dying! . . .

THOMAS.   [*He slips out of* ASEL'S *grasp. He shakes the man's shoulders*]   I'll give you water!

MAN.   Like a hungry rat!

THOMAS.   [*Shouting*]   I won't stand for it! . . .

TULIO.   Shut up! They're going to come check! [THOMAS *runs toward the alcove curtain.* ASEL *catches him.*]

ASEL.   Quiet!

THOMAS.   Turn loose! [*They struggle.*] I'm going to give him a drink! [*They all attempt to restrain him.*]

LINUS.   Shut your mouth!

ASEL.   Silence! All of you!

MAN.   [*In a very weak voice.*]   It's too late . . . now.

[THOMAS *struggles. Aided by* ASEL, LINUS *subdues him with a wristlock.*]

ASEL.   Do you hear them? They're at the door.

[THOMAS *works loose. Motionless, they all fix their eyes on the door. A few seconds of absolute silence. Suddenly we hear a harsh metallic sound, and the door opens very rapidly toward the right. The interior light changes instantaneously. A gray, oppressive glow replaces the bright iridescence. The* SUPERINTENDENT *bursts in, followed by his* AIDE *who remains in the doorway with his hand suspiciously hidden in his jacket pocket. The* SUPERINTENDENT *surveys the scene, runs to*

the bed, and jerks the cover from the man who is revealed in poor and
worn underclothes. He shakes the body a bit and turns around.]
SUPERINTENDENT.   How long has this man been dead?
[*The lights suddenly change, becoming brighter and harsher. Only the*
corners of the room and the overhead fixture remain in a dull, indis-
tinct half-light.]
THOMAS.   Dead? . . . Why, he just spoke.
SUPERINTENDENT.   You be quiet! [*To the others*] Answer!
ASEL.   Six days.
THOMAS. [*Mumbling*]   It's not possible.
SUPERINTENDENT.   Why didn't you report it? [*Silence. An evil smile*
   comes over the SUPERINTENDENT'S *face.*] You wanted to keep his
   ration. Right? [*Silence. He directs his words toward the door.*] Get
   this carrion out of here! [THE WAITERS, *now dressed in white hospital*
   jackets, appear with a stretcher which they put down just outside the
   door. Without disguising their revulsion, they enter, take the rigid body
   out, place it on the stretcher and exit with it.] His personal effects. [*To*
   the AIDE] And you, roll up the mattress. [MAX *hastens to take one of*
   the duffel bags from its hook. The SUPERINTENDENT *takes it from him.*
   The AIDE *puts the pillow and blanket on the mattress, rolls it all up,*
   puts it on his shoulder, and takes it into the corridor.] Plate, cup, and
   spoon. [TULIO *goes to the shelves and, to* THOMAS'S *surprise, takes*
   down a plate, a metal tumbler and a crude metal spoon, which he
   hands over to the SUPERINTENDENT. *The* SUPERINTENDENT *points*
   downstage.] Keep the window open! [*From the doorway, in an icy*
   voice] And depend on the consequences. [*He exits. The door closes*
   with a loud clank. Its surface has changed. It is no longer of wood but
   of studded metal plate, and the knob has disappeared. Silence.
   THOMAS *rushes to the door, which he pushes to no effect. He looks in*
   vain for the brass knob. His face distorted, he caresses the cold sheet of
   metal. He turns around and stands with his back glued to the door,
   looking aghast at his companions. ASEL *watches his every movement.*
   The others wearily find a place to sit down.]
TULIO.   It finally happened. I'm almost glad.
LINUS.   I'm not. Six days aren't very much.
TULIO.   Better than nothing.
MAX.   Now they'll take us downstairs to the hole.
ASEL. [*Fervently*]   That's what I'm hoping for.
MAX.   Do you mean . . . you wanted this?
ASEL.   I didn't say that.
LINUS.   Will it be long before they move us?
TULIO.   Within a couple of hours. Or maybe tonight.
   [*Silence again.* THOMAS *slowly moves away from the door, shaking his*
   head.]
THOMAS. [*In a veiled voice*]   He wasn't dead. [*Taking a few more steps*]
   We all heard him speak. He asked for something to eat.

LINUS. [*Hostile*] No one heard him. Except you.

THOMAS. [*Frightened*] Are you insinuating that . . . I'm sick?

LINUS. [*After a moment*] He's been dead for six days.

THOMAS. But it can't be . . .

LINUS. Of course it can! Why do you suppose it smelled so bad in here? [*With a mordant laugh*] They've fixed the plumbing for you! [*A new and instantaneous increase in the harsh illumination, except in the corners.*]

ASEL. Be sensible, Linus.

LINUS. What does it matter now? It's all finished.

ASEL. Not for him.

THOMAS. Is that true, Asel? Was I the only one who heard him? [ASEL *bows his head.*] You didn't hear him? Tell me the truth. . . .

ASEL. [*Sad, he goes and sits on the bed.*] No, Thomas. I didn't hear him. [THOMAS *goes to the foot of the bed and leans against it.*]

THOMAS. Why did you kill him? [LINUS *represses a retort.*]

ASEL. Nobody killed him. He died of starvation. [THOMAS *straightens up. Perplexed, he runs his fingers over the bedframe. He studies the room, the overhead fixture, the harsh new light. He goes over to the bedrolls and touches one of them.*]

THOMAS. It's stifling in here . . . I think I'll have a beer. [*He has hardly dared to say this. Unsteadily, he goes to the refrigerator. When he gets close, he stops in amazement and steps back. The light suddenly becomes even harsher and stronger. At the same moment, a panel the same color as the wall descends and completely hides the porcelain door.* THOMAS *turns around.*] It's not . . . possible. [*He goes to the wall unit and holds out an unsure hand. The light makes its final leap and remains fixed in a hard and almost unbearable whiteness that only respects the shadows in the corners. A panel descends, gradually hiding the bookshelves until they disappear completely. With increasing anxiety,* THOMAS *goes to the telephone and stands looking at it. Undecided whether to pick up the receiver or not, he puts his hand on it. Then he withdraws his hand very slowly and places it against his other hand. Suddenly he turns toward the window and toward the sundrenched landscape. He then goes downstage and takes a deep breath as he looks through the invisible window. Without turning around, he appeals to* ASEL.] Am I sick, Asel?

ASEL. No more than the rest of us. [*He gets up and goes to his side. They look through the invisible window together.* ASEL *points with his pipe to the exterior.*] The afternoon is beautiful.

THOMAS. Yes. [TULIO, LINUS, *and* MAX *watch them.*]

ASEL. Look. A band of swallows.

THOMAS. They're playing

ASEL. The world is marvellous. And that is our strength. We can recognize its beauty even from here. These bars can't destroy it. [THOMAS *reacts with a start. His hands seize two invisible bars.*]

THOMAS.   Where are we, Asel?
ASEL. [*Gently*]   You know where we are.
THOMAS. [*Unconvinced*]   No . . .
ASEL.   Yes. You do know. And you'll remember.
   [*They stand looking through the window.*]

Curtain

PART TWO
Scene 1

The light has stabilized—harsh and garish, although less intense than before. The strange gray half-light persists in the curtained area and down-stage left. The dazzling panorama still glows behind the large window. All of the smaller armchairs have disappeared; around the table, only three bedrolls which serve as seats. The folding bed at right is still in its place. The table is no longer of fine wood but of cast iron similar to the wall shelves, and it is fixed into the floor. The bed has also been transformed: a simple cot of the same cast iron, built into the left wall, with two wide metal legs at the foot. On the small table, only the telephone. No expensive dishes, no fine crystal or linens on the shelves; only the dull shine of metal tumblers and a stack of spoons. In the doorway, a small pile of trash.

THOMAS *is still wearing his dark trousers, but his four companions are dressed in wrinkled pants of the same color as their numbered shirts, which they now wear loose like blouses. On the bare bed and propped against the head, another bedroll on which* ASEL *is seated savoring his old pipe.* TULIO, *seated on the bedroll nearest to the left wall, is reading, bored, in his eternal old book.* LINUS *is drying, with a greasy cloth, five dented metal plates which are stacked on the table.* MAX *is not visible. Leaning against his folding bed,* THOMAS *watches* LINUS, *who smiles and shows him the plate he is drying. Their faces are all more emaciated now.*

LINUS.   Fine china! Worthy of the exquisite meal we've just bolted
   down.
   [THOMAS *lowers his head.*]
MAX'S VOICE. [*From behind the curtain*]   I've got the runs!
LINUS.   You too?
MAX'S VOICE.   A minor complaint.
   [LINUS *goes on with his task and becomes immersed in his peculiar humming. Without turning to look at it,* THOMAS *touches the piece of furniture he is leaning against like a blind man trying to identify its shape. Afterwards, he goes to the table and studies its metal form. He looks at* LINUS *and then at the others*]
THOMAS.   Have you always worn those pants?

TULIO. [*Without looking up from his book*]   Ever since we came here. [THOMAS *sneaks a look at his own to compare. He then walks slowly behind* LINUS *to the small table. Doubtful, he places his hands on it.*]

ASEL.   The ration was worse than ever today.

MAX.   Little more than slop.

ASEL.   I wish I knew if it was punishment for us or if everybody got the same.

MAX'S VOICE.   I don't think they're giving us any special treatment. . . . They haven't even shaved our heads.

ASEL.   No, and it's odd. [*Brief pause*]

THOMAS. [*To himself*]   The magazines were here.

[ASEL *looks at him.*]

TULIO. [*Offering his book to* THOMAS]   If you want to read, this is all there is.

THOMAS.   No, thanks.

[TULIO *goes back to his reading.* THOMAS *turns his head and contemplates the radiant light of the landscape outside. The light in the room is dimming very slowly.*]

LINUS. [*Carrying the plates and the cloth to the shelves*]   Now you can sweep under the table. We're due for a room inspection.

TULIO.   They opened the doors a minute ago.

LINUS.   All except ours, of course. [*He looks for the broom behind the curtain and glances at the floor under the.table.*] It's not worth the bother to sweep. Nobody ever drops a crumb around here. [*He goes to the door, sweeps the trash into a more compact pile and, still holding the broom, leans against the wall with his arms crossed.*]

THOMAS. [*Facing forward*]   It's growing dark. [*He turns back toward the landscape, where the glorious morning still gleams.*]

TULIO.   You can't see a thing. They're taking their time to turn on the light. . . .

LINUS. [*Toward the curtain*]   Finish up, Max! They'll be coming soon.

MAX'S VOICE.   I'll be right there.

[*There is the sound of a toilet flushing.* THOMAS *notices it. Then he goes to the bed and sits at* ASEL'S *feet. He runs his fingers over the metal work of the bedframe. The light suddenly comes on over the bed.*]

TULIO.   Speaking of the devil . . . [*He tries to go on reading.*]

THOMAS.   This metal is strong.

ASEL.   Very strong.

THOMAS.   And the bed is fastened into the wall.

TULIO.   What a pitiful light! [*He drops the book on the table with a dull thud.*]

THOMAS. [*Standing up hurriedly*]   Maybe if I turn on . . . [*He starts to the left to turn on the overhead fixture. Silently the great glass shade rises and disappears; the light in the area that it occupied is now the same as in the room.*]

TULIO.   The what?

[THOMAS *watches the shade disappear without too much surprise and passes his hand over his forehead. He then goes to the head of the bed to turn on the reading lamp attached to the wall. He extends his hand only to see the little lamp sink into the wall.* MAX *comes out of the curtained alcove fastening his trousers under his loose shirt.* THOMAS *returns to downstage left.*]

THOMAS.   Asel . . . weren't any of those things ever here?

[MAX *sits on his bedroll.*]

ASEL.   Did you see something?

LINUS. [*Caustically*]   Of course he did. He even turned it on sometimes. A lamp.

THOMAS.   It's hard for me to think . . . that they only existed in my imagination.

TULIO.   You're to be congratulated, Asel. The mental confusion is clearing up. And a bit of extra food was all it took. You were right.

ASEL. [*Gravely*]   I'm not so sure.

TULIO.   The boy's better and it seems there've been no relapses.

ASEL. [*Hesitating*]   Yes . . . unless . . . something else is involved.

THOMAS.   Are you talking about me?

[ASEL *does not answer him.*]

TULIO.   I don't understand what you mean.

MAX.   Neither do I. What are you talking about?

ASEL. [*Measuring his words*]   Yesterday . . . Thomas had a visit from his girlfriend. Not here, but in the visiting room. At least that's what they said when they summoned him.

THOMAS. [*Surprised*]   And what about it?

[*They all look at him. We begin to hear doors slamming consecutively; each time the sound is closer.*]

LINUS.   The inspection! [*He takes a position against the wall beside the door.* MAX *and* TULIO *get up quickly and go to the door, stationing themselves at attention on the other side.* ASEL *puts away his pipe, leaps from the bed and lines up next to* LINUS. THOMAS *moves more slowly and takes a place, facing the door.*]

THOMAS.   The doors slamming . . .

MAX.   You hear them every day.

THOMAS.   Yes . . . I know that.

[*The sound of the slamming doors grows louder, recedes, and becomes louder again until it can be heard very near. Suddenly it ceases.*]

LINUS.   Attention. [*He stiffens. We hear the noise of a heavy key, and the door opens. The* SUPERINTENDENT *and his* AIDE, *in their elegant attire, are in the doorway. The fragment of remote countryside that could still be seen through the doorway has been eclipsed; now we glimpse another long gallery, several yards away and parallel to the familiar one, with a railing identical to the other. It projects over a gray wall in which the dark steel rectangles of numerous identical doors are visible.*]

SUPERINTENDENT. The garbage.

LINUS. Yes, sir. [*He quickly sweeps out the little pile and leaves it at left of the door, returning immediately to his rigid position. The* SUPERINTENDENT *enters and brushes* THOMAS *aside. With quick fingers, he inspects the utensils on the shelves; he pokes a bit at the duffel bags, runs his hands over the table, the bed. . . . His eyes investigate every corner of the room.* THOMAS *is struck by anxiety when he notices the new panorama through the door.*]

THOMAS. [*To the* SUPERINTENDENT] Why don't they let us go out? [*The* SUPERINTENDENT *turns around like a flash and studies him for a moment. From the gallery, the* AIDE *lets out a faint guffaw.*]

SUPERINTENDENT. [*Opting to smile*] The Foundation offers you once more its apologies, Mr. Novelist. It is necessary to open an investigation into what has happened here. And in the meantime . . . [*His hands complete his apology. He goes out into the corridor and speaks over the stifled laughter of the* AIDE.] We wish you gentlemen a peaceful repose. [*He exits left. The* AIDE *closes the door with a dull thud. Immediately the sounds of successive doors closing resume. The noise gradually diminishes for a few moments.* LINUS *leaves the broom behind the curtain.* TULIO *starts toward the most distant bedroll;* MAX *sits again where he was;* ASEL *walks slowly downstage and looks through the invisible window.*]

ASEL. It's night now.

TULIO. I'm going to unfold my sumptuous divan and lie down.

MAX. We have to conserve our strength.

[LINUS *sits on another bedroll and starts to hum absentmindedly.* THOMAS *hasn't moved. Suddenly he goes to the door and pushes in vain. Then he studies the brilliant landscape.* ASEL *notices what he is doing, moves back to the table, and sits on its edge with his arms folded.* TULIO *unrolls the bedroll at left and extends it along the wall after spreading the wrapping on the floor. He pounds the mattress without much effect and also softens up the pillow, which he puts in its place. He then tosses the narrow blanket over it all.*]

THOMAS. [*Mumbling*] I can't believe it.

MAX. [*Softly*] Can't believe what?

THOMAS. When they opened the door . . . you couldn't see the countryside.

MAX. What did you see?

THOMAS. A lot of doors . . . like ours.

TULIO. [*Sitting on his thin mattress*] And you heard them open and close.

THOMAS. Yes.

TULIO. [*To* ASEL] You must surely recognize that the process continues.

MAX. You believe you're seeing odd things, right? The Superintendent was probably dressed differently. In a uniform, for example . . .

THOMAS. No, no. He was dressed the same as always. But those doors . . . are incomprehensible.

[TULIO *stretches out with a sigh of relief.*]

ASEL. Something else is incomprehensible. And I wonder if you've all noticed how incomprehensible it is.

TULIO. I know.

ASEL. So what's your opinion?

TULIO. Perhaps they're thinking it over.

ASEL. There's nothing to think over. It's been three days since they discovered the dead man. They should have transferred us to the hole immediately. And we're still here.

[LINUS *stops humming.*]

MAX. But we're cut off from the rest and denied the right to take exercise.

ASEL. The transferral hasn't happened, and it always does, even for the slightest infraction. They haven't even searched us for weapons. [THOMAS *hears these words with amazement.* ASEL *turns to look at him.*] And even our isolation isn't complete.

[TULIO *sits up and looks at him.*]

MAX. Are you referring to what happened before the inspection?

ASEL. Thomas was called to the visiting room yesterday. Yesterday, two days after they discovered what we had done.

THOMAS. It was Berta. . . . You heard him say so.

ASEL. [*Without looking at him*] Isn't that unusual? Max, your mother has moved to a town nearby to see about you better, and she visits you frequently. It's certain that she must have tried to see you during these three days of isolation, and they haven't called you.

MAX. Special treatment . . .

TULIO. Like we've given him.

MAX. It's the only thing that they are in agreement with us about.

ASEL. You don't understand what I'm saying. Let's suppose for a moment that his mysterious girlfriend . . . didn't come, as she never came here.

THOMAS. But she did visit me! And she's here!

ASEL. [*Without looking at him*] She doesn't come, and they call him. And when he returns, he tells us about her visit.

[*They all look at* THOMAS *and he, astounded, at* ASEL.]

TULIO. What are you thinking?

ASEL. [*Twisting his hands*] The worst part of our situation is that we can't even speak frankly. I'm thinking what you are.

TULIO. [*After casting a glance at* THOMAS, *he murmurs.*] It's hard for me to believe.

MAX. [*Calmly*] And me.

ASEL. But you are thinking it.

MAX. Even if it were true, how can you explain that they don't move us?

THOMAS. [*Disturbed*] You're leaving me out of things again!

MAX. [*To* ASEL] You seem to be sorry that they haven't taken us to the hole. [ASEL *and* TULIO *exchange looks.*] We wouldn't be better off down there than here. Or would we?

TULIO.   We'd be worse off.

LINUS.   Then what does it matter?

ASEL. [*Irritated*]   It matters because it's not logical! And I don't like that at all.

MAX.   Given our situation, maybe they haven't considered the infraction so serious.

ASEL.   With Thomas, at least, they've acted differently.

LINUS. [*Laughing*]   Are you losing your confidence in him? You've changed in a hurry.

[THOMAS *sits on Asel's bedroll and hides his face in his hands.*]

ASEL.   I just wonder why they called him. That's all.

LINUS.   That I don't know. [*He gets up and disappears behind the alcove curtain.*]

MAX.   He must have had a visitor. . . .

ASEL. [*Sharply*]   We're not allowed visitors.

MAX.   Maybe they're making exceptions.

ASEL.   And what about your mother? [*Silence. The toilet is flushed.* ASEL *turns around slowly and faces* THOMAS.]

MAX.   Thomas, tell us about your visit with Berta.

THOMAS. [*Uncovering his somber face*]   I've already told you.

ASEL.   But not in detail.

THOMAS.   What difference does it make?

[LINUS *reappears and leans against the wall.*]

ASEL. [*Holding back his anger*]   Please.

THOMAS.   You think I'm lying.

ASEL.   Then tell us and don't lie.

THOMAS.   I've never lied!

TULIO. [*Mildly*]   Thomas, tell us about your visit. . . . I believe you.

THOMAS. [*Sighing*]   They called over that speaker. [*He points over the door.*] All of you heard it.

TULIO.   And then?

THOMAS.   Berta was waiting for me in the visiting room.

ASEL.   Behind a metal screen?

THOMAS.   No.

ASEL.   What do you mean no?

THOMAS.   Didn't you want details? Behind two screens. Our fingers couldn't even touch. They apologized for that.

LINUS.   What did they say?

THOMAS.   That they were doing it to avoid possible contagion. Because of the work she does in the laboratory and because of what had happened here.

TULIO.   What did your girlfriend say to you?

THOMAS.   She asked me how I was. I said fine. I reproached her for not coming to see me more often, or hardly ever phoning me.

MAX.   And she? . . .

THOMAS. [*Bowing his head*] She started to cry. She wouldn't tell me why. I told her she couldn't fool me, that something was wrong. Because . . . she was not wearing the clothes of the Foundation . . . but an old suit, without a number. She said that she was dressed that way because . . . she had gone into town to do some shopping . . . and she promised to visit me soon, or call me. But she hasn't come. . . . And she left in tears . . . really sobbing. And now you . . . I don't know what you suspect or what you're up to. And I don't understand anything about what's going on!

[ASEL *goes to the bed and sits at its foot.*]

ASEL.   And what did you say to them?

THOMAS.   A half-dozen words. They insisted on escorting me back.

MAX.   Perhaps they asked you about your novel. . . .

THOMAS.   And about your work . . . They expressed regret for the atrocity we had committed; they asked me if some medical experiment had been involved. . . .

ASEL.   Medical?

THOMAS.   They know that you're a doctor.

[ASEL *looks at the others.*]

ASEL.   Did you tell them?

THOMAS.   They already knew, didn't they? And they asked if it was a medical experiment.

ASEL   Mine?

THOMAS. [*Thinking*] I don't recall that they mentioned you specifically. They only asked me what our purpose was in doing it.

[ASEL *gets up and takes a few steps. He turns around.*]

ASEL.   And what did you answer them?

THOMAS.   That I wasn't well and that I didn't remember a lot of things . . . that, in my judgment, the absurd thing had been done to have something more to eat. Then they apologized again for the shortage of supplies and assured me that it would get better very soon.

LINUS.   They spend their lives promising.

TULIO.   But it hasn't gotten better.

THOMAS.   No. [*Silence.* THOMAS *looks at the landscape and notices that it is fading. It frightens him but he says nothing.*]

LINUS.   I'm going to make my bed. They'll be turning off the lights soon.

ASEL.   Wait. [*He goes very close to* THOMAS *and speaks to him.*] What else did you tell them?

THOMAS. [*Intimidated by the hardness of his tone*] I think . . . that's all.

ASEL.   You think. But your head doesn't always work so well. . . . You admit that yourself. You see things the rest of us don't see, you speak of people we don't know. . . . Let's suppose for a moment that your memory is false . . . a false memory that conceals the real one.

THOMAS.   She was in the visiting room. And she was crying.

ASEL.   Let's suppose . . . you didn't go to the visiting room; they take

you to an office. And they ask you why we concealed the death
of our companion.

THOMAS.   I told them on the way back!

ASEL. [*Forcefully*]   What else did you tell them?

THOMAS. [*Sitting up*]   You have no right to suspect me like this! [*He
leaps from the bed and* ASEL *grabs him by the arm.*]

ASEL.   Berta didn't come! Why did they call you?

TULIO. [*Intervening*]   Asel, you're going too far. . . .

THOMAS.   Let go of me!

ASEL.   What did you talk to them about?

THOMAS. [*Struggling*]   Let me go! . . .

ASEL. [*Angrily*]   Why don't they transfer us?

[THOMAS *pulls free and goes downstage angrily.*]

MAX.   An interesting question.

THOMAS.   Let someone answer that who knows. The Foundation is
very strange, I do know that. But the Superintendent has just
apologized! That was real! [*He points upstage.*] As real as that
landscape!

ASEL.   Which never changes!

THOMAS. [*With his finger extended toward the window*]   It's growing
dark! Night's falling and it's growing dark! Don't you see it?

TULIO.   The relapse.

ASEL.   Or a stupid lie.

THOMAS. [*Making an effort to remain calm as he speaks.*]   I'm not lying.
And Berta is here. She'll come tonight. Because I'm going to tell
her to right now.

ASEL. [*Ironically*]   By telephone?

THOMAS.   Yes! Before someone makes it vanish too. [*He goes slowly to
the phone and puts his hand on it; he watches the others suspiciously.
With an angry movement,* ASEL *extends his bedroll on the bed; without arranging it further, he observes* THOMAS *with deep distrust.*]

MAX. [*Meanwhile, being conciliatory*]   We all lose our calm sometimes,
and today it was Asel's turn.

LINUS. [*Looking at him*]   Not everyone.

MAX.   Everyone! You included. Asel's a very rational man, and if
something seems to him incomprehensible, he loses patience.
. . . Maybe your call will explain things. Pick up the phone. [MAX
makes a pleading gesture to ASEL *to keep calm.* ASEL *then lies back
against the edge of the bed and folds his arms.* TULIO *sits on his mattress.* THOMAS *glances around and picks up the telephone. He dials. A
long pause. He jiggles the phone several times and continues to listen
nervously.*]

THOMAS.   Nobody answers. [*The others watch him suspiciously. He
hangs up slowly, with a look of puzzlement. He withdraws his hand
and stands contemplating the telephone. Then he moves away without looking at anyone.*]

ASEL. [*Softly*]   I don't know what to think.

TULIO. [*Sitting on the bed beside* ASEL]   Now I'm the one who tells you: keep quiet and give it some thought.

ASEL. [*Keeping an eye on* THOMAS]   I'll try.

TULIO.   Maybe he is sincere and the process is still going on. It appears that the telephone is still here, but it no longer works.

LINUS. [*Softly*]   And it's possible that his girlfriend really did visit him. [*Unhappy with himself,* ASEL *arranges his mattress on the bed.* TULIO *goes closer to* THOMAS, *who notices him and proceeds to the folding bed and begins to open it up. Once his meager bed is ready,* ASEL *stretches out and enjoys his pipe.*]

TULIO. [*To* THOMAS]   You'll see your girl again, just as I'll see mine. At least I hope so.

[ASEL *shows interest in what* TULIO *has said.*]

MAX.   Yours?

TULIO.   I've never mentioned her to you. Why? I don't know. But tonight I can't get her out of my mind. I'm almost twenty years older than she is. I adored her and couldn't tell her so. Just imagine: I felt so ridiculous before that girl . . . [*He laughs.*] She had to propose to me.

[MAX *smiles.* LINUS *sits on his bedroll.*]

ASEL. [*Putting his pipe away*]   Where is she now?

TULIO.   Abroad. We decided that she should take advantage of the fellowship she'd won . . . [THOMAS *listens as he finishes arranging his bed.*] That was a real fellowship! When she came home, we were going to get married. I don't know where she is now. Her trip saved her.

THOMAS. [*Timidly*]   From what?

TULIO. [*Looking at him and smiling*]   From me . . . [*He sits.*] You don't know how much it means to me that she's safe and able to use her time productively. She has a doctorate in physics; she knows a lot more than I do. She came to me to find out what all the fuss about holograms meant . . . because I am a good technician. [THOMAS *is leery of this topic.*] If we were together again, there's an excellent university that would hire us . . . in another country. We spent a year there: the best year of our lives. We had all the equipment we needed, they built whatever we requested . . . and we approached it like a game . . . For us, the most fascinating of games.

ASEL.   Holographics? [*He goes toward them.*]

TULIO.   Yes. We played jokes on each other. We would project three-dimensional objects to fool the other. . . . We had achieved enormous perfection in the images and in disguising the projection source.

[THOMAS *stops what he is doing. He feels nauseated.*]

I fell for it more often than she; I've always been a little naive.

And she would burst into laughter, with that laugh of hers . . . that I'll hear always.

THOMAS. [*Very softly.*]   Stop talking.

TULIO.   One day she was waiting for me in the laboratory, sitting very quietly in a chair reading. I started to kiss her . . . [*He laughs.*] It was a hologram!

MAX. [*Astonished and amused.*]   A hologram?

TULIO.   From top to bottom! Even the chair! She had hidden behind a table, she began to laugh like crazy. [*He laughs.*] And I . . .

THOMAS. [*Shouting*]   Shut up! [*They all look at him. Silence.*]

TULIO.   Patience, boy. You'll have Berta in your arms again.

ASEL.   Don't tell him that.

TULIO.   Let's dream a little, Asel! [*Standing*] He'll be reunited with his girl, and I'll be with mine! Life would have no meaning if that didn't happen. I understand you very well, Thomas.

[THOMAS *shakes his head without turning around.*]

One day we'll have them in our arms! And they won't be illusions, they won't be holograms! [THOMAS *buries his face in his clenched fists.*] It will be a reality we can touch . . . of flesh and blood. [*He goes toward* ASEL.] That's why I'll do all that you say, Asel. It must happen!

LINUS.   What?

ASEL. [*Quickly*]   His reunion with her, man. [*He and* TULIO *exchange looks.*] You'll invite us to the wedding, won't you?

MAX. [*Looking at* ASEL *curiously*]   Now you're starting to dream.

ASEL. [*Laughing*]   Just a little unburdening, before the lights go out.

LINUS.   They're taking their time tonight.

ASEL.   Then what's wrong in using the time that's left to dream a little? Yes. Maybe one day we will toast the health of the happy couple.

TULIO.   We'll drink a lot of toasts on a lot of occasions. [*He paces.*]

MAX.   What occasions?

TULIO. [*Very seriously*]   When they give my girl and me the Nobel Prize.

[MAX *laughs broadly.* THOMAS *manages a smile and turns toward them slowly. The others laugh too; and* TULIO *laughs in turn.*]

Well, here we are in a madhouse and all happy. But I warn you that it was already being talked around the university . . . when we had the bright idea of coming back here.

MAX.   Homesickness.

TULIO.   Stupidity.

MAX. [*Laughing*]   I swear I'd like to have a beer now.

[THOMAS *looks instinctively at the place where the refrigerator had been.*]

LINUS.   So would I!

MAX.   To toast your Nobel Prize and the one that Thomas will get for his novel!

THOMAS. [*Smiling, he goes to the table and sits on the end.*]   Don't talk like children.

TULIO. [*Slapping him on the shoulder*]   Why not! We're all children, like you! Dream, Thomas. I'm sorry I criticized you for it. It's our right. To dream with our eyes open! And you're opening yours now. If we dream that way, we'll get somewhere.

ASEL.   If they give us time. [*He sits on* THOMAS'S *bed.*]

LINUS.   Sentences can be commuted, Asel! They could commute ours!

ASEL.   I prefer not to hope for that.

MAX.   What else can we hope for?

ASEL. [*He and* TULIO *exchange looks again.*]   True.

THOMAS.   What would they have to commute for us?

[*A burst of laughter from the others*]

TULIO.   Asel, that is the voice of innocence!

ASEL. [*Coldly*]   Perhaps.

THOMAS. [*He gets up; his manner is more outgoing.*]   I'm glad you said all that, Tulio. We've had our disagreements, but I am your friend. You'll be with your girl again! [*With strength and seriousness*] Life, the happiness of creating, awaits us all.

TULIO.   That's how it will be, Thomas. They won't destroy us. One day we'll remember all this, over a beer. [*He puts his arm around his shoulders.*] We'll say: it seemed impossible then. But we dared to imagine it, and here we are.

ASEL. [*Gravely*]   You said it. Here we are.

TULIO.   No, no! We shall be, we shall say: here we are. [*He presses* THOMAS'S *shoulder affectionately.*] And you, with your fantasies, have made me understand that. You're not so crazy. You're alive. Like me.

THOMAS. [*Moved*]   But . . . do you understand, Tulio? If we believe in that future it's because, in some way, it already exists. Time is another illusion. We don't hope for anything. We remember what is going to happen.

ASEL. [*With a melancholy smile*]   We remember that time does not exist, . . . if they give us time to.

TULIO. [*Laughing*]   Don't ruin this night for us, Asel. Not tonight!

THOMAS. [*Almost like a child*]   Not tonight, Asel. [*And he laughs too.*]

ASEL.   Agreed, agreed. Long live the eternal present! [*He takes out his pipe.*]

MAX.   Bravo! Smoke your pipe filled with air, Asel!

[ASEL *laughs and puts the pipe back in his mouth. But he puts it away at once and sits up, tense.*]

ASEL.   Shhh. Be quiet. [*Brief pause*] Don't you hear footsteps?

TULIO.   Footsteps?

[ASEL *gets up and looks toward the door.* LINUS *rushes to the door and listens with his ear against the metal.* TULIO *becomes tense.*]

LINUS.   They're coming closer.

MAX.   Maybe they're only passing by.

[*Absolute silence. A few seconds pass.*]

LINUS.   They're not going by. [*He steps back toward the right wall. The sound of a key. The door opens quickly. On the threshold, the* SUPER-INTENDENT *and his* AIDE. *Behind them the gallery full of closed doors. Both men have their right hand in their jacket pocket; the* SUPERIN-TENDENT *has a piece of paper in his other hand. He enters.*]

SUPERINTENDENT.   C-81.

TULIO. [*His hand touches the inscription on his breast.*]   That's my number.

SUPERINTENDENT. [*Reading*]   Tulio? . . .

TULIO. [*Interrupting him*]   That's me.

SUPERINTENDENT.   Come with us and bring all your possessions.

ASEL.   No one else?

SUPERINTENDENT. [*Irritated by the question*]   From here, no one else.

[TULIO *gives a deep sigh and crosses to take his bag from its hook.*]

LINUS.   I'll help you. [*He turns around and takes a plate, a tumbler, and a spoon from the shelf.* TULIO *crosses with his duffel bag and leaves it on his mattress.* ASEL *goes to his side and bends over to help him.* LINUS *starts to cross; he hesitates and looks at the* SUPERINTENDENT.]

SUPERINTENDENT. [*Sharply*]   What's wrong with you?

LINUS.   Are they taking him below?

SUPERINTENDENT.   Why below?

LINUS.   Because of what happened here . . .

SUPERINTENDENT.   No.

[LINUS *goes on to* TULIO'S *mattress, opens the duffel bag, and puts the utensils in it. He immediately goes to the foot of the mattress and looks at* ASEL, *who is at the other end.*]

TULIO. [*In a weak voice*]   Let me do it.

LINUS.   No. Not you. [*With* ASEL'S *help, he rolls up the mattress and ties it with some cords attached to the cover.*]

THOMAS. [*At the same time, to the* SUPERINTENDENT]   Are they transfer-ring him to another room?

[LINUS *gives him a hard look;* TULIO *is motionless, with his eyes down; the* SUPERINTENDENT *smiles.*]

SUPERINTENDENT.   To another place.

THOMAS.   I never went so far as to request it, Tulio . . .

TULIO.   I know. Don't worry.

THOMAS. [*Puzzled*]   Come back to see us. . . .

SUPERINTENDENT. [*To* ASEL *and* LINUS]   Get a move on you!

ASEL.   It's ready. [*He and* LINUS *stand at attention.*]

SUPERINTENDENT. [*To* TULIO]   Pick it up.

TULIO. [*Disdainfully*]   Not without saying goodbye first.

[*The* SUPERINTENDENT *shows his impatience but he says nothing.*]

Thomas, we'll always be friends.

[*He embraces him.*]

THOMAS. [*Smilingly*] I swear we'll not have any more arguments. I'll see you soon.

TULIO.   In case we don't see each other, just a word of advice. . . . Wake up from your dreams. It's a mistake to dream. [*He releases* THOMAS.]

THOMAS. [*Surprised*] But . . . I thought we . . .

TULIO. [*He cuts him off with an affectionate pat on the shoulder.*]   Good luck. [*Turning to* MAX] Max . . .

MAX. [*Embracing him*]   Keep your courage.

TULIO.   I will. Thanks for your help, Linus.

LINUS. [*Embracing him*]   We won't be any luckier than you.

TULIO.   Who knows? [*To* ASEL] Who knows, Asel? They haven't given me enough time, but it can all still work out. [*They embrace warmly.*]

ASEL. [*His voice breaking*]   Tulio . . . Tulio.

TULIO.   No. Don't weaken now. [*They separate. Their hands are still firmly clasped.*]

SUPERINTENDENT.   Come along!

[LINUS *and* ASEL *hoist the bedroll onto* TULIO'S *shoulder. He walks to the door and turns around.*]

TULIO.   Luck to all of you!

THOMAS. [*Affected in spite of himself*]   I hope you see your girl soon, Tulio! [*For* TULIO, *this is like a stab in the back, and a look of desperation comes over his face. But he grits his teeth and exits rapidly, disappearing at left. The* SUPERINTENDENT *exits behind him, and the door is closed. Silence.* ASEL *throws himself down on his bedroll.*]

LINUS. [*Striking his hand with his fist*]   That's why they didn't turn off the light!

MAX. [*Mumbling*]   I'll make my bed. [*He goes to his bedroll.*]

LINUS.   Do you prefer his place? It's more private.

MAX.   You take it.

[LINUS *takes his bedroll and begins to spread it out in the place that* TULIO'S *had occupied.* MAX *extends his between the bed and the table.* ASEL *begins to undress very slowly: first, his shoes, which he places under the bed. Then his shirt, which he puts at the foot of the bed. He is deep in thought.*]

We'll try to sleep. [MAX *takes off his shoes and unbuttons his blouse.*]

LINUS.   Will they deprive Tulio of light also?

ASEL.   At dawn.

LINUS.   You didn't understand me.

ASEL.   You didn't understand *me*.

LINUS. [*Taking off his shoes*]   We'd better hurry. They're going to turn it off. [*He continues undressing.* THOMAS *sits on his bed and takes off his shoes.*]

THOMAS.   We're all sorry to see Tulio leave. . . . He was a good companion in spite of his moods. [*He starts placing his clothing on the bed.* LINUS *watches him closely.*]

ASEL.   Just be quiet, please!

MAX.   Don't pay any attention to him.

ASEL.   None of you can understand how alone I feel.

THOMAS. [*Fondly*]   You're not alone, Asel. And it won't be long before
we see Tulio again. [*He has finished undressing and remains in
immaculate underwear, which contrasts with the tattered and not
very clean underclothes of his companions.*]

ASEL. [*Harshly*]   If you were pretending, you would not be forgiven.

LINUS.   I don't think he's pretending. He just doesn't want to wake up.

THOMAS.   Wake up?

LINUS. [*Bitterly*]   The last thing Tulio said to you . . . don't forget it,
because you won't see him again.

THOMAS.   What do you know about it?

LINUS.   They're going to kill him!

[THOMAS'S *expression suddenly changes, and he stands up. The light
over the door goes out. The only illumination is the pale moonlight
that penetrates through the invisible window.*]

MAX.   At least there's a moon. [*He finishes undressing hurriedly.*]

THOMAS. [*To* LINUS]   What did you say?

LINUS.   They're going to kill him, you fool! Like all of us! [*To* ASEL] He
has to be told, Asel, even if you don't wish it!

ASEL. [*Seated on his bed, he looks at* THOMAS.]   I have nothing more to
say.

THOMAS.   Are we all losing our minds? [*Suddenly he runs to the telephone.*]

LINUS.   Where are you going?

[THOMAS *starts to pick up the phone as the instrument slides across the
table and disappears through an opening in the wall which then
closes.*]

THOMAS.   Are you all trying to destroy me? . . . Asel, can't I even trust
in you? [*In the face of* ASEL'S *silence, he returns to his bed and sits
down, trembling.*]

ASEL. [*In a voice like ice*]   What else did you tell them when they called
you?

[*With a desperate gasp,* THOMAS *hurriedly climbs between his clean
sheets. He contracts his body and pulls the sheet up until only his staring eyes are visible over the edge.* ASEL *lifts up his legs, props them on
the bed and hides his face in his hands.* MAX, *seated on his bedroll,
can hardly be seen behind the table; his arms crossed over his knees,
he rests his head on them.* LINUS *sighs and crawls under his blanket;
half sitting up on one elbow, he stares straight ahead. A long pause.*]

LINUS.   What else could he have told them? And what can it matter to
you?

ASEL. [*Without lifting his head*]   Very little now. This is the end.

LINUS.   You shouldn't think the worst. . . .

ASEL.   You're young. . . . Is this the first time?

LINUS.   Yes. And you?

ASEL.   The third. The second was very long. This one won't be so long. And there won't be a fourth time.

LINUS.   You can never say that.

ASEL.   Even if I escaped from this one, there wouldn't be another. I've used up my strength. For some time now I've been asking myself if it wouldn't be preferable to hear music, to see television sets, cars, refrigerators, all around me. . . . If Thomas wasn't pretending, his world was real for him, and a lot more bearable than this horror in which we insist that he live too. If life is so short and so poor, and he enriched it this way, perhaps there is no other wealth, and we're the crazy ones for not imitating him. . . . [*With sad humor*] It's curious. I would like for all that I've fought against, because it's a lie, to be true. [*He laughs feebly.*] These are the things you think when you know it's all over.

LINUS.   Only when you're tired. Tomorrow you'll see things differently.

MAX.   Shall we try to rest then? It's all we can do. [*He crawls into bed and covers up.*]

LINUS.   Are you asleep, Thomas? . . .

[THOMAS'S *eyes are wide open but he doesn't answer.*]

MAX.   At least there won't be any more visits tonight.

LINUS.   I hope you all get some rest. [*He stretches out, turns toward the wall and covers himself up.*]

ASEL.   Poor Tulio. [*He lies down. Without changing his position,* THOMAS *closes his eyes. A long pause. Very soft, almost inaudible, a faint melody begins: Rossini's "Pastorale." At the same time, and with no change in the spectral moonlight inside the room, the gentle light of dawn brightens the landscape behind the window.* THOMAS *opens his eyes and listens, ecstatic, to the soft notes. A silent silhouette appears slowly from behind the bathroom curtain.* THOMAS *sits up suddenly and sees* BERTA, *dressed in the white outfit of her first appearance.*]

THOMAS.   [*Very softly*]   Berta.

[*She motions to him to be silent and advances cautiously, looking at the sleeping men. Then she sits on the edge of* THOMAS'S *bed.*]

BERTA.   Keep your voice down.

THOMAS.   How did you get in? The door is locked.

BERTA.   Not for me.

THOMAS.   You certainly took your time.

BERTA.   [*Ironically*]   If you wish, I'll leave.

THOMAS.   [*Grabbing one of her hands*]   No. You're my only certainty.

BERTA.   Certainty?

THOMAS.   I'm going to wake them up. I want them to see you.

BERTA.   They're tired. Let them sleep.

THOMAS.   They've moved Tulio.

BERTA.   I know that.

THOMAS. The others told me that they're going to kill him. But it's not true. If you're here, it's not true.

BERTA. I suppose you know.

THOMAS. I don't know anything, Berta. Why is the Foundation treating us this way? Do you know?

BERTA. Yes, and so do you.

THOMAS. I don't.

BERTA. Well, then you don't.

THOMAS. [*He embraces her and she allows it passively.*] Won't you answer me? Have you come to tease me? . . . You used to love me. It's not the same now.

BERTA. [*With a little laugh*] No?

THOMAS. Please don't laugh.

BERTA. [*Serious*] As you wish. [*She looks into space.*]

THOMAS. Why were you crying in the visiting room?

BERTA. For Thomas.

THOMAS. For the mouse?

BERTA. He's very sick.

THOMAS. Is he going to die?

[*Silence*]

He'll be a martyr.

BERTA. For science.

THOMAS. If you've inoculated him with something . . .

BERTA. No, nothing. I don't even know if there'll be any research. [*They look into each other's eyes.*]

THOMAS. Then what is Thomas going to die of?

BERTA. [*Sharply*] I don't know if he's going to die.

THOMAS. He's alive, so he'll die. He'll die, Berta. And we don't even know if there will be any research. Come here. [*He pulls her toward him.*]

BERTA. What do you want?

THOMAS. [*He lifts the bed covers.*] Lie down beside me.

BERTA. [*She lies back.*] What about them?

THOMAS. What does it matter? Let's devour each other. Consume me, kill me.

BERTA. [*With a little laugh*] Is that all you want me for?

THOMAS. What difference does it make? You're not Berta anymore. [*They look at each other. She throws herself on him and bites his lips. As they kiss, his hands become bolder. They fall back together on the bed; he lifts the covers so that she can get under them. The kiss goes on; he moans softly. The music suddenly stops and* ASEL'S *voice is heard.*]

ASEL. What's wrong with you, Thomas?

BERTA. [*Sitting up quickly and whispering*] I told you so!

THOMAS. [*Whispering*] Go into the bathroom.

[BERTA *gets up and steps back toward the curtained alcove. She disappears.* ASEL *sits up on the side of his bed.*]

ASEL.   Whom were you talking to?

THOMAS. [*Not sitting up*]   Nobody.

ASEL.   You're not going to tell me that you thought we were asleep. No
one could sleep after what happened to Tulio. Not even you.

THOMAS.   I wasn't asleep.

[MAX *sits up in his bed.*]

ASEL.   Then were you trying to fool us?

[THOMAS *sits up, sullen.*]

To show us that Berta, in spite of everything, had come. Was that
it?

MAX.   Even if he wasn't asleep, maybe he was imagining it.

ASEL.   That's what I say.

MAX.   You don't get my meaning. I'm talking about . . . the compensa-
tions of loneliness. Relieving the senses by imagining a pleasant
intimate encounter . . .

THOMAS. [*Unsure*]   I wasn't imagining.

ASEL. [*Bitterly*]   He wasn't imagining. Berta has come . . . and gone.

THOMAS. [*Unsure*]   . . . She hasn't gone.

LINUS.   What?

THOMAS.   She's . . . in the bathroom. [*A loud laugh from* LINUS. *Exasperated,* THOMAS *puts his hands to his head.*] Yes, and you're going to
see her! I won't let her leave until you see her! It's time to put an
end to all this secrecy.

ASEL.   If they took Tulio because of something you said . . .

MAX.   What could he say to them?

THOMAS. [*Putting on his pants quickly, he gets up.*]   Berta is listening to
every word you say! You're going to see her now!

ASEL. [*Getting up too*]   Fine! Have her come out!

[LINUS *gets up, intrigued.*]

Call her!

THOMAS. [*stammering*]   You want me to call her?

LINUS.   Yes! Call her!

THOMAS.   Berta! Come out, Berta! Now! [*He waits a few instants; he
runs toward the curtain. Angry,* ASEL *stops him.*]

ASEL.   Is it your fault that they haven't transferred us?

THOMAS.   Let me go!

ASEL.   Answer!

[THOMAS *evades him and runs to the curtain, lifts up a portion of it
and looks behind it. Demoralized, he looks again. He turns around.*]

THOMAS. [*Very softly*]   She's not here.

MAX. [*Calmly*]   But the door hasn't been opened.

[THOMAS *rushes to the door and pushes it in vain. Then he beats on it
in a frenzy.*]

THOMAS.   I want to get out! . . . I want to get out! [*They all run to subdue him.*]

LINUS   Quiet, you lunatic! They'll hear you!

THOMAS. [*Sobbing*]   . . . get out!
[LINUS *gives him a slap.* THOMAS *falls to his knees as they release him.*
He cries silently. MAX *withdraws and sits on the table.*]
MAX.   He's beginning to disgust me.
[*The landscape is growing darker, almost to total blackness.*]
THOMAS.   She . . . hasn't come. [*He looks toward the window.*]
ASEL.   Do you admit that?
THOMAS.   She never came. [*Absorbed in the night that inundates the*
landscape] I've been delirious.
MAX.   Spare us your playacting. You're not going to fool us any longer.
[THOMAS *hides his face in his hands.* LINUS *walks away and sits on his*
bedroll. Silence.]
ASEL. [*Who has been watching* THOMAS *with the keenest attention*]   It's
not playacting.
MAX.   Please, Asel! It's impossible to believe him now.
ASEL.   On the contrary. Now is when he can be believed. And I'm
sorry for all I've said to him.
MAX.   Don't defend him anymore!
ASEL.   If his hallucinations were invented, he would have maintained
that Berta was in our presence, even when we didn't see her. Or
that the door was being opened and she was running away, even
if the door remained closed. A liar who was caught in the act
would have done that. The disappearance of Berta is the reality
that overtakes him in spite of himself. . . . That meeting may
have been the last attempt to escape into his delusions and the
final crisis.
LINUS.   Why final?
ASEL.   He said himself that she never came here. . . . Believe him. He
can't be lying.
[*Silence. Perplexed,* LINUS *gets up and looks at* THOMAS, *who has*
been listening to ASEL *with increasing emotion.* ASEL *goes over to*
THOMAS.]
Thomas, do you know where you are?
THOMAS. [*Humbly, his head down*]   You tell me.
ASEL.   No. You say it.
[*A short pause*]
THOMAS.   We're in . . . jail.
ASEL.   Why?
THOMAS.   You say it.
ASEL.   No. You.
THOMAS.   I . . . don't remember very well . . . yet.
ASEL.   Then go to bed. Rest.
[THOMAS *stands up and walks toward his bed. For a second, he looks*
at the landscape, now dark and faint. He unfastens his pants, sits on
the bed, and takes them off. LINUS *stretches out again on his bed.*]
THOMAS.   Is it true . . . that they're going to kill Tulio?

ASEL.   Yes. [*He sits down on his bed.*]

THOMAS.   Was he . . . condemned to death?

LINUS.   Yes.

[THOMAS *crawls into bed. Silence.*]

THOMAS.   Couldn't it be just a transfer?

ASEL.   Those who are condemned to death are no longer taken to another prison.

LINUS.   If they take only one, it's because they're going to carry out an order of execution.

MAX.   [*Returning to his bed*]   And besides, they ordered him to leave with all his belongings.

THOMAS.   I don't understand. . . .

ASEL.   In every prison they have their own way of doing things. In this one, when you go to be executed, you have to take all your possessions . . . and leave them in the office.

LINUS.   If they transfer you to the special punishment cells, they also tell you: "With all your possessions." When you hear that, it won't be too difficult for you to figure out what's in store for you.

MAX.   If they order you to leave and bring nothing with you, either it's for a visitor or for business.

THOMAS.   Business?

ASEL.   Interrogation . . . very hard . . . unbearable.

[THOMAS *sits up and looks at him. A brief pause.*]

THOMAS.   Are we condemned to death?

[ASEL *hesitates.*]

LINUS.   All of us.

[*Silence*]

THOMAS.   Yes . . . I seem to remember. You explain it to me, Asel.

ASEL. [*Enigmatically*]   Why me?

THOMAS.   I don't know.

[ASEL *goes to his side.*]

ASEL.   Our individual cases matter little. You'll remember yours, but that's the least of it. We live in a civilized world that still finds the very old practice of killing the most intoxicating sport of all. They murder you for fighting established injustice, for belonging to a detested race: they let you starve to death if you're a prisoner of war, or they shoot you for supposed attempts to incite revolt; secret tribunals condemn you for the crime of resisting in your own occupied nation. . . . They hang you because you don't smile at the one who decrees smiles, or because your God is not theirs, or because your atheism is not theirs. . . . Throughout time, rivers of blood. Millions of men and women . . .

THOMAS.   Women?

ASEL.   And children . . . The children pay too. We've burned them, suffocating their terrified cries to their mothers, for forty centuries. Yesterday the god Moloch devoured them in a brazier in his belly; today napalm eats at their flesh. And the survivors can't congratulate themselves either: children who are crippled or blind. . . . Their parents have destined them for that. Because we are all their parents.

[*Short silence*]

Am I supposed to remind you where we are and which of those killings we face? No. You'll remember.

THOMAS. [*Somberly*] I already remember.

ASEL.   Then, now you know . . . [*He lowers his voice.*] This time it has been our turn to be victims, my poor Thomas. But I'm going to tell you something . . . I prefer it. If I saved my life, perhaps one day it would be my turn to play the role of executioner.

THOMAS.   You no longer want to live?

ASEL.   We must live! To put an end to all the atrocities and all the outrages against humanity. But . . . in so many terrible years, I've seen how difficult it is. It's the hardest struggle: the struggle against oneself. Combatants sworn to carry out a violence without cruelty . . . and incapable of distinguishing, because the enemy doesn't separate them either. That's why a strange calm comes over me at times . . . almost a kind of happiness. The happiness of ending up as the victim. The truth is, I'm tired. [*Silence*]

THOMAS.   Why . . . everything. . . ?

ASEL.   The world is not the landscape you envision. It's in the grip of plunder, of lies, of oppression. It's one long calamity. But we do not resign ourselves to endless calamity, and we must abolish it.

THOMAS.   We?

ASEL.   Yes. Even though we're exhausted. [*He lowers his voice.*] Even though we may fear to dirty our hands and lie.

THOMAS. [*Thinking*]   Was I fighting too?

ASEL.   Yes.

THOMAS.   With you?

ASEL   In a sense.

THOMAS.   Yes. I'm beginning to remember. [*He rubs his hand over his forehead.*] But I don't remember you.

ASEL.   You never saw me before coming here. But we had a certain relationship.

THOMAS.   What kind?

ASEL. [*Pressing his shoulder*]   If you remember it, I'll help you understand what happened.

THOMAS. [*After a moment*]   Victims . . .

ASEL.   That's how it is.

THOMAS.   Poor Tulio.

[*The light begins to dim.*]

LINUS.   The moon has gone behind a cloud. Let's try to sleep. [*He covers up with his blanket.*]

ASEL.   Rest, my boy. [*He goes upstage and gets into bed. Almost complete darkness. Distant and faint, the monotonous chant of a sentry is heard: "Station One, all is well." A few seconds later, a second voice, closer, responds: "Station Two, all is well."]*

THOMAS.   The sentries.

ASEL.   Like every night.

THOMAS.   But I refused to hear them.

[*Another voice, still closer: "Station Three, all is well." On the dark background behind the window, a faint figure emerges little by little. It is* BERTA, *and she seems to be holding something in her hands. Very tall, almost floating, the apparition captures* THOMAS'S *attention. He doesn't need to turn his head to see it. A fourth voice, very close, is heard: "All is well, Station Four." The arms of* BERTA'S *image separate and her right hand is extended. From it, a motionless white mouse hangs suspended by the tail. Another voice, farther away: "Station Five, all is well." With a sorrowful expression, the image releases the mouse and it falls. The feminine head turns toward* THOMAS *and looks at him with the deepest pain. The light that illuminates the fig-ure fades completely and darkness prevails, while the calls of the sixth, seventh, and eighth sentries are heard, each more distant than the last. The curtain falls for a few moments or blackout.*]

Scene 2

Harsh daylight. The large window has disappeared behind a flat identical to the other walls. At right, in the space the folding bed occupied, there is now another bedroll. The only thing that remains from THOMAS'S *imagina-tion is the curtain over the alcove, which is still in an indistinct half-light.*

THOMAS *is seated on his bedroll, deep in thought. His gray pants are identi-cal to those of the others; his blouse hangs loose.* ASEL, *seated at the head of the bed on his bedroll, sucks on his empty pipe. Seated on his bedroll at the left end of the table,* LINUS *strums on the metal frame.* MAX *is similarly seated near the right end, with his hands folded on the table. A few seconds of silence.* THOMAS *touches his bedroll pensively; then he takes a pinch of his pants and examines the cloth.*

THOMAS.   My mind has been full of amazingly clear images. And they were all false. And others, which according to you are the real ones, were simply erased.

[MAX *looks at him with mistrust;* ASEL *watches him with interest.*]
Am I crazy, Asel?

ASEL.   I suppose you've suffered what doctors would call an episode of schizophrenia. Still, I can't tell you for certain because . . . [*He smiles.*] I'm not a doctor.

THOMAS. [*Astonished*]   It's not the first time I've heard someone say that. Who said it before? . . . [*He points to* LINUS.] Yes. The engineer.

LINUS.   I'm not an engineer, Thomas.

THOMAS.   You aren't?

LINUS.   I'm a lathe operator.

THOMAS.   A lathe operator?

[LINUS *nods.*]

ASEL.   You always thought of him as an engineer. You changed our professions for us . . . Because I really am an engineer.

THOMAS.   You?

MAX.   Don't look like that. You've always known it.

THOMAS.   I assure you I didn't. . . .

MAX. [*To the others*]   I can't believe him.

THOMAS.   And you aren't a mathematician either?

MAX. [*Ironically*]   It depends on how you look at it. Numbers everywhere, yes . . . But as for integral calculus, not a bit. I'm an ordinary accountant, as you well know.

LINUS.   You believed him before.

MAX.   Well, I don't any longer.

[*Brief pause*]

THOMAS. [*To* ASEL]   Why would I insist that you were a doctor?

ASEL.   I suspect that you invented a doctor because you needed to. [*Smiling*] And I tried not to be too bad a doctor for you.

LINUS.   Did Berta really come to the visiting room?

THOMAS. [*He stands up anxiously; he takes a few steps.*]   Yes. It was hard for me to recognize her. Poorly dressed . . . she looked unwell. [*Holding back his emotion*] She was studying to be a laboratory technician. But there was no fellowship from any Foundation. . . . She had just lost her job when they arrested me.

ASEL.   Do you remember that?

THOMAS. [*He looks through the invisible window.*]   She's all I have in the world. I lost my parents when I was a child, and there was no one to pay for my education. I took all sorts of jobs, and I read everything I could. I wanted to write. And she encouraged me. I didn't dare involve her in anything. They would have questioned her and even abused her physically. I may never see her again.

[*A pause.* LINUS *starts humming. A metallic voice comes from the grill over the door.*]

VOICE.   Attention. Number C-96, prepare for the visiting room.

[LINUS *stops humming.* THOMAS *looks up.*]

MAX. [*Standing up*]   It's for me!

VOICE.   Attention. Prepare for the visiting room, C-96.

MAX. [*Smoothing down his hair with his hands to make himself more presentable*]   I have a visitor!

THOMAS. [*To the others*]   It must be his mother. . . .

MAX.   Of course! My mother! [*He runs to the door to listen.*]

LINUS. [*Thinking*]   Then we're not forbidden contact with the outside.

MAX.   Well, no! Thomas had a visitor, and now mine proves it. Maybe your parents will come tomorrow, Linus!

LINUS.   How I wish.

MAX. [*Listening*]   Be quiet.

ASEL. [*To himself*]   It still doesn't seem logical.

MAX.   I think it is. They've limited our isolation to a few days in view of the fact that we're under the death penalty.

[ASEL *looks at him dubiously.*]

LINUS.   Maybe she's bringing you some food. . . .

MAX.   It would certainly be welcome, but I don't know. The poor thing hardly has enough for herself.

LINUS. [*Pessimistic*]   Or maybe she brought it and they won't let her give it to you.

MAX.   They're here!

[*Sound of a key. The door opens halfway. The panorama of cells can be glimpsed in the background. The* AIDE *is in the doorway and is wearing a black uniform, visored cap, and a holster belt with pistol.*]

AIDE.   C-96, to the visiting room.

MAX.   Yes, sir. [*He exits and the door closes. A pause.*]

THOMAS. [*Sitting on* MAX'S *bedroll*]   In a uniform.

LINUS.   The aide?

THOMAS.   Yes.

LINUS.   He always came in a uniform. [*He gets up and walks about, still skeptical.*]

ASEL.   Now you see that your episode was temporary.

[LINUS *jumps onto the iron bed in a single leap and sits at* ASEL'S *feet.*]

LINUS.   Asel . . . [ASEL *motions to him to keep quiet.*]

THOMAS. [*Continuing the thread of his reflection*]   Was it because of my weakness?

LINUS.   Listen, Asel . . .

ASEL.   Afterwards. [*To* THOMAS] Because of weakness and wanting to escape from a reality that seemed unacceptable to you.

THOMAS.   Don't continue. . . .

LINUS. [*Impatiently*]   You tried to kill yourself. Everyone in the prison knows it.

ASEL.   No, Linus! Not that way.

LINUS.   Yes, man!

THOMAS. [*Standing up*]   It's true! I tried to throw myself over the railing. [*He points toward the door.*]

ASEL. [*Leaping to the floor and going to him*]   And I stopped you! [*Very affected,* THOMAS *looks at him and steps back.* ASEL *follows him and takes him by the arm.*] Easy. If you remember everything, stay calm.

THOMAS. [*Pulling away, in great distress*]   I informed on you!

LINUS. [*He sits on* ASEL'S *bedroll.*]   What? . . .

ASEL.   Yes, you informed on us. And you were closer to the head of our group than you realized.

THOMAS.   And you were arrested because of me, Asel!

ASEL.   I and the others, yes.

THOMAS. [*Choking*]   And they condemned you to death!

ASEL. [*Holding him by his arms*]   I told you I'd help you to understand! Get control of yourself!

THOMAS. [*Bowing his head*]   I have understood!

ASEL.   You haven't understood anything! You need twenty more years to understand. [THOMAS *leans on the table for support, and his face is convulsed with pain.*] What's wrong with you?

THOMAS.   I feel sick . . . I hurt . . .

ASEL.   It'll pass.

THOMAS.   My stomach. [*His face contorted, he looks toward the alcove curtain. He staggers over to it as if drunk and hides behind it.* ASEL *shakes his head sadly and leans on the table.*]

ASEL.   Don't go to pieces, boy. They caught you handing out leaflets, you told who gave them to you; he in turn informed on us, and they captured us all. Do you hear what I'm saying, Thomas?

THOMAS'S VOICE. [*From behind the curtain*]   Yes.

ASEL.   You talked because you couldn't endure the pain.

THOMAS'S VOICE.   I'm a despicable person.

ASEL. [*Shaking his head*]   You're a human being. Strong sometimes; weak at other times. Like almost everyone.

LINUS.   But he did inform on us.

ASEL. [*Sharply*]   And what about it?

[LINUS *shrugs: he has already passed judgment.*]

THOMAS'S VOICE.   A traitor.

ASEL.   We're close to death. Words like that no longer have any meaning to me.

THOMAS'S VOICE.   I can't forgive myself!

ASEL.   That's why you tried to kill yourself. And that's why, when I prevented it, your mind created the immense fantasy of the Foundation: from the beautiful landscape you saw on the wall to the shiny bathroom. [*The alcove curtain rises and disappears. At the same time, the light in the area becomes identical to that in the rest of the room. In the dirty corner, crusty with dampness, there is only a lidless commode with its high water tank, a button to flush it and, waist-high, a faucet over a metal drain. At one side, the old broom; on the other, crumpled pieces of paper on the floor. Very pale,* THOMAS *is sitting on the toilet, with a piece of paper in his hand. No sooner has the alcove curtain risen than he sees his companions and jumps up in embarrassment. He throws the paper in the toilet and pulls up his pants.*]

THOMAS. [*Fastening his pants clumsily*]   You saw me . . .

LINUS.   And you saw us. We're all tired of seeing each other's butt around here.

ASEL.   You believed that you were hidden by a door or some kind of
    curtain . . . [THOMAS *nods.*] Until now?

THOMAS.   Yes.

LINUS.   Modesty . . . what a luxury!

ASEL.   You've just lost your last refuge. Now you're cured.

LINUS.   Flush the toilet.

[THOMAS *pushes the button. The water is released. Not daring to look
at* ASEL, THOMAS *faces* LINUS *with humble eyes, and* LINUS *gives him a
severe look in return. Then he crosses and sits on the bedroll at left,
with his back to the others.*]

ASEL.   No one can be strong if he doesn't first know how weak he is.

THOMAS.   You were captured because of me.

ASEL.   I and the best who remained. [*He goes over to him.* THOMAS *hides
    his face in his hands.*] A catastrophe. [*He moves a little closer.*] But
    you couldn't endure the pain.

LINUS.   It was his duty to endure it!

ASEL.   Duty? [*He smiles.*] Categorical positions, solemn words:
    betrayal, duty, informer . . . You throw them around and he
    picks them up. In the final analysis, you're both alike: two young-
    sters. Have they ever tortured you?

LINUS.   They gave me a good working over when they brought me
    here.

ASEL.   Then keep quiet, because that's nothing. [*He sits at the table.*]
    And listen to what I say to Thomas. [*To* THOMAS] They tortured
    me. The first time, many years ago . . . Like you, I knew my duty
    was to keep silent. [*Brief pause*] But I talked, and my accusations
    cost at least one life. [THOMAS *looks up without turning around.*
    LINUS *does not miss a word.*] Are you surprised? A steadfast man
    like Asel confessing under physical pain? Hard to believe! But
    Asel informed. His flesh informed, after screaming like a tor-
    mented mouse. And now, tell me what Asel is: a lion or a mouse?
    [*Brief pause*] The courtyard of this jail fills up every day with
    naive souls who consider him a lion. But he knows that he can
    always be dangled like a mouse. It all depends on what they do
    to him. [*He sits a bit closer to* THOMAS.] His greatest fear is still
    that. Year after year, he lies awake knowing that he's like some
    soft-shelled mollusk between steel pincers. He's toughened a bit,
    to be sure. But he knows he can't resist indefinitely. And so he
    lives a half-life . . . afraid . . . feeling remorse for the poor man
    his words killed. [*To* LINUS.] I know what you're thinking, my
    young friend. [*He goes to his side.*] I've been like you as well as
    like Thomas. . . . You think that a man who is so afraid is incapa-
    ble of action. [LINUS *looks away.*] Of course. You have to believe
    that you can keep silent even under torture. But we're all afraid,
    and we all carry within us an informer and, still, we must act. I
    know very well I shouldn't be saying it, and I shouldn't demoral-

ize you! But on a very special occasion, like this . . . it's a time to be humble and sincere. [*He paces a bit and turns toward* THOMAS.] I saw it in you, and I wanted to save you. I did my part, and you must do yours. [*He puts his hand on* THOMAS's *shoulder.*] Don't be ashamed of your weakness in front of me. You're no weaker than I am. [LINUS *looks at him suspiciously; he jumps out of bed and turns on the faucet in the corner to get a drink of water.* THOMAS *breaks into quick sobs. Without turning around, he clasps the hand that* ASEL *has placed on his shoulder.*] No, man! None of that! [ASEL *steps away.* LINUS *turns off the faucet, turns around to look at them, and wipes his mouth with his sleeve. Then he goes downstage and looks through the invisible window. As* ASEL *passes behind him, he reaches out and grasps his arm for an instant without turning around.*]

LINUS.   You'd make a great legislator.

[ASEL *gives him a pat on the shoulder and stands beside him looking out.*]

ASEL.   Not very likely now. What did you want to tell me before?

LINUS.   A little thought that was bothering me . . . but I got side-tracked. It's evident that Thomas told the guards something. If he informed before, he must have also been the informer this time.

[THOMAS *looks up with surprise.*]

ASEL. [*Slowly*]   Informed about what?

LINUS.   You must know . . . I'm not in on the game.

[THOMAS *stands shaking his head.* ASEL *seizes* LINUS *by the arm and pulls him back.*]

ASEL.   What are you referring to?

LINUS.   You asked him several times if he was the reason they hadn't transferred us to the isolation block. If he had told them some-thing . . . that worries you and I don't know about . . .

THOMAS. [*Stepping forward*]   No! Asel, my head is clear. I remember the plan. But I never told them anything.

LINUS.   A plan?

THOMAS.   That you don't know about. Tulio did, and I remember it too. [*To* ASEL] I swear I didn't say anything.

LINUS.   Who knows about that. . . .

ASEL.   He's telling the truth.

LINUS. [*Going to the table and sitting on the bedroll at right*]   Possibly. But what I was thinking was not so farfetched.

ASEL. [*He sits on the edge of the table.*]   Explain yourself.

LINUS.   You wanted them to move us to the punishment cells in the basement.

[THOMAS *sits at the other side of the table.*]

ASEL.   It was just that the lack of logic troubled me. . . .

LINUS.   Do you think I'm a fool? It troubled you because they didn't move us. You were nervous, irritable, and you let some suspi-cious words slip out.

ASEL. [*He looks at him uneasily, smiles and sighs.*]   Well . . . let's say that
I proposed the scheme of passing off the dead man as sick for
two reasons: the first, to help us out a little with his food, and,
the second . . . yes, to get us moved to the hole.

LINUS.   And they didn't move us, so you think that someone put them
on guard.

ASEL.   It couldn't have been Tulio. Nor Thomas . . .

LINUS.   That leaves only two of us.

ASEL. [*Shaking his head and thinking*]   It wasn't you either, that's evident . . . [*Murmuring*] Could it be possible? . . .

LINUS.   There's no doubt in my mind: Max. I've suspected him for several days.

ASEL. [*With a gesture of concern.*]   Why?

LINUS.   Why is a squealer a squealer? [ASEL *looks at him with suspicion.*
LINUS *lowers his voice.*] One day I saw him talking with a guard.
They were laughing. They had called him, like today. But he
wasn't in the visiting room. I saw him pass by from the courtyard
door, not going in the direction of the visiting room but toward
the prison headquarters.

THOMAS.   They could have called him for a number of reasons. . . .

ASEL.   But he didn't tell us.

LINUS.   No. He only said that he'd come from seeing his mother.

ASEL.   Are you sure that's who it was?

LINUS.   Absolutely. But there's more.

ASEL.   Well, out with it!

LINUS.   Pegleg, the cripple fellow who's in one of the cells opposite us
. . . he's a wizard at opening the peephole from inside. About ten
days ago he told me something in the courtyard. And he's not one
to make things up.

ASEL.   He's a sensible man.

LINUS.   Well, the day before, Max had had one of his visitors. And
Pegleg saw him come back to this cell . . . very slowly . . . stuff-
ing himself with food from his package . . . while the guard
waited for him to finish, very amused by it all.

ASEL.   Any hungry man could have done that.

LINUS.   And what about the guard? He wouldn't have waited for any
of us.

ASEL.   That's for certain. . . .

LINUS.   He's the one who squealed. All of us have lost control here at
one time or another. Including you, Asel! But never Max. Always
calm, joking . . . He had a sureness about him that we lacked.

ASEL.   Why didn't you tell us about this before?

LINUS. [*Muttering angrily*]   I never trusted anyone. [*He lowers his voice.*]
Not even you.

[*Pause*]

ASEL.   He's going to return.

LINUS.   And soon. [*He goes to the door to listen.*]

ASEL. [*Nervously*]   We don't have much time left. [*Standing*] You have to be in on the plan, Linus. If they had moved us, I would have explained it down there. But they obviously suspect something. They suspect me. You were the last to come, Linus; and as for Thomas . . . they think he's crazy. Max has probably told them that I want to go to the hole. I've been imprudent, and they won't let me set foot there now. But they may let the rest of you, later, if you can figure out some way to get them to punish you. If you manage it, you have a possibility of escaping. [*He stops to listen beside the door.*]

LINUS. [*Excited*]   To get away? Now you're talking!

ASEL. [*He brings them together.*]   My profession gave me the chance to become familiar with the construction plans for this entire zone. And for this building. The isolation block is not near the outside wall; there's no worry about thick concrete. The cells are at basement level, with tiny windows that face one of the courtyards. Only ten feet below and some six feet behind the wall opposite the window . . . do you follow me? . . . [*He sketches in the air with his hand.*] . . . a sewer crosses. If a tunnel is burrowed from the edge of that wall, with a twenty-seven degree slope . . . [*His hands trace the triangle in the air.*] at seven feet and four inches, more or less, it will reach the sewer wall. If that is bored through, you must follow it to the right. Sixty feet further, it's almost certain there's a grating. It will be necessary to file through it. Once you're on the other side, you enter the northern collector. The best thing would be to walk left and try one of the exit shafts. It's a spot that's not closely guarded.

LINUS. [*Astounded*]   Are you out of your mind?

ASEL.   No.

LINUS.   What would you do it with? Your fingernails?

ASEL. [*Leaning on the table between the two of them.*]   Do you remember the angle, the direction?

THOMAS.   The hole, half in the floor and half in the wall opposite the small window, so that it can be covered with a bedroll. Is that right?

ASEL.   Exactly.

THOMAS.   Twenty-seven degree slope and some seven feet and four inches to the sewer line.

ASEL.   One other point: it can only work from cells 14 or 15. If they take you to any other, it will be impossible.

LINUS.   Why?

ASEL.   They are the only two with windows that face the same courtyard as the latrine windows of the second block.

LINUS.   What has that got to do with it?

ASEL. [*Lowering his voice*]   In that block there are two prisoners we can trust. There's no need for you to know their names. They have managed to smuggle in and hide a file, a cord, and a wicker basket. The bar is for excavating the tunnel. Spoons can be used too. Every night, after the final check, one of them goes to the latrine and stays there half an hour. If he hears on the floor three blows and one more, like this: pam-pam-pam; pam. . . , he'll determine which of the two cells they're coming from and lower the basket with the tools to the little window.

LINUS.   What about the noise?

ASEL.   You'll have to work all night and nap whenever you can during the day. All that subsoil is very cloddy; once you're on the other side of the wall and the floor, the sound will be negligible.

THOMAS.   And the rubble?

ASEL.   The basket will take up all the loads it can during the night. The others won't be sleeping either.

LINUS.   What if they search?

ASEL.   They usually don't in those cells. They think they're very secure.

THOMAS.   Where will they put all the dirt and rocks?

ASEL.   All that can't be gotten rid of in the latrine and through the outside windows will be put in the trash containers. They're building a new wing, so there's always debris in the common collection.

LINUS.   How many days will it take to dig the tunnel?

ASEL.   With two people working . . . six nights maybe.

THOMAS.   We'll be in constant danger of being discovered, of our friends in the cell block being caught. . . .

ASEL.   There's one greater danger: being executed before the transfer is carried out.

LINUS.   We can at least try! And if we succeed, I know where to go.

THOMAS. [Standing up and pacing anxiously]   It's absurd, Asel! That's not freedom; it's a hell! To dig into the earth only to die smothered in darkness, or under a cave-in. It's incredible . . . an illusion.

ASEL.   As incredible as freedom! That tunnel will be hell only if you don't believe in it.

THOMAS.   They'll hear us, they'll catch us!

ASEL.   Do you prefer the firing squad?

    [THOMAS stops, altered.]

LINUS.   Get it into your head, novelist. If something can be thought, it can be done.

THOMAS.   We can't even get them to transfer us.

LINUS.   We'll see about that.

    [His energy exhausted, THOMAS sits down on the iron bed.]

THOMAS. [To ASEL]   If you could come with us . . .

ASEL.   I suspect I've lost this game. But you two can win it. Try!

    [Silence]

LINUS.   What do we do with Max?

THOMAS.   We have to make sure. . . . If we were wrong . . .

LINUS.   After what I told you?

ASEL.   And Berta's visit to Thomas confirms it.

THOMAS.   Why?

ASEL.   He was informing on us when they called him to the visiting room. So that they could keep on calling him without arousing our suspicions, they first authorized your girlfriend's visit.

LINUS.   And he's informing this very minute . . . although he knows nothing concrete, fortunately.

ASEL.   Both of you, listen carefully: we have to pretend. Being at a disadvantage, we have to use our wits. If we show our hand . . . [A slight smile to THOMAS] The Foundation will eliminate us without a second thought.

LINUS.   Asel, we have to neutralize the informers! If they are an arm of the Foundation . . . [He interrupts himself.] Fine! Now I'm talking about the Foundation too!

ASEL.   Go on.

LINUS.   Exactly because we are at a disadvantage, we must deal relentlessly with any arm of the enemy!

ASEL.   Not here! The reprisals are always more severe!

LINUS.   But don't you understand?

ASEL.   You don't understand! You're young and you're impatient for action. I've been at this for years, and I know that in this case we have to be cautious . . . to protect our comrades in the cellblock, to avoid detection.

LINUS.   But it makes sense to unmask him and give him a scare! If they find out that we've discovered one of their stoolies, they'll eliminate him, because he's of no use to them anymore. And we diminish their strength!

ASEL.   We double it! We incite them to take away the little breathing space we have left. [He smiles sadly.] Linus, I've lived through many defeats that were the result of not having measured well the poverty of our means . . . But no one learns from another's mistakes. You're very quiet, Thomas. What do you think?

THOMAS.   I don't know what to say. It's all so complicated.

LINUS.   We must confront him now! As soon as he returns from that supposed visit with his mother.

THOMAS.   Why?

LINUS.   I think I've hit on a way to trap him.

ASEL.   How?

LINUS.   Let me think it out! [He sits, wary of ASEL's reaction.]

THOMAS.   We don't have much time. . . .

ASEL.   Linus, listen to me! Don't do it!

LINUS.   Just let me think!

ASEL.   Then think . . . but think hard. [Pause]

THOMAS.   It won't be long before he comes back.

ASEL.   No. [*He sucks on his pipe.* LINUS *hums very softly.*]

THOMAS.   Asel . . .

ASEL.   What?

THOMAS.   Have you ever wondered if all this is . . . real?

ASEL.   The jail?

THOMAS.   Yes.

ASEL.   Do you want to go back to the Foundation?

THOMAS.   I know that wasn't real. But I wonder if the rest of the world is any more so. . . . It happens to those outside too: a television set suddenly vanishes, or a glass that they're holding in their hand . . . or a beloved person . . . And they keep on believing, nevertheless, in their comfortable Foundation. . . . And sometime, from afar, they'll see this building and they won't say: it's a prison. They'll say: it looks like a great research center, a Foundation . . . and they'll pass on by.

ASEL.   Quite true.

THOMAS.   Then, isn't the prison perhaps equally an illusion? Our sufferings, our death penalty . . .

ASEL.   And we ourselves?

THOMAS. [*Avoiding his eyes*]   Yes, even that.

ASEL.   Everything, inside and out, like a gigantic hologram displayed before our perceptions, not knowing if they're our own, or what they are. And you, a hologram for me, and I, another one for you . . . Something like that?

THOMAS.   Something like that.

ASEL.   It had occurred to me before. [LINUS *has listened to them in astonishment. He brushes off their speculations with a gesture of his hand to follow his own train of thought.* ASEL *smiles.*] It seems silly to Linus . . . but I have indeed thought that.

THOMAS.   And if it were true, why escape from here to find freedom or a prison that are equally illusory? The only freedom would be in destroying the hologram, to find the authentic reality . . . which is here too, if it does exist . . . or in us, wherever we are . . .

ASEL.   No.

THOMAS.   Why not? [*A long silence*] Why not, Asel?

ASEL.   Maybe everything is one immense illusion. Who knows? But we won't find the hidden truth by turning our backs on it. We must immerse ourselves in it. [*With a penetrating look*] I know what your problem is at this moment.

THOMAS.   What is it?

ASEL.   It's not that you scorn escape as another fantasy, but you're cowered by the risks.

THOMAS.   My Foundation still has me entrapped. [*He sits down.*]

ASEL.   No, you've left it now. And you've discovered a great truth, even though it still may not be the definitive truth. Once you've been in jail, you come to understand that no matter where you go, you are in jail. You've come to that realization without escaping.

THOMAS. Then . . .

ASEL. Then you must exit into the other jail! [*Walking about.*] And when you're in it, go into another, and from it, to still another. Truth awaits you in all of them, not in inaction. You found it here, but only by making yourself see the lie of the Foundation you imagined. And it waits for you in the effort of that dark tunnel in the basement . . . in the hologram of that escape.

THOMAS. I'm ashamed that what I imagined was so absurd.

ASEL. You were afraid . . . you invented a rose-colored world. And not so absurd at that. . . . One day they'll build better prisons of metal and bars. The cells will have a television set, a refrigerator, books, and background music. . . . To the inmates it will seem like freedom itself. Then you'll have to be very intelligent indeed not to forget that you're a prisoner.

[*Pause*]

THOMAS. We have to think up some way to get the three of us to the punishment cells. With you beside me, I'll prefer the tunnel to the landscape.

ASEL. [*Putting his hand on* THOMAS's *shoulder*] Never forget what I'm going to say. You dreamed some foolish things, but the landscape you saw . . . is real.

THOMAS. [*Not understanding*] It has been erased too. . . .

ASEL. I know. It doesn't matter. The landscape was truly real.
[THOMAS *looks at him in astonishment.* LINUS *looks up and listens; he gets up and runs to the door.*]

LINUS. They're coming! And I have my trap set. You must tell him that they also called me to the visiting room and . . .

ASEL. [*He runs to him and grabs him by the arm.*] That's too flimsy to work.

LINUS. [*Pulling free.*] Just let me do it!

THOMAS. I won't be able to look him in the eye. [*He searches on the small table for the old book and sits at the left of the table, opening the book in front of him.*]

LINUS. They're here! [*He moves back from the door and leans on the edge of the table. The sound of a key. With a gesture of disapproval,* ASEL *gets on the bed and sits on his bedroll. The door opens halfway, and* MAX *enters smiling. The door closes.*]

MAX. Hello!

ASEL. How was your mother?

MAX. Weak and exhausted. But her spirits are good. [*Sadly*] She's convinced that she'll get my sentence commuted.

LINUS. Did she bring you anything to eat?

MAX. [*He laughs, steps forward, and pats him on the shoulder.*] You had to ask that, you hungry fellow! [*Sighing*] They wouldn't let her

bring the package in. [*He crosses and leans on* THOMAS'S *shoulder.*]
Are you reading that?

THOMAS. [*Without looking up*]   What do you expect? I'm bored.

MAX. [*Sitting beside him*]   The art books were prettier, weren't they?

THOMAS. [*Embarrassed*]   Please . . .

MAX.   Did you really see them?

THOMAS   I thought I did.

MAX. [*Sarcastically*]   You thought you did . . . Well, have it your way.
[*He looks skeptically at* ASEL. *He walks toward the right. Behind him,*
LINUS *sits up; he starts to speak.* ASEL *gives him a warning look,*
leaps from the bed, and grabs him. But LINUS *pulls free.*]

LINUS.   Have you been in the visiting room all this time, Max?

MAX.   Of course. Where else?

LINUS.   That's strange.

MAX.   Why?

LINUS.   Because I didn't see you.

MAX.   You?

LINUS.   They called me right after you. My parents came. And you
weren't there. Or your mother either.

[*Brief pause.* ASEL *pretends to be arranging something on his bedroll.*]

MAX.   What kind of game is this, Asel?

ASEL.   Why, I don't know, Max. . . . Linus just got back too.

MAX. [*He crosses and puts his hand on* THOMAS'S *shoulder.*]   Thomas,
did Linus have visitors?

THOMAS. [*With difficulty*]   Yes.

MAX. [*He no longer doubts that they suspect; he tries to throw them off the*
track.]   Fine. Now you can explain it to me.

LINUS. [*Curtly*]   What?

MAX.   The joke. Obviously all three of you are in on it. [*Laughing*]
Even our fantastic novelist. [*He gives* THOMAS *a pat on the shoul-*
der.] Because I was in the visiting room. And the one who wasn't
there was you, Linus.

LINUS. [*Turning to face him, he leans on the table.*]   Then one of us must
be lying.

MAX.   You weren't there, Linus! [*He starts walking nervously.*] And I
don't like your joke anymore, if it is a joke! Because it strikes me
more like some . . . foul suspicion, that I can't explain!

ASEL.   But if he didn't see you there . . .

MAX. [*Facing him*]   You're lying too! He hasn't left this cell.

LINUS.   And you went to the visiting room.

MAX.   Yes! [*He stops, breathing hard.* LINUS *approaches him with a smile*
and puts his hands on his shoulders.]

LINUS.   It's all right, Max. It was stupid of me to think you'd bite the
bait. My parents didn't come. Now, what about your mother?

MAX. [*Pale*]   Take your hands off me.

LINUS. [*He gives him a shove.*]   Go on, sit down. We're going to talk frankly. [*He forces him to sit on the bedroll.*] A few days ago we were in the courtyard, and they called you. An unexpected visitor! Do you remember? [*He sits on the table.*]

MAX. [*Coolly*] Yes.

LINUS. But you were in the office.

MAX. That's a lie!

LINUS. The guard with the mustache was with you. Both of you were laughing your heads off. . . . You looked like two lovers.

MAX. I won't put up with any more of your lies! [*He tries to stand up.*]

LINUS. [*Shoving him back down*] Sit down!

MAX. It's not true! Who saw me? Another madman like Thomas? Maybe it was Thomas himself. [*To* THOMAS] Did you see me? Or did you tell them you saw me so that they wouldn't suspect you?

THOMAS. What are you making up?

LINUS. [*Seizing his arm tightly*] Shut up, squealer! That tactic won't work. You're only getting youself in deeper. . . . I saw you!

MAX. You?

LINUS. From the door to the courtyard. [*He gets up.*]

MAX. You mistook someone else for me!

LINUS. My sight's good. And others saw you too. Ten days ago they saw you from one of the peepholes on the opposite side . . . [*He places himself behind Max and puts his hands on his shoulders.*] . . . returning to the cell. You were carrying the package you had received, and we shared it.

MAX. At least you remember that. I did share my package!

LINUS. After you'd stuffed yourself outside before you came in. And they saw the guard with the mustache too, laughing and waiting for you to get your fill. [*He laughs softly.*] Has the cat got your tongue?

MAX. [*Bowing his head*] It was weakness on my part, and I beg your forgiveness. We're all hungry, and the package was mine. . . . But I'm not an informer!

LINUS. Then you just like to chat with the guards. Now you can tell me what you talk about.

MAX. No . . . you're mistaken. That guard . . . he must be queer. He smiles at me, and takes me aside to tell me a lot of pointless things . . . You can understand why I didn't tell you about all the attention he was showing me . . . because I was embarrassed.

LINUS. [*Sitting on the table beside him*] No, you're not a fool. But if you're not an informer, who is? They didn't transfer us to the hole, they allow us to have visitors. . . . Someone from this cell is giving them information. Asel is a very important prisoner, and they've put a spy in his cell. [ASEL *makes a warning gesture.*] Who squealed? Thomas?

MAX. I have nothing more to say. You're all crazy.

LINUS. Because there's nothing you can say. A Judas like you has a difficult job. There are thousands of eyes watching you. Sooner or later they find you out.

MAX.   You haven't found out or proven anything.

LINUS.   No? . . . All right. Then we agree that your mother visited you.

MAX.   That's the truth; all there is!

LINUS.   And they didn't let her give you the package.

MAX.   No . . . not this time.

LINUS.   [*He leans toward him.*]   Let me smell your breath.

MAX.   What?

LINUS.   [*Seizing him by the hair and twisting his head back.*]   Open your mouth!

MAX.   Turn loose, you fool! If you think I'm going to put up with any more of your dirty tricks . . . [*He tries to get up, to get loose, but* LINUS *grabs his jaw and forces him to open his mouth.* MAX *lets out a groan.* LINUS *smells his breath.*]

LINUS.   [*Still holding on to* MAX, *he looks up at the others.*]   Get a whiff, Asel. And you, Thomas. [THOMAS *gets up.*] He reeks of wine. He gave them his report and got his customary payment in food and drink.

[MAX *flails his arms and moans.* LINUS *gives him a knee thrust in the stomach, causing him to scream in pain and become motionless.* THOMAS *goes over and sniffs* MAX's *breath.* ASEL *nods without making the test.*]

THOMAS.   You're right. [*He steps back.* LINUS *releases* MAX, *who doubles up.*]

MAX.   The guard with the mustache gave me a glass of wine . . . that's all.

LINUS.   Listen, you clown: this isn't a trial. We've had enough proof already.

[*Silence*]

THOMAS.   Did they beat you . . . to make you talk?

[MAX *looks at him askance and doesn't reply.* THOMAS *steps back, observing him; then he goes to the invisible window and takes a deep breath.*]

ASEL.   It's not the same thing, Thomas. He's only a small-time spy. They tell him that he may save his life, they offer him a few scraps, some cigarettes. . . . Above all, they provide him with the reassuring feeling that the ones in power are counting on him, that he's going to be a person again instead of a worm. I don't hate you, Max. You're a frightened child and you've sold yourself. No one would be a spy in a human world.

LINUS.   But now our little friend is going to tell us, willingly or by force, what he told them. And what they said to him. [*He sits down beside* MAX *again.* MAX *looks at him with fright. Worried,* THOMAS *goes back to sit on his bedroll.*] I also know how to make people talk.

ASEL.   No, Linus. No more violence.

LINUS.   You leave him to me. [*He leans over him.*] Come on, sweetie, loosen your tongue. [MAX *gets up, his eyes staring.*] Where're you going?

[MAX *steps back toward the right.* LINUS *stands up in a threatening manner.* ASEL *restrains him.*]

ASEL.   Leave him alone! It would only make matters worse!

LINUS.   You bet it's going to be worse! [MAX *runs to the door and starts pounding on it frenziedly.* THOMAS *gets up.* ASEL *rushes over and tries to pull* MAX *away from the door.* MAX *resists and pounds harder.* LINUS *hasn't moved.*] Let him call them, Asel! They're not going to be very happy about our little discovery. They'll toss him on the garbage heap now that he's of no use to them. [MAX *stops beating on the door. A pause.* MAX'S *heavy breathing can be heard.*] Come over here. You can clear up a few things. [*Desperate,* MAX *starts pounding again.*] Oh! You fear me more than you do them? There must be a reason.

ASEL.   Shut up, Linus! [*He struggles with* MAX.] Thomas, help me!

[THOMAS *goes to his assistance.*]

LINUS.   Why it's very easy! [*He goes over and seizes* MAX *by the neck with one hand.*]

MAX.   [*Choking*] No! . . .

[LINUS *leads him to his bedroll and shoves him down on it.* MAX *is gasping for breath.*]

THOMAS.   [*Listening near the door*]   They're coming!

LINUS.   [*He strikes* MAX *on the neck.*]   You damn snake! Don't open your mouth! [*He crosses and sits on his own bedroll.* ASEL *leans on the edge of the bed.* THOMAS *retreats downstage. After a few seconds, we hear the sound of a key in the door. The door opens. In the background, the closed cells. The* SUPERINTENDENT *and his* AIDE *appear in uniform, their expressions impenetrable. The* AIDE *remains in the doorway. The* SUPERINTENDENT *enters.* LINUS *gets up too but not quickly enough to restrain* MAX.]

MAX.   It was me! I was the one shouting! Take me out of here, please! Take me out!

SUPERINTENDENT.   [*Pushing him aside roughly.*]   You be quiet! C-73.

ASEL.   [*His expression changes; he stiffens.*]   I'm C-73.

SUPERINTENDENT.   Come with us.

[ASEL *looks at the others with an expression of dread. Then he addresses the* SUPERINTENDENT.]

ASEL.   With everything?

SUPERINTENDENT.   You were told to leave; nothing more.

LINUS. [*To* ASEL]   They didn't call you over the loudspeaker. . . .

ASEL.   It's for questioning. [*With a deep sigh*] I have nothing to say and I'll say nothing.

SUPERINTENDENT.   Get going!

ASEL.   Can I say goodbye?

SUPERINTENDENT.   For what, if you're coming back?

ASEL.   Who knows? [*He takes* LINUS'S *hand.*] Good luck, Linus.

LINUS. [*His voice husky*]   Courage.

[ASEL *looks at* MAX *with profound sadness.* MAX *aviods his eyes. Then he goes to* THOMAS *and clasps his hand.*]

ASEL.   Don't forget, Thomas. Your landscape is real. [*He exits to the gallery. The* AIDE *directs him to the left. The* SUPERINTENDENT *exits in turn.* ASEL *stops an instant.*] Yes . . . Yes . . . [*Suddenly he breaks into a run toward the right and disappears.*]

AIDE.   Stop! [*He takes out his pistol and aims it.*]

SUPERINTENDENT.   Where's he going? [*To the* AIDE] Don't fire. [*He disappears running to the right. We hear his voice.*] Stop! There's no way out! [THOMAS, LINUS, *and* MAX *go closer to the door.*]

ASEL. [*We hear his victorious exclamation.*]   There is a way!

SUPERINTENDENT. [*His voice farther off*]   What's he doing? Don't move! [THOMAS, LINUS *and* MAX *crowd into the doorway.*]

AIDE.   Get back, all of you! [*He pushes them back. We immediately hear the* SUPERINTENDENT'S VOICE.]

SUPERINTENDENT'S VOICE.   Come here, but don't fire! [*The* AIDE *disappears running.*] And you, don't move! [*Urgent blasts from a whistle. The* AIDE *is hardly out of sight when* MAX *goes out onto the gallery and looks to the right, holding on to the railing. With more caution,* THOMAS *and* LINUS *look out the door. We hear the* SUPERINTENDENT'S VOICE.] Get back inside! [THOMAS *and* LINUS *step back into the room;* MAX *doesn't move. The commotion increases. More whistle blasts, followed by shouting.*] Stay where you are! Get down from there!

AIDE'S VOICE. [*From a distance.*]   Don't do anything stupid! Nothing's going to happen to you! . . .

MAX.   He's going to jump!

SUPERINTENDENT'S VOICE.   Don't!

AIDE'S VOICE.   No!

MAX.   Asel! . . . He threw himself over.

THOMAS.   To keep from talking.

[*A dull banging far off. We begin to hear the prisoners pounding on the cell doors. Soon the sounds become more frequent and more intense until they are thunderous. Added to the clamor are numerous voices shouting: "Murderers! Murderers!"*]

SUPERINTENDENT'S VOICE.   Damn bastard! [*Shouting*] You two down there! Pick him up, quickly!

[*Cries, whistle blasts, running, the thunder of the doors. In a fit of outrage,* LINUS *lurches toward* MAX.]

LINUS.   You too! [*He seizes him by the legs, and with a quick herculean push, he throws him over the railing.*]

THOMAS. [*Crying out from the door.*]   Linus!

[*We hear* MAX'S *scream as he falls.* LINUS *enters rapidly.*]

What have you done?

LINUS.   They didn't see me.

THOMAS.   We're going to pay dearly for that!

LINUS.   He was guilty!

THOMAS.   But you've ruined everything!

LINUS.   I couldn't help myself. Those cries went to my head. [*He listens at the door.*]

THOMAS.   Linus, I can no longer pass judgment on anything . . . except myself. But that murder was wrong!

LINUS.   They're coming!

[*The sound of footsteps running toward the cell.*]

THOMAS.   I'll try to fix things. Go over there! Quickly! [*He points left. LINUS runs to his bedroll. The SUPERINTENDENT and his AIDE enter hurriedly. The din outside goes on.*]

SUPERINTENDENT.   [*He grabs THOMAS roughly.*]   What happened here? [*LINUS stands up.*]

THOMAS.   [*Displaying the greatest indignation*]   That's what I'd like to know! What's going on in the Foundation?

SUPERINTENDENT.   Don't talk nonsense!

THOMAS.   [*Pulling free violently*]   Let go of me! How dare you lay hands on the holder of a fellowship in the Foundation? I'm not talking nonsense and I demand that you explain what's going on! For days now, very strange things have been happening, and you are to blame! Yes, you! [*He goes from the SUPERINTENDENT to the AIDE reprimanding them.*] Have your jobs gone to your head? You're nothing but arrogant subordinates! [*He shouts at the AIDE.*] Put away that pistol! How dare you carry arms in the Foundation? I'll have you fired! I said, put away that pistol!

SUPERINTENDENT.   Put it away.

[*The AIDE puts it in his holster.*]

THOMAS.   That's better. And now, tell me: why have you permitted those noises, those terrible accidents? Why did Asel fall? Did you two push him? [*He takes the SUPERINTENDENT by the holster belt.*] What horrendous conspiracy is this?

SUPERINTENDENT.   [*Looking at him hard*]   Don't touch me. [*He pushes his hand away.*]

THOMAS.   [*In an emotional outburst*]   A conspiracy against me?

AIDE.   [*Stepping forward with a vicious look on his face*]   And who pushed C-96?

THOMAS.   No one!

AIDE.   What do you mean no one?

THOMAS.   He climbed up on the railing and jumped! I saw him from here. And it's your fault! You'll have to answer for that misfortune too! The good name of the Foundation demands it! Now get out! [*The SUPERINTENDENT brushes him aside with disdain and faces LINUS.*] Don't push me, you swine.

[*The banging and shouting have been dying down.*]

AIDE.   They seem to be getting tired. . . .

SUPERINTENDENT. [*To* LINUS]   Who threw C-96 over the railing?

LINUS.   Since I was forbidden to watch, I didn't see anything.

AIDE. [*In a low voice*]   Could he have done it?

SUPERINTENDENT. [*To the* AIDE]   Too afraid, maybe. Start collecting
their belongings.

AIDE.   Yes, sir.

[*The banging has ceased. The chorus of voices goes on, deliberately
and monotonously: "Mur-der-ers! . . . Mur-der-ers!" The* AIDE *goes
out and signals. Then he comes back in and takes two plates, two
tumblers, and two spoons from the shelves.*]

SUPERINTENDENT.   Why did C-73 want to be moved to a punishment
cell?

[*The* AIDE *stops and listens.*]

LINUS. [*Pretending surprise*]   That's the first I've heard of it.

SUPERINTENDENT.   Don't try to fool me!

LINUS. [*Laughing*]   Why would he want to go down to those rat-
infested holes? [*He and the* SUPERINTENDENT *are looking at each
other fixedly. The two waiters appear in the doorway and wait. They
are dressed as when they appeared as janitors. The accusing voices
begins to die down.*]

AIDE. [*Harshly*]   Which are their bedrolls?

LINUS. [*Pointing*]   That one and this one.

[*Only a few voices are now repeating the accusation. Soon almost all
are silent.*]

AIDE.   Their duffels!

THOMAS. [*He goes to the rack and takes down two.*]   Take them and get
out of here now. [*The* AIDE *collects them and starts to put one of
them on* MAX'S *bedroll.*] That belongs to the other one!

[*The* AIDE *puts down the other bag and carries* ASEL'S *to the bed. A single
voice says: "Mur-der-ers!"*]

AIDE. [*To the two at the door*]   Take these things.

[*The waiters enter; each one picks up a bedroll and bag. They exit
with them to the gallery and go off left.*]

SUPERINTENDENT.   Let's go. [*The* SUPERINTENDENT *and the* AIDE *exit. The
latter slams the door shut. Pause. Very faintly and for the final time,
we hear the accusation of a single voice: "Mur-der-ers!" Silence.
Exhausted,* THOMAS *goes to the table and sits on its edge.* LINUS *sits
on his bedroll again.*]

LINUS.   They fell for it.

THOMAS.   It seems so.

LINUS.   You were admirable. . . . Thank you.

[THOMAS *responds with a gesture of indifference.*]

I'll cede the bed to you. I prefer the floor.

THOMAS.   There won't be any need for that.

LINUS.   Why not?

THOMAS.   If they believe that Max lied to them, they no longer have anything to learn from us. If they think he didn't deceive them, they probably believe that you and I don't know what Asel was up to either. In any case, they have no reason to wait. They'll take us out of here today.

LINUS.   To execute us?

THOMAS.   Maybe.

LINUS.   [*With a motion of rebellion*]   I hope they all get what's coming to them!

THOMAS.   They will. These administrators of death will also fall one day. And if the hour has come for us, it doesn't matter much. [*He turns and looks at* LINUS.] Linus, we'll face them like Asel. With courage. Asel wasn't a coward. He sacrificed himself for us, to save our comrades, and to give us one last chance.

LINUS.   You and me?

THOMAS.   Don't you see? [*He gets up and goes over to him.*] Within an hour, or a minute, they'll take us out of here. Yes, to kill us. Almost for certain. [*Brief pause*] But they might decide just to move us to a punishment cell. Even if they believed that Max threw himself over the railing, they would have to set an example with those in the cell where it started.

LINUS.   Are you sure you aren't fantasizing?

THOMAS.   Perhaps. It's only the tiniest of possibilities; maybe only an illusion. If it happens, tonight we'll give the signal. And for six days . . . [*Ironically*] if they don't send us to the firing squad first . . . we'll live that other curious fantasy of hands blistered from digging, of anxiety in a dark tunnel, of exhaustion from lack of sleep, of the hope of embracing Berta again one day . . . of life and a struggle which goes on.

LINUS. [*Standing up; tense*]   How I wish . . .

THOMAS.   I won't be driven insane by that illusion, or by any other. If the time has come to die, I'll face it. For Asel this strange cinema has vanished. And for Tulio. We have no right to survive them. [*A smile transfigures his face.*] But as long as I live, I'll hope! Until the last second! [*He takes a few steps and looks through the invisible window.*] I'll hope in the face of the rifle barrels . . . for all that will have been a hologram! [*Brief pause*] We owe that strength to Asel. And I thank him . . . I no longer feel fatherless. [*With a glance upstage, he murmurs.*] Yes, the landscape is real. [*He goes toward* LINUS.] If he were still here, he would repeat it to you, Linus. Prudence, cunning, since they force us to use it. But not one mistake more. Throwing that poor devil off the gallery was a useless atrocity, and very dangerous.

LINUS.   Not so useless . . . if they take us below.

THOMAS.   It's not certain. We barely saved the day. Your fit of anger could have ruined everything. We must learn to dominate even the most just indignation. If we don't succeed in separating violence from cruelty, we'll be destroyed. Asel was right, Linus. He knew more than we . . . and I'll never forget his words.

[*Pause*]

LINUS.   We have the right to our indignation. . . .

THOMAS.   And the duty to conquer it.

[*Brief silence*]

LINUS.   Yes, I've ruined everything. I still have to learn to think.

THOMAS.   And I . . .

LINUS.   . . . to understand what all this is. Do you know?

THOMAS. [*Ironically*]   The hologram . . . of the wild beasts.

LINUS.   Maybe it is what you call it. But it's so obscene, so cruel. . . . Aren't we ever going to succeed in changing it?

THOMAS. [*He goes closer and presses his shoulder.*]   It's changing already. Even within us. [*He walks away and sits down.*] And now, let's wait.

[LINUS *sits down.*]

LINUS.   For death?

THOMAS.   Or the punishment cell. The frightening tunnel toward freedom.

[*A long pause*]

LINUS. [*Lowering his voice*]   Don't you hear footsteps?

THOMAS. [*He lifts his smiling face.*]   Yes. [*They look toward the door.*]

LINUS.   They've stopped. [*They both stand up. Softly.*] They won't tell us where they're taking us.

THOMAS.   We'll know soon.

[*Sound of a key. The door opens. The* AIDE *enters.*]

AIDE.   C-46 and C-72. Leave with all your possessions.

[THOMAS *and* LINUS *look at each other.*]

LINUS.   Yes, sir. [*He goes to the wall rack, takes down the two duffel bags that are left, hangs his over his arm and leaves the other one on* THOMAS'S *bedroll.* THOMAS *goes to the metal shelves and takes down plates, tumblers, and spoons.*]

THOMAS.   Here. [*He hands* LINUS *his.* LINUS *puts them in his bag.* THOMAS *does the same with his, hangs the bag over his shoulder, and casts a circular glance around the cell.*]

AIDE. [*Sarcastically*]   You seem very happy.

THOMAS. [*With a faint smile*]   Naturally. Shall we go, Linus?

LINUS.   Yes. [*They hoist their bedrolls to their shoulders and exit. The* AIDE *goes out behind them and closes the door. A brief pause. We begin to hear, very softly and far away, Rossini's pastorale. The light grows iridescent. The alcove curtain descends and hides the corner with the toilet. The left wall rises to reveal again the bookshelves, the television set. The telephone reappears on the table. At the head of the bed, the little lamp comes out. The lower panel at right slips back*]

*and the refrigerator door gleams again. The large, multicolored shade
descends slowly until it reaches its former position. Finally, the large
window is revealed, and behind it the marvelous landscape is glow-
ing. The music grows louder. The door opens. The* SUPERINTENDENT
*appears and immediately stations himself in the doorway. In the
background, behind the railing, is the distant countryside. The* SUPER-
INTENDENT *is wearing his formal attire, and with his most obsequious
smile he invites new occupants, who are approaching, to enter the
room.*

Curtain

IN THE BURNING DARKNESS

Drama in Three Acts

Characters (in order of appearance)
ELISA
ANDRES
PEDRO
LOLA
ALBERTO
CARLOS
JUANA
MIGUEL
ESPERANZA
IGNACIO
DON PABLO
THE FATHER
DOÑA PEPITA

ACT ONE

The student lounge of a modern institute for the blind. In warm weather large glass doors open out onto a terrace overlooking the field where the blind students engage in sports. At stage right there is a doorway leading to the terrace and to the outside. Upstage left, another door or passageway. Downstage right there is a small table with several chairs; centerstage a sofa and two armchairs around another small table. At far left, an isolated table with an armchair. Ashtrays on all the tables. In the first act, trees lush with foliage can be seen beyond the terrace, giving a rich submarine effect to the scene.

Eight carefully attired students are seated calmly onstage. Some of them are smoking. In spite of their cheerful and alert manner, there is something in their appearance that seems strange to us; and after continued observation, we realize that all of them are blind. Several are wearing dark glasses, no doubt to hide a spectacle that would be too unpleasant for the others; or, perhaps, simply from vanity. Apparently they are happy. They are so confident that when they stand up they move about easily and find their places with only the slightest suggestion of hesitation or groping. The illusion of normality is frequently complete, and the audience would end up forgetting about the affliction of these young people if it were not for the one unavoidable detail to remind them: they never look directly at the person who addresses them. CARLOS *and* JUANA *are seated at right. He is a sturdy young man dressed in a light-colored suit; his tie is carefully arranged.* JUANA *is quite pretty and her manner is gentle.* ELISA *occupies the chair at left. She is unexceptional in appearance and tends to be impulsive and emotional.* ANDRES, PEDRO, *and* ALBERTO *are seated on the sofa; seated nearby are* LOLA *and* ESPERANZA.

ELISA. [*Impatiently*] What time is it now? [*Most of the other students laugh broadly as if they had been expecting the question.*] I don't know what you're so amused about. What's wrong with asking the time? [*The laughter is louder.*] All right. I won't say another word.

ANDRES. You heard the clock strike ten-thirty a moment ago.

PEDRO. And we don't have to be at the opening ceremony until eleven.

ELISA. I was only asking if you'd heard it strike a quarter of eleven.

LOLA. It's only the third time you've asked.

ELISA. [*Furious*] Well, did it strike or not?

ALBERTO. [*Teasingly*] We don't know. . . .

ELISA. You're all terrible!

CARLOS. That's enough. Don't tease the poor child.

ELISA. I am not a poor child.

JUANA. [*Gently*] It's not a quarter of eleven yet, Elisa.

[MIGUEL *enters from left. He is a very animated boy who wears dark glasses because he knows from experience that people who can see are embarrassed by his quick movements when they contrast them with his dead eyes.*]

ANDRES.   Just calm down. You know very well that Miguel will get here at the last minute.

ELISA.   Who said anything about Miguel?

MIGUEL. [*With pretended distress*]   If no one says anything about Miguel, I shall surely weep.

ELISA. [*Standing up quickly*]   Miguel! [*She runs to his side. Most of the other students, with the exception of* CARLOS *and* JUANA, *get up and go to greet him affectionately.*]

ANDRES.   Damn if it isn't Miguel!

PEDRO.   About time.

LOLA.   Elisa was on pins and needles.

ESPERANZA.   How was your vacation?

ALBERTO.   How are things? [*With his arm around* ELISA, MIGUEL *moves confidently toward the sofa.*]

CARLOS.   Don't you remember your friends?

MIGUEL.   Carlos! [*He goes to shake his hand.*] And Juana's with you, I'll bet.

JUANA.   Right you are. [*She takes his hand.*]

MIGUEL. [*Finding* ELISA *again*]   Uf! I thought I wouldn't get back for the opening. I've had a marvelous time, absolutely marvelous! [*He sits down on the sofa with* ELISA *beside him.* ANDRES *joins them. The others gather around.*] But I missed all of you. A street can seem very long when you're alone. It's easy to breathe here. The moment I got back I gave my cane to the guard. "Am I late?" "You've still got twenty minutes." "That's good." And everyone was delighted to see me. "Miguel!" "Miguel's back!" My importance must be obvious to everyone.

[*Laughter from the students*]

ELISA. [*Convinced of his importance*]   You're conceited!

MIGUEL.   Silence! No interruptions, please. I shall continue. "Miguel, where are you headed?" "Miguel, Elisa is on the terrace."

ELISA. [*Embarrassed, she nudges him.*]   Idiot!

MIGUEL. [*Loudly*]   Ouch! . . . [*Laughter*] Now I'll continue. "What do you mean, where am I headed? To be with my friends in our own private castle." And here I am. [*He gives a sigh.*] Well, aren't we supposed to be in the auditorium? [*He starts to get up.*]

LOLA.   Not yet. There's plenty of time.

ANDRES. [*Holding him back*]   Go on. Tell us about your vacation.

ESPERANZA. [*Applauding*]   Please tell us.

ELISA. [*Irritated, she imitates* ESPERANZA'S *action.*]   Do tell the child everything!

ESPERANZA. [*Upset*]   And just what does that mean?

ELISA.   Oh, nothing. Just that I know how to clap my hands too.
   [*The boys laugh.*]
ESPERANZA. [*Irritated*]   Really!
MIGUEL.   Control yourself, Elisa. The ladies and gentlemen want a
   full account of my activities. So, gather round.
   [*They settle down to listen to an amusing narration.*]
PEDRO.   What are you waiting for?
MIGUEL.   Lend an ear. [*Laughing*] One morning I took up my faithful
   cane to venture into the street, and . . . [*He stops. In a tone of sur-
   prise*] Didn't you hear something?
ANDRES.   Go on and stop joking.
MIGUEL.   I'm not joking. I tell you I heard something odd. I hear a
   cane tapping. . . .
LOLA. [*Laughing*]   It's your own. You still have it in your ears.
ELISA.   Go on, silly.
ALBERTO.   No, he's not joking. You can hear a tapping.
JUANA.   I hear it too.
   [*They all listen. Pause. From left,* IGNACIO *appears, feeling his way
   with a cane. His face reveals his uncertainty. He is a very slender boy,
   serious and introverted. He is carelessly dressed; his collar is unbut-
   toned, his tie loose, and his hair disheveled. Although the weather is
   still warm, he is wearing black and continues to do so throughout the
   play. He advances a few steps hesitatingly and stops.*]
LOLA.   How strange.
   [IGNACIO *steps back.*]
MIGUEL.   Who are you?
   [*Frightened,* IGNACIO *turns around to leave the way he came in. Then
   he changes his mind and moves rapidly toward the right.*]
ANDRES.   Aren't you going to speak?
   [IGNACIO *stumbles over* JUANA'S *chair; he holds out his arm, and she
   takes his hand.*]
MIGUEL. [*Standing up*]   Wait, fellow! Don't go away. [*He goes over to
   touch him.*]
JUANA. [*Uneasily*]   He's taken my hand . . . I don't recognize him.
   [IGNACIO *releases her hand, and* MIGUEL *grabs his arm.*]
MIGUEL.   Neither do I.
   [ANDRES *crosses and takes his other arm.*]
IGNACIO. [*Afraid*]   Let me go.
ANDRES.   What are you looking for here?
IGNACIO.   Nothing. Leave me alone. I . . . I'm blind.
LOLA. [*Laughing*]   You've got competition, Miguel.
ESPERANZA.   Competition? This one can teach Miguel a thing or two.
ALBERTO.   He must be some clown from the lower school.
MIGUEL.   Leave him to me. What did you say you were?
IGNACIO. [*Frightened*]   I said . . . I'm blind.
MIGUEL.   You poor fellow! Do you want me to help you cross the

street? [*The others are greatly amused.*] Out, idiot! Take your jokes
back to your own kind.

ANDRES.   Really, it was in very bad taste. Go back where you came
from.

[*They shove him.* IGNACIO *retreats downstage.*]

IGNACIO. [*Violently, perhaps on the verge of tears*]   I tell you I'm blind!

MIGUEL.   You've certainly learned your lines well! Out!

[*They advance toward him threateningly.* ALBERTO *joins them.*]

IGNACIO.   But can't you see it?

CARLOS.   I think we've made a great mistake. He's telling the truth. All
of you, sit down again.

MIGUEL.   How do you like that!

CARLOS. [*Approaching* IGNACIO]   We, too, are . . . as you call it . . .
blind.

IGNACIO.   All of you?

JUANA.   All of us. Don't you know where you are?

[ELISA *takes* MIGUEL'S *arm. He is nonplussed. The other students
whisper to one another; then they listen.*]

IGNACIO.   I know where I am. But I can't believe that you're all . . .
like me.

CARLOS.   Why not?

IGNACIO.   You walk around without hesitating. And you talk to me
. . . as if you were looking at me.

CARLOS.   You'll soon be doing the same things. You've just arrived,
haven't you?

IGNACIO.   Yes.

CARLOS.   Alone?

IGNACIO.   No. My father is in the office with the director of the
school.

JUANA.   And they left you outside?

IGNACIO.   The director said that I shouldn't be afraid to walk around.
My father didn't want me to, but the director told me to take a
stroll around the building. He said it would do me good.

CARLOS. [*In the role of protector*]   And he's right. You have no reason to
be afraid.

IGNACIO. [*With pride*]   I'm not.

CARLOS.   What just happened isn't important now. Sometimes Miguel
gets carried away.

MIGUEL.   I'm really sorry, fellow. Don Pablo will have to take the
blame for my mistake this time.

ALBERTO. [*Laughing*]   And his "Applied Educational Psychology."

MIGUEL.   That's what he calls it. He was using it on you from the
moment you arrived. You'll have further encounters with our
director's psychology. Don't worry about it. [*He and* ELISA *sit at
right. They quickly become involved in each other.*]

CARLOS.   If you wish, we'll walk you back to the office.

IGNACIO.   Thanks, but I know how to go by myself. Goodbye. [*He takes a few steps upstage*]

CARLOS.   No, I don't think you do. That's not the way out. [*He takes him affectionately by the arm and turns him toward the left. Passively and with bowed head,* IGNACIO *lets himself be led.*] Wait for me here, Juana. I'll be right back.

JUANA.   I'll wait.

[*From the left, Ignacio's* FATHER *and* DON PABLO, *director of the institute, enter.* THE FATHER *walks rapidly because of his anxiety over his son. He is prematurely old and dresses with the drab correctness of an office worker. Smiling and relaxed,* DON PABLO *follows him. He is about fifty years old, with graying temples; but age has failed to erase a certain air of boyish exuberance. His attire is conservative and elegant. He is wearing dark glasses.*]

THE FATHER.   Here is Ignacio.

DON PABLO.   I told you we'd find him safe and sound. [*Smiling*] And in good company, I believe. Good morning, boys and girls.

[*At the sound of his voice, all of the students stand up.*]

STUDENTS.   Good morning, sir.

[THE FATHER *goes to his son and takes him paternally but timidly by the arm.* IGNACIO *doesn't move, but he is obviously annoyed by this contact.*]

CARLOS.   We've already gotten acquainted with Ignacio.

JUANA.   Carlos was about to bring him back to you.

DON PABLO. [*To* THE FATHER]   As you see, nothing has happened to him. Your boy has found friends right off. And good ones at that. Carlos, one of our finest students. And Juana.

THE FATHER. [*Shyly*]   Pleased to meet you.

JUANA.   It's our pleasure.

DON PABLO.   Your son will be fine with us, you may be sure. He'll have good companions, sports, and healthy attitudes.

THE FATHER.   Yes, of course. But the sports . . . The games I've seen are marvelous, no doubt of that! I never would have supposed that blind people could play ball, much less guide a toboggan. [*Timidly*] Do you really think my son will be able to do those things without getting hurt?

DON PABLO.   He'll do all that and more. Never doubt it.

THE FATHER.   He won't fall?

DON PABLO.   No one learns without falling occasionally.

THE FATHER.   It's amazing that they can run and play without cause for concern. . . .

DON PABLO.   We've never had an unfortunate incident here. No, my friend. These and other activities have been a part of our life for quite a while.

THE FATHER.   But all these boys and girls . . . poor creatures . . . are blind! They can't see at all!

DON PABLO.   But they hear, and you must not think of them as objects
    of pity. . . . Don't you agree, Andrés?

ANDRES.   Yes, sir, I do.

DON PABLO.   And you boys, Pedro, Alberto?

PEDRO.   There's no reason to pity us.

ALBERTO.   We're anything but pitiable.

LOLA.   If you will permit me, sir . . .

DON PABLO.   Yes, what would you like to add?

LOLA.   Only that Esperanza and I feel the same way.

THE FATHER.   You must forgive me.

DON PABLO.   You must forgive us for what may seem a censure but is
    only an explanation. The blind or, simply, the non-seers, as we
    prefer to say, can go as far as other people in life. We have our
    jobs. Some are writers and journalists; others are teachers. We
    are strong, healthy, and socially aware. And we possess a morale
    of steel. But enough of this. [*To the students*] I must remind you
    that assembly was scheduled for eleven. [*Smiling*] I think you
    should be on your way.

ANDRES.   Yes indeed, sir. Let's go, fellows.

    [ANDRES, PEDRO, *and* ALBERTO *exit right accompanied by* LOLA *and*
    ESPERANZA.]

STUDENTS.   Good day. Good day, sir.

DON PABLO.   I'll see you shortly, my friends.

    [ELISA *is about to follow them, but* MIGUEL *takes hold of her arm and
    makes her sit down. Holding hands, they become engrossed in each
    other again.* JUANA *and* CARLOS *remain standing at right, listening to
    the conversation that follows. Brief pause*]

THE FATHER.   I feel embarrassed. I . . .

DON PABLO.   You shouldn't. You came with the prejudices of those
    who are not acquainted with our life. For example, you probably
    think that marriage is out of the question for us.

THE FATHER.   Not at all. Among yourselves, of course.

DON PABLO.   No, my friend. Unions between persons who see and
    those who don't are becoming more common all the time. I
    myself . . .

THE FATHER.   You?

DON PABLO.   Yes. I am a non-seer from birth and I'm married to a
    woman with sight, a seer.

IGNACIO. [*Slowly, with amazement*]   A seer?

THE FATHER.   You refer to yourselves in that way?

DON PABLO.   Yes, indeed.

THE FATHER.   Forgive me, but . . . since we speak of people who look
    into the future as "seers."

DON PABLO. [*Rather curtly*]   Naturally. But we—more modest from
    necessity—use the expression to describe those who have, sim-
    ply, vision.

THE FATHER. [*Who feels completely inadequate at this point*]   Once again you must forgive me. . . .

DON PABLO.   There is nothing to forgive. I would be delighted to present you to my wife, but she hasn't arrived yet. At any rate, your son will meet her, for she is my secretary.

THE FATHER.   Perhaps another day. Well, my boy . . . I'm going now. I'm satisfied that you're in good hands. I'm certain that you're going to be happy here. [IGNACIO *is silent. To* CARLOS *and* JUANA] And you two, please cheer him up. [*With unaccustomed joviality*] Help him to acquire that morale of steel that all of you seem to have.

IGNACIO. [*Greatly annoyed*]   Father.

THE FATHER. [*Embracing him*]   Yes, my son, you'll leave here a man.

DON PABLO.   Assuredly. In just a few years . . . with an education you'll be proud of.

[*The tension between father and son is less obvious now.* CARLOS *intervenes, taking* IGNACIO *by the arm.*]

CARLOS.   With your permission, we'll take charge of our friend.

THE FATHER.   Yes, thank you. [*Moved*] Goodbye, my boy . . . I'll be back . . . soon . . . to see you.

IGNACIO. [*Indifferently*]   Goodbye, father.

[THE FATHER *is deeply affected; he looks at the others with tears in his eyes, which they cannot see. His movements reveal his indecision. He is on the point of embracing his son again, of saying goodbye to the two students. He starts to consult* DON PABLO *with a sheepish glance that is lost in the air.*]

DON PABLO.   Shall we go?

THE FATHER.   Yes, yes.

[*They start upstage.*]

DON PABLO. [*Pausing*]   Take him to assembly now, Carlos. Ah, yes! And introduce him to Miguel, because they're going to be roommates.

CARLOS.   I certainly shall, sir.

[DON PABLO *exits with* THE FATHER, *who pays scant attention to what is being said to him. He is worried about his son and looks back several times with a troubled expression. Finally they disappear through the doorway at left. Meanwhile,* CARLOS, IGNACIO, *and* JUANA *have situated themselves downstage right.*]

CARLOS.   It's a shame you didn't come here earlier. Are you just beginning your studies?

IGNACIO.   Yes. This is my first year.

CARLOS.   Juana and I will help you. Don't hesitate to come to us if you have problems.

JUANA.   Any time.

CARLOS.   That's understood. Miguel can help you get your things arranged in the dormitory. First you have to memorize this building. Listen carefully: this corner is our private preserve, to which you'll be admitted from now on. There's nothing in the way. [*He leads him around.*] So you don't have to worry about tripping. We'll walk you around so that you can learn the positions of the chairs and tables. [*The three are now at left.*] But you must get rid of that cane right now. You won't be needing it.

JUANA. [*Trying to take it from him*] Give it to me. We'll leave it with the guard.

IGNACIO. [*Resisting*] No, no. I'm . . . rather clumsy when I try to walk without it. And you needn't bother to show me the building. I don't intend to memorize it.

[*A moment of silence*]

CARLOS. I'm sorry. Do what you want. But you should try to overcome your clumsiness as quickly as possible. You did study in our lower school, didn't you?

IGNACIO. No.

JUANA. You weren't born blind?

IGNACIO. Yes, I was. But . . . my family . . .

CARLOS. Well, it's not important. All of us have been this way from birth, and most of us have studied in these centers under men like Don Pablo.

JUANA. What did you think of our director?

IGNACIO. An absurdly happy man.

CARLOS. Like any other person who achieves the fulfillment of his professional dreams. That's not absurd.

JUANA. If Doña Pepita heard you say that . . .

CARLOS. You'll meet other teachers who are just as happy.

IGNACIO. Blind men too?

CARLOS. We prefer to say "non-seers" when we speak of the sightless . . . [*Brief pause*] For example, the biology professor is a non-seer and he's married to the language assistant who is a seer. The physics teacher is a seer, and the one in . . .

IGNACIO. Seers . . .

JUANA. Seers. What's so special about that?

IGNACIO. Listen, Carlos; and you, too, Juana: Is love between a blind man and a seer really possible?

CARLOS. Does it seem so improbable to you?

JUANA. Why, there are so many cases!

IGNACIO. And between a seer and a blind woman? [*Silence*] Eh, Carlos? [*Brief pause*] Juana?

CARLOS. Juana and I know a couple who've been married for years.

IGNACIO. One.

JUANA. And Pepe and Luisa. They're certainly happy!

IGNACIO. Two.

CARLOS. [*Smiling*] Ignacio . . . don't be offended, but you're a little upset by the newness of all this. How should I say it? A little . . .

abnormal. Relax. There's more than enough happiness for you here, and you'll find your share. [*He gives him a warm pat on the shoulder.* JUANA *smiles.*]

IGNACIO. Maybe I am . . . abnormal. All of us are.

CARLOS. [*Still smiling*] We'll talk about that some other time. Right now we need Miguel, don't we, Juana? Something tells me he didn't go to the auditorium. Miguel! Miguel! [MIGUEL *reacts with annoyance but does not move.*] Don't play dead with me. I know you're here. [*He feels his way toward* MIGUEL *who presses closer to* ELISA. *Finally, with a laugh, he touches him.*]

MIGUEL. I'll remember this one day when you want to be alone with Juana.

CARLOS. Come over here.

MIGUEL. I don't feel up to it.

CARLOS. Come along and stop playing the fool. I have instructions for you from Don Pablo.

MIGUEL. [*Pulling himself together reluctantly*] I'll cooperate only if your instructions include Elisa.

ELISA. Can't you leave me out of your jokes?

MIGUEL. No. I can't.

JUANA. You come too, Elisa.

MIGUEL. If it has to be. [*He sighs.*] Come along. [*Taking* ELISA *by the hand, he follows* CARLOS.] Well, what is it?

CARLOS. [*To* IGNACIO] This is Miguel, the school lunatic. You heard him before. Our seventeen-year-old mascot. But, with all his shortcomings, a remarkable fellow. Elisa takes care of him.

MIGUEL. Wiping my brow continually.

ELISA. Can't you keep quiet even for a minute?

MIGUEL. For me it's impossible.

CARLOS. Come on, shake hands with our new student.

MIGUEL. [*Obliging*] Now it's my nursemaid's turn.

[ELISA *takes* IGNACIO'S *hand and is startled by the touch.*]

CARLOS. [*To* IGNACIO] By decree from above, Miguel is to be your roommate. If he gives you any trouble, just let us know.

IGNACIO. Why shouldn't we get along well? We're both blind. [JUANA *and* ELISA *are now standing together at one side.*]

MIGUEL. Did you hear that, Carlos? I told you we had a comic in our midst.

IGNACIO. I didn't intend it to be funny.

MIGUEL. Oh, really? Well, thanks for your sympathy. But I don't consider myself as unfortunate as you do. My only real misfortune is having to endure this . . .

ELISA. Don't say it, silly! I know you too well. [*They all laugh except* IGNACIO.]

MIGUEL. [*To the girls*] Why don't you two go off somewhere and talk about us? The secrets of women, Ignacio! The most frightening

thing in the world. [JUANA *and* ELISA *attack him in mock fashion.*]
What did I tell you? [*More laughter*] Very well. Carlos, Ignacio, I
propose a retreat en masse to the pub; without the girls. Let's
have a beer.

CARLOS.   Motion seconded.

JUANA.   A common front? I'll have a word to say later.

CARLOS.   It's only for a little while. . . .

MIGUEL.   Don't capitulate now, coward. Let's escape while we can.
Women! You can cut us up into little pieces while we're gone.

JUANA.   Well, go . . .

ELISA.   Yes, go on . . .

[*With* IGNACIO *between them,* CARLOS *and* MIGUEL *exit left.*]
Now we can talk.

JUANA.   Let's. [*They sit down quickly side by side on the sofa while* DON
PABLO *crosses behind the terrace window and enters from right. He
goes close to the girls, stops for a moment, and listens.*] It's been a
long time since we've had a chance to talk.

ELISA.   And I have so many things to tell you.

DON PABLO.   I hope I'm not interrupting.

JUANA.   Not at all, sir. [*The girls stand up.*] We were only chatting.

DON PABLO.   About the new student, perhaps?

ELISA.   I believe we were more concerned about two of the old students.

JUANA.   Elisa!

DON PABLO. [*Laughing*]   A pleasant topic of conversation, I imagine.
[*Becoming serious*] But this bothersome old man has arrived, and
he prefers to speak about the new boy. No doubt Elisa has met
him too.

ELISA.   Yes, I have, sir.

[DOÑA PEPITA *has crossed the terrace and stands in the doorway
watching her husband affectionately. She is about forty and carries a
briefcase under her arm.*]

DON PABLO. [*He is immediately aware of her presence and turns his head
into the emptiness to locate her.*]   Just a moment . . . my wife.

DOÑA PEPITA. [*Going toward him*]   Forgive me, Pablo, I know that I'm
late.

DON PABLO. [*Taking her hand with a tenderness that seems undiminished
by the passing years*]   You're wearing a lovely scent today, my
dear.

DOÑA PEPITA.   The same as always. Good morning, girls. Where did
you leave your knights errant?

ELISA.   They left us for a new friend.

JUANA.   A sad boy. But he's nice.

ELISA.   I don't think so.

DON PABLO.   You mustn't speak of a classmate that way, young lady.
Especially since you've had so little time to get to know him. [*To*

DOÑA PEPITA] Carlos and Miguel are with the new boy who has just come to us.

DOÑA PEPITA.   Ah, yes? What kind of a boy is he?

DON PABLO.   You've heard the opinions of the girls.

JUANA.   Elisa spoke too hastily.

DON PABLO.   Yes, a bit. And, for that very reason, I'm going to give the two of you some special instructions.

JUANA.   Concerning Ignacio?

DON PABLO.   Yes. [To DOÑA PEPITA] And, incidentally, you must lend a hand in this.

DOÑA PEPITA.   A difficult case?

DON PABLO.   A familiar story. Lack of morale.

DOÑA PEPITA.   A typical problem.

DON PABLO.   Typical, yes; but perhaps a wee bit more complicated this time. A sad boy, harmed by the misdirected love of his parents. Pampered, private tutors. An only child. Well, you understand the type. As on other occasions, it requires the intelligent aid of a few students.

JUANA.   We've already tried to persuade him to give up his cane, and he refused. He feels helpless without it.

DON PABLO.   Well, we must convince him that he is a useful human being and that he has every road open to him if he'll only take the first step. He has good examples here, but you must deal with him tactfully. Carlos has the most important task of all: the development of an easy-going friendship that will draw him out of his shell. I don't think it will be so difficult. . . . Boys like this one are starved for affection and happiness. They seldom reject the person who knows how to reach them.

DOÑA PEPITA.   Why don't you assign him to Miguel's room?

DON PABLO. [Nodding and smiling]   I already have. But, Elisa, there's no reason for Miguel to be told of my recommendations. If he took this as an obligation, it might turn out badly.

ELISA.   I won't say a word about it.

DOÑA PEPITA.   Fine. Then it's simply a question of developing in this boy, with the least possible delay, some of the confidence the other students have. Are we agreed?

DON PABLO.   Precisely. But enough talk for now. You young ladies are already late for assembly. And don't forget; I'm putting this matter in your hands.

JUANA.   You can count on us, sir.

DOÑA PEPITA.   I'll see you later, dears.

JUANA.   Yes, Doña Pepita.

DOÑA PEPITA.   Pablo, with your permission, I'll have the loudspeakers turned on. The students can have a bit of music until assembly begins.

[They exit right, engrossed in their conversation. JUANA and ELISA, *clinging to each other, walk rather awkwardly downstage.*]

JUANA. We can talk now. [ELISA *doesn't reply. She seems worried.* JUANA *insists.*] Talk to me, Elisa!

ELISA. [*Hesitating*] I don't like being involved in this. There's something about Ignacio that frightens me. Do you believe in intuition?

JUANA. Of course. Who doesn't?

ELISA. A lot of people have told me it doesn't exist.

JUANA. People who've never been in love.

ELISA. [*Laughing*] You're right. But that's another kind of intuition. I'm talking about a premonition of evil.

JUANA. For example?

ELISA. [*Seriously*] The evil in Ignacio. When he was with us, I seemed to feel a choking sensation, an uneasiness. And when I gave him my hand, it increased terribly. He has a dry . . . burning hand, full of bad intentions.

JUANA. I didn't notice anything like that. He seemed nice to me. [*Short pause*] You must remember that he's an unhappy person. He simply needs to adapt. So forget all that nonsense about intuition and evil.

ELISA. Well, I prefer the sensation I get from Miguel!

JUANA. I understand. But listen; I have an idea. . . .

[*Silence. Then from distant loudspeakers we hear the Adagio from Beethoven's* Moonlight *Sonata.*]

ELISA. Yes?

JUANA. Listen. The music is so beautiful! [*Pause*]

ELISA. Can't we go on talking?

JUANA. Yes, yes. I wanted you to be quiet because I had found . . . the answer to Ignacio's problem.

ELISA. Yes? Tell me.

JUANA. The answer to his problem is . . . someone to care for. And we must find that person for him. [*Brief pause*] Don't you like my idea?

ELISA. Yes, but . . .

JUANA. It's the perfect solution! Don't you remember how we used to be, before we found Carlos and Miguel? You won't deny that we were sad enough ourselves. . . . We hadn't discovered yet what Carlos calls the region of bliss. [ELISA *gives her a kiss on the cheek.*] Remember when I told you: "He loves me, Elisa!"?

ELISA. And I asked you: "How did he tell you?"

JUANA. Yes. And when I questioned you about Miguel, you said very sadly: "He doesn't love me."

ELISA. But the next day he told me he did . . . [*She is suddenly startled by a cry from* MIGUEL.]

MIGUEL. Elisa! Elisa! Elisa! [*He appears at left.*]

ELISA. [*Running toward him frightened*] Here I am, Miguel! What's wrong?

MIGUEL.   Come here! . . . [*His anguished tone changes suddenly to one of joking.*] I want to hug you.

ELISA.   Why must you always be teasing me?

JUANA.   There are secret agents lurking here, Miguel.

MIGUEL.   Oh, I know. Collecting incriminating evidence on lovers. But we're on to them. Come along, Elisa.

JUANA.   Where's Carlos?

MIGUEL.   He won't be long. He wants you to wait for him here.

JUANA.   Where did you leave Ignacio?

MIGUEL.   In my room. He says he's tired and won't go to assembly. Well, little Elisa, shall we go? Let's see if we can still find seats.

ELISA.   Yes, let's go. Are you staying, Juana?

JUANA.   I'll wait for Carlos. Save us a place, if you can.

MIGUEL.   We'll try.

[ELISA *and* MIGUEL *exit right.* JUANA *is left alone. She walks back and forth, listening to the sonata. A new sound suddenly intervenes: the unmistakable tap-tap of a cane.* JUANA *stops abruptly and listens.* IGNACIO *enters from left and moves slowly downstage.*]

JUANA.   Ignacio? . . .

[*He stops.*]

You are Ignacio, aren't you?

IGNACIO.   Yes, I'm Ignacio. And you're Juana.

JUANA.   I thought you were in your room.

IGNACIO.   I was . . . for a while. Goodbye. [*He starts to exit.*]

JUANA.   Where are you going?

IGNACIO. [*Coldly*]   Home.

[JUANA *is dumbfounded.*]

Goodbye. [*He takes a few steps.*]

JUANA.   But . . . you were going to study with us!

IGNACIO.   I've changed my mind.

JUANA.   In less than an hour?

IGNACIO.   It's enough.

[JUANA *goes to him and touches his lapels affectionately.* IGNACIO *stiffens.*]

JUANA.   Don't let yourself be carried away by an irrational impulse . . . How are you going to get home?

IGNACIO. [*Nervously pulling back from the contact*]   That's easy enough.

JUANA.   But your father will be very upset! And what will our director say?

IGNACIO. [*Contemptuously*]   Your director . . .

JUANA.   And us. We'll all miss you. We already think of you as one of us . . . someone to share our experiences, our happiness.

IGNACIO.   Shut up! All of you get on my nerves. You most of all. "Happiness" is the motto of this place. You're all obsessed with happiness. And that's not what I expected to find here. I thought I'd find . . . people like myself . . . not a flock of deluded sheep.

JUANA. [*Smiling in spite of his words*]   Poor Ignacio. I sympathize with you.

IGNACIO.   Keep your sympathy!

JUANA.   Don't be angry! What you feel is very natural. We've all been through this, but it's over after the first day. And I know a remedy. [*Brief pause*] If you'll just listen to me calmly, I'll tell you what it is.

IGNACIO.   I am calm.

JUANA.   Listen . . . you need to find yourself a girl. [*Pause.* IGNACIO *begins to laugh lightly.*] You're laughing! I was right!

IGNACIO. [*He stops laughing.*]   You are obsessed with happiness. But you're dull and sad without even realizing it . . . especially the girls. Here, just as in the outside world, you repeat your lines pitifully, whether you're blind or not. You're not the first to suggest that childish solution. There were girls on my street who said the same thing.

JUANA.   Silly! Don't you understand what they meant?

IGNACIO.   No! Like you, they had found their great loves. They were simply giving me the stupid advice that their own infatuation had put in their mouths. It is an . . . insincere kindness. They would all say: "Why don't you find yourself a girl?" But not one of them ever said, with unmistakable sincerity in her voice: "I love you." [*Furious*] You're not saying it, are you? Or perhaps you are? [*Pause*] I don't need your help. I need someone to say "I care" and mean it. "I care for you with your torment and your anguish. I will suffer with you. I will not carry you to any false kingdom of happiness." There is no one like that.

JUANA.   Maybe you've never asked anyone.

IGNACIO. [*Harshly*]   A seer, you mean?

JUANA.   Why not?

IGNACIO. [*With irony*]   A seer?

JUANA.   What difference does it make? Any woman! [*Brief pause*]

IGNACIO.   To hell with all of you! Keep your happiness and your Carlos, who's so very good and so very wise . . . and an utter fool to think that he's happy. And Miguel and your director are just like him. All of them are! What right have you to live this way, determined not to suffer? You refuse to face up to your tragedy, pretending a normalcy that doesn't exist; trying to forget and forever prescribing showers of happiness to cheer up the dejected ones. [*A reaction from* JUANA] Do you think I don't understand? I see through you. Your director was naive enough to suggest it to my father, and he shamelessly asked you to help me . . . [*Sarcastically*] You are the model students, the faculty's faithful collaborators in the fight against desperation . . . which is waiting for you in every corner of this building. [*Pause*] Blind people! Not non-seers, but blind people!

JUANA. I don't know what to say to you . . . I don't want to lie to you either . . . But at least respect and be grateful for our good intentions. Stay! Try it. . . .

IGNACIO. No.

JUANA. Please. You can't leave now. I don't know how to reach you with words. I don't know how to convince you.

IGNACIO. You won't convince me.

JUANA. [*Excitedly; with her hands clasped*] Don't go. I know I sound very stupid. You've managed to make me feel my own helplessness. But if you go, they'll all know that I spoke with you and that I failed. Stay.

IGNACIO. Such vanity!

JUANA. [*Hurt*] It's not vanity, Ignacio. [*Sadly*] Shall I beg you on my knees?

[*Brief pause*]

IGNACIO. [*Coldly*] Why on your knees? They tell me that pose impresses seers immensely . . . But we can't see it. Don't be silly. Don't speak of things you know nothing about. Don't imitate people who are really alive. And spare me your disgusting helplessness, please. [*Long pause*] I'll stay.

JUANA. Thank you!

IGNACIO. For what? You're making a bad bargain. Because all of you are too neutral, too cold. And I am burning inside; burning with an awful fire which I can never forget. I'm burning in this thing that seers call darkness, which is so frightening because we can't even understand the word. It's not peace that I'll bring you . . . but a fight.

JUANA. Don't talk like that. It hurts me. The important thing is that you're staying. I'm certain it will be good for us all.

IGNACIO. [*Mockingly*] Dull and foolish. Your optimism and your blindness are the same. The struggle that is destroying me will destroy you.

JUANA. No. You must not disrupt our lives. Isn't it possible for all of us to live in peace? I don't really understand you. Why must you suffer so much? What's wrong with you? What do you want?

[*Brief pause*]

IGNACIO. [*With tremendous pent-up energy*] To see!

JUANA. [*She backs away from him, amazed.*] What?

IGNACIO. Yes. To see! Even when I know it's impossible! Even if my whole life is left barren by this desire, I want to see! I cannot conform. We must not conform, much less smile at our own predicament. Reconcile myself to your world of happy blind men? Never! [*Pause*] And if no one has the courage to go with me on my dark journey, I shall go alone. I refuse to live resigned, because I want to see!

[*Pause. We still hear the music from the distant loudspeakers.* JUANA

*seems paralyzed, with a hand on her mouth and anguish showing on
her face.* CARLOS *enters rapidly from left.*]

CARLOS. Juana! [*Silence.* JUANA *turns toward him instinctively; then, confused, she turns back to* IGNACIO *without managing to speak.*] Aren't
you here, my Juana? . . . Juana! [*She neither moves nor answers.*
IGNACIO, *absorbed in his bitterness is also mute.* CARLOS *loses his
instinctive assurance; he feels strangely alone. Blind. He raises his
arms uncertainly in the eternal gesture of groping the air and
advances cautiously.*] Juana! . . . Juana! . . . [*He exits right, still calling her name.*]

Curtain

ACT TWO

*The lounge. The trees in the background are now bare skeletons except for
a few yellow leaves still clinging to the branches. On the terrace are piles of
dry leaves which the wind stirs up.*

ELISA *is leaning against the terrace doorway at right. Her hair has been
disheveled by the wind; her posture reveals the dejection she feels. After a
moment* JUANA *and* CARLOS *enter arm in arm from left. They try in vain to
hide their concern from each other.*

CARLOS. Juana . . .
JUANA. Yes . . .
CARLOS. What's bothering you?
JUANA. Nothing really.
CARLOS. Don't try to hide it from me. You've been this way for days.
JUANA. [*Attempting to pass it off*] This way? What way?
CARLOS. I mean . . . you've been ill at ease. [*He sits on one of the chairs
centerstage.* JUANA *sits nearby on the sofa.*]
JUANA. It's nothing. . . .
[*Brief pause*]
CARLOS. We've always told each other our troubles. . . . Don't you
want to please me now and tell me what you're worried about?
JUANA. I'm not worried about anything.
[*Brief pause*]
CARLOS. [*Caressing her hand*] Yes you are. And so am I.
JUANA. You? You're worried? About what?
CARLOS. About the situation that . . . Ignacio has created.
[*Pause*]
JUANA. Do you think it's serious?
CARLOS. [*Smiling*] What about you? Come on, tell me the truth. You
always have.

JUANA. I don't know what to think. I consider myself partly to blame.

CARLOS. Why?

JUANA. I told you how I managed to persuade him not to leave that first day. And now I think it might have been the best thing.

CARLOS. Maybe it would have been better, but it's still possible to work things out, isn't it?

JUANA. Perhaps.

CARLOS. Yesterday I had to tell Don Pablo the same thing. I was surprised to find him so upset. He admitted his concern to me. He finds the students more withdrawn, not as sure of themselves as before. They seem to have lost all sense of competition. I tried to reassure him. It hurt me to see him so indecisive . . . and I experienced an odd sensation.

JUANA. What kind of sensation?

CARLOS. I'm almost afraid to tell you. . . . It's so new to me. . . . A feeling of . . . contempt for Don Pablo.

JUANA. Carlos!

CARLOS. I couldn't help myself. And he also asked me what was wrong with Elisa, if she had quarreled with Miguel. Out of consideration for Miguel I didn't give him the details.

JUANA. Poor Elisa! When we were eating, I could tell that she hardly touched her food. [*Brief pause*] It's unusual not to find her here. [ELISA *does not react to these words although she is not too far away to hear them. She remains absorbed in her thoughts.* CARLOS *and* JUANA *do not sense her presence either. The bond between the blind students seems to have been destroyed.*]

CARLOS. It's late. She must be all alone in some corner. [*Suddenly impassioned*] For her sake, and for everybody's well-being, we have to do something.

JUANA. But what?

CARLOS. Ignacio has shown us that kindness and understanding mean nothing to him. He's bitter and unsociable. He's a sick person!

JUANA. He's restless; he needs to come to terms with himself. . . .

CARLOS. He doesn't want to come to terms with himself or anyone else. [*Brief pause*] Well, we'll give him the fight he wants!

JUANA. [*She gets up suddenly and moves away nervously.*]   Fight . . .

CARLOS. What's wrong with you?

JUANA. [*From downstage*]   What you have just said. Isn't it better to be kind to him?

CARLOS. You don't understand Ignacio. Inside he's a coward. We have to stand up to him. Who would have thought when he arrived here that instead of our helping him he would disrupt our own lives! Juana, he has a power to attract that we didn't count on.

JUANA. I thought he only needed someone to love. It seemed to be the answer.

CARLOS.   It isn't. Ignacio is not susceptible to love. Here he's been surrounded with potential friends, as you well know. He attracts the
girls like a magnet. And he ignores them. There is only one way;
discredit him in the eyes of the other students with simple logic;
make him undesirable to the others. Force him out!

JUANA.   That would be bad for the school!

CARLOS.   Bad? There's nothing bad about it if we have a just cause.
And we do.

JUANA.   Yes . . . but someone could still help him.

CARLOS.   [*With affection*]   Come here . . . Come! [*She goes to him slowly
and takes his hands.*] My Juana, your goodness pleases me so
much. If you were a doctor, you would always heal and never
hurt. [*He kisses her.*] We are the only ones left to fight him. You
mustn't desert me too.

[*Brief pause*]

JUANA.   Why do you say that?

CARLOS.   No reason. It's just that now I need you more than ever.
[IGNACIO *enters upstage with three students. He has not given up his
cane, and his attire is more untidy than ever. He refuses to wear a tie
like the others.*]

ANDRES.   This way, Ignacio. [*He leads him toward the chairs at right.*]

IGNACIO.   Are the girls coming?

ALBERTO.   I don't hear them.

IGNACIO.   That's a relief. They're getting to be unbearable.

ANDRES.   Don't concern yourself about the girls. Sit here. [*Taking a cigarette from his pocket*] Have a cigarette.

IGNACIO.   No, thanks. [*He sits down.*] Why should I smoke? To imitate
seers?

ANDRES.   You're right. That's the reason we have our first smoke. Then,
of course, you get the habit. Help yourselves. [*He offers cigarettes
to the other two students. They sit down. Each lights his cigarette with
his own match and throws it into an ashtray.* CARLOS's *hands tighten
on the arms of his chair.* JUANA *takes a seat on the sofa.*]

CARLOS.   [*With a hint of challenge in his voice*]   Good afternoon, my
friends.

IGNACIO, ANDRES, AND ALBERTO. [*Indifferently*]   Hello.

PEDRO.   Oh, hello, Carlos. What are you doing here?

CARLOS.   I was talking with Juana.

[IGNACIO *looks up.*]

IGNACIO.   It's a pleasant place to be. We've had a beautiful autumn.

ANDRES.   It's still early. I can feel the sun from the terrace.

PEDRO.   Ignacio, go on with your story.

IGNACIO.   Where were we?

ALBERTO.   We were at the point where you stumbled.

IGNACIO. [*Making himself comfortable and taking a deep breath*]   Oh,
yes. It was when I was feeling my way down the steps. I imagine

the same thing has happened to all of you. You count and think you've passed the last step. Then you put your foot out confidently and there is nothing there. I put my foot down hard and I felt terror. My legs were like cotton. And the girls who were watching me started to laugh. Their laughter was innocent enough but it went right through me. And I felt my face burning. The girls tried to stop but they couldn't, so they started all over again. Have you ever noticed how women become almost hysterical at times and are helpless? I was on the verge of crying. Well, I was only fifteen at the time! Then I sat down on the steps and started thinking. For the first time I tried to understand why I was blind and why there should be blind people in the world. It is abominable that the majority of people – without being more worthy than we are – enjoy a mysterious power that emanates from their eyes, with which they can encompass our bodies, while we are helpless to prevent it. The power to perceive things at a distance has been denied to us, without reason! We are less than those who live in the outside world. Do you know that chant of the blind beggars who stood on street corners in the old days asking for alms? "There is no treasure like sight, dear brothers." Perhaps it doesn't harmonize very well with our tranquil existence in this school, but I consider it much more honest than our pretense. Because those beggars didn't fall into the stupid error of believing themselves normal.

[*While* CARLOS *has been listening to* IGNACIO, *his expression of repressed anger has become accentuated.* JUANA *shows in her expression a strange identification with the incidents which* IGNACIO *has described.*]

ANDRES. [*Reserved*]   Perhaps you're right. I've thought a lot about this, too. I believe that blindness is not only the lack of a power to perceive from a distance but also the absence of a kind of pleasure. A marvelous kind of pleasure, surely. What do you suppose it's like?

[MIGUEL, *who has not lost his playful air completely, enters from the terrace at left. He passes near* ELISA *without sensing her presence and arrives in the lounge in time to hear* IGNACIO'S *words.*]

IGNACIO. [*Unconsciously underlining the tactile qualities of his assumption with hand movements full of yearning and intensity*]   I think it's like a tickling sensation entering through our eyes to reach deep into our bodies, touching our nerves . . . calming and reassuring us.

ANDRES. [*Sighing*]   It must be something like that.

MIGUEL.   Hello, fellows.

[ELISA *looks up, puts her hand to her breast, and begins to move toward* MIGUEL.]

PEDRO.   Hello, Miguel.

ANDRES.   You're in time to tell us what you think the pleasure of seeing is like.

MIGUEL.   Ah, well, not the way Ignacio has explained it. But that's not really important, because I've hit on a brilliant idea – don't laugh! – it's this: We don't see. Fine. Can we conceive what sight is? No. Then sight is inconceivable. Therefore, seers don't see either.

[*All but* IGNACIO *laugh loudly at this discovery.*]

PEDRO.   Then what do they do if they don't see?

MIGUEL.   Don't laugh, idiots. What do they do? They suffer collective hallucination. A madness known as vision! The only normal beings in this world of lunatics are ourselves.

[*Another burst of laughter.* MIGUEL *laughs too, but* ELISA *suffers.*]

IGNACIO. [*Whose deep and melancholy voice silences the laughter of the others*]   Miguel has found a solution for you – a rather absurd one. It would allow you to live unperturbed if you didn't know only too well that sight does exist. That's the reason your great discovery won't work.

MIGUEL. [*With a sudden sadness in his voice*]   But, truly, wasn't it clever?

IGNACIO.   Yes. You've learned to hide the hopelessness of our condition with laughter.

ELISA. [*Unable to hold back any longer*]   Miguel!

JUANA.   Elisa!

MIGUEL. [*Casually*]   Well, Juana, you were here? And how about Carlos?

CARLOS.   Carlos too. And if you'll permit me . . . [*Pressing* JUANA's *hand on the chair arm in silent warning*] I'll join you. [*He sits down at the right of the group.*]

ELISA.   Miguel, listen to me! We were going for a walk. It's very nice out today. Wouldn't you like to go now?

MIGUEL. [*Harshly*]   Dear Elisa, I've just come from a walk. And this happens to be a very interesting conversation. Why don't you stay here with Juana?

JUANA.   Come over here, Elisa. There's a place for you.

[ELISA *sighs and says nothing. She sits beside* JUANA *who caresses her and comforts her until they too are caught up in the conversation between* IGNACIO *and* CARLOS.]

ALBERTO.   Were you listening to us, Carlos?

CARLOS.   Yes, I was, Alberto. I found it all very interesting.

ANDRES.   And what do you feel about it?

CARLOS. [*Calmly*]   There are some things I don't understand clearly. You know that I'm a practical person. To what reasonable end could this talk lead you? That's what I don't understand. Especially when I find in your words nothing but dissatisfaction and hopelessness.

MIGUEL.   Hold it! There was also a suspicion of laughter . . . [*Again with involuntary sadness*] provoked by the irreparable misfortune of your humble servant.

[*Laughter from the students*]

CARLOS. [*With growing determination*] I must tell you, Miguel, that at times you aren't very amusing. But let's drop that subject. [*With emotion*] It's for you, Ignacio, that I have a question. [IGNACIO *is taken aback by the tone of* CARLOS'S *voice.*] Did you mean to say that we sightless people live in a world apart from seers?

IGNACIO. [*He appears frightened and clears his throat.*] Well, I meant . . .

CARLOS. [*Cutting him short*] No evasions, please. Did you mean it or not?

IGNACIO. Well . . . yes! A world apart . . . a more wretched world.

CARLOS. Well, it isn't true! Our world and theirs are one and the same. Don't we go to school as they do? Aren't we as socially useful as they are? Don't we compete in sports? Don't we have fun? Don't we love, don't we get married?

IGNACIO. [*Softly*] And don't we see?

CARLOS. [*Violently*] No, we don't see! But there are other afflictions in the world. Some people are cripples, paralytics; some have sick minds or a weak heart or a failing kidney. Some even die at twenty of tuberculosis or they are murdered in wars . . . or they die of hunger.

ALBERTO. Those are facts.

CARLOS. Of course they're facts! Misfortune is spread among all men; but we don't live in a separate camp. Do you want definite proof? Marriage between us and seers. There are many cases; someday it will probably be commonplace. We would all have been better off long ago if we'd dared to think in these terms instead of chanting: "There is no treasure like sight," that you were talking about before. [*Severely, to the others*] And it amazes me that those of you who've been here a long time could doubt it for a moment. [*Brief pause*] We can understand why Ignacio has his doubts. He doesn't know yet how free and beautiful our life can be. He lacks confidence; he's afraid to part with his cane. . . . You are the ones who should help him achieve that confidence! [*Pause*]

ANDRES. What do you say to that, Ignacio?

IGNACIO. Carlos's reasoning is very feeble. But this conversation is like a boxing match. Wouldn't it be better to end it? I have a high regard for you, Carlos, and I shouldn't like . . .

PEDRO. No, no. You must answer him.

IGNACIO. It's just that . . .

CARLOS. [*Mockingly, believing that he has won*] Don't worry about it, man. Answer me. There's nothing more annoying than a problem half resolved.

IGNACIO. I'm afraid that great problems are never completely resolved. [*He gets up and moves away from the group.*]

ANDRES. Don't leave!

CARLOS.   Let him go, Andrés . . . It's understandable. He still isn't sure of himself.

IGNACIO.   [*Beside the small table at the left*]   And that is why I need my cane, isn't it?

CARLOS.   You said so yourself.

IGNACIO.   [*Without making a sound, he takes the ashtray from the small table and puts it in his jacket pocket.*]   We all need one not to stumble and fall.

CARLOS.   You stumble because you're afraid. You'll carry a cane all your life and you'll still stumble all your life. Dare to be like us! We never stumble!

IGNACIO.   You're very sure of yourself. Maybe one day you'll stumble and fall and do yourself some bodily harm. . . . Perhaps sooner than you think. [*Pause*] Anyhow, I wasn't intending to leave. I want to answer you, but allow me to move around while I do. . . . I think more clearly that way. [*He has taken the table by its pedestal and is walking, tapping firmly with his cane, to centerstage. He places the table there without making the slightest sound.*] You, Carlos, seem to think that confidence comes through daring, and that life can be the same for us as for seers.

CARLOS.   Precisely.

IGNACIO.   You are too confident. Your sureness is an illusion. The slightest obstacle would trip you. You laugh at my cane, but this cane permits me to move back and forth in this room, as I'm doing now, without fear of obstacles. [*He moves downstage left and turns around. The table is now exactly on a line between him and* CARLOS.]

CARLOS.   [*Laughing*]   What obstacles? There aren't any here. Don't you realize your own cowardice. If you weren't afraid to rely on your own knowledge of this place, as we do, you'd throw that stick away.

IGNACIO.   I don't want to fall.

CARLOS.   [*Excitedly*]   But you can't fall! Everything is foreseen here. There isn't a corner of this building that we don't know. The cane is for the street, but here . . .

IGNACIO.   Here it's necessary too. How can we pathetic blind people know what lies in wait for us?

CARLOS.   We're not pathetic! And we know perfectly! [IGNACIO *laughs loudly.*] Don't laugh.

IGNACIO.   Forgive me, but your optimism struck me as being so . . . naive. For example, if I asked you to stand up and walk very quickly to where I'm standing, could you convince us that you'd do it without fear?

CARLOS.   [*Standing up impulsively*]   Of course! Do you want me to? [*Pause*]

IGNACIO.   [*Gravely*]   Yes, please. Don't forget: quickly.

CARLOS.   As quickly as you wish.

[*All the blind students lean closer to listen.* CARLOS *takes a few rapid steps; but, suddenly, uncertainty causes his face to contract and he slows his movement, extending his arms. It does not take him long to find the table, and an expression of brutal hatred crosses his face.*]

IGNACIO.   You're walking very slowly.

CARLOS.   [*Skirting the table, he advances with clenched fists until he is face to face with* IGNACIO.]   Don't believe it. I'm right here beside you.

IGNACIO.   You did hesitate.

CARLOS.   Not at all. I walked directly to your side to show you the pointlessness of your fears. And . . . you must surely be convinced that there are no obstacles in the way.

IGNACIO.   [*Triumphant*]   But it frightened you. Don't deny it! [*To the others*] It frightened him. Didn't you hear him hesitate and stop?

MIGUEL.   It's true, Carlos. We all noticed it.

CARLOS.   [*Flushed*]   But it wasn't from fear! I did it because suddenly I understood . . .

IGNACIO.   What? That there might be an obstacle after all? Well, if that's not fear, call it what you like.

MIGUEL.   A point for Ignacio!

CARLOS.   [*Controlling himself*]   Granted. But it wasn't fear; there was a reason . . . that I can't explain. This test is meaningless.

IGNACIO.   I have no objections to conceding that. [*As he speaks, he moves back to the group and sits down.*] But I still must answer your arguments. . . . We do go to school, yes; and we study ten percent of the things that seers study. We engage in sports – all except nine-tenths of them. [CARLOS, *who has remained downstage, crosses his arms tensely to control himself.*] And as for love . . .

ALBERTO.   You can't refute that.

IGNACIO.   Love can be a marvelous thing. The love between Carlos and Juana, for example. [JUANA, *who has followed the events of the confrontation, is visibly shaken.*] But with us it is never more than a sad parody of love between those who see! Because they possess the beloved one entirely. They are capable of enveloping each other in a glance. We possess . . . merely pieces. A caress, a momentary tenderness in the voice. In reality we don't love each other. We feel pity for another blind person and try to mask that sad pity with cheerful nonsense, calling it love. I think it would be more bearable if we didn't pretend.

MIGUEL.   Another point for Ignacio.

CARLOS.   [*Holding his temper*]   It seems to me that you have forgotten something very important.

IGNACIO.   That may be.

CARLOS.   Marriages between seers and non-seers. Don't these prove that our world and theirs is the same? Don't they prove that the love we feel and the love we inspire in others is not a parody?

IGNACIO.   Pure compassion, like the others!

CARLOS.   Are you going to try to tell me that Don Pablo and his wife have never loved each other?

IGNACIO.   Ha! I shouldn't want to have my words misinterpreted by anyone. . . .

ANDRES.   We all promise not to repeat what you say.

[DOÑA PEPITA *moves across the terrace toward the entrance, observing them through the glass. On hearing her name spoken, she stops.*]

IGNACIO.   The land of optimism where Carlos dreams keeps him from appreciating reality. [*To* CARLOS] For that reason, you have failed to discover a very significant detail that some of us have learned from outsiders who've come here. Very significant. Doña Pepita and Don Pablo got married because Don Pablo needed a cane. [*He strikes the floor with his.*] But, most of all, for a reason that blind men can't appreciate . . . one that is very important to seers. Because . . . Doña Pepita is very ugly!

[*A silence. Little by little the idea takes hold, and some of the students begin to laugh.* CARLOS *is speechless.*]

MIGUEL.   A third point for Ignacio! [*The laughter increases.* CARLOS *clenches his fists.* JUANA *covers her face with her hands.* DOÑA PEPITA, *who has bowed her head in sadness, masters her emotions and speaks.*]

DOÑA PEPITA.   [*Cordially*]   Good afternoon, my friends! You seem to be in good spirits. [*At the sound of her voice, the laughter stops abruptly.*] One of Miguel's jokes, no doubt. . . . Am I right?

[*They all stand up; some of them are still trying to hold back their laughter.*]

MIGUEL.   You're right, Doña Pepita.

DOÑA PEPITA.   Well, I was going to scold you for wasting time this way. It's almost three and you haven't gone out to practice. We'll never win the skating championship at this rate. Come along! All of you outside!

MIGUEL.   I'm sorry.

DOÑA PEPITA.   No harm done. Now go out and make a good showing on the rink. And you, young ladies, can come outside with me. [*The students file out toward the terrace and disappear at right amid repressed giggles.* CARLOS, IGNACIO, JUANA, *and* ELISA *remain behind.* DOÑA PEPITA *speaks to* CARLOS *with a special tenderness: this student is her favorite, perhaps the substitute for the real son she never had with her husband. She may even be in love with him a bit without realizing it.*] Carlos, my husband wants to speak with you.

CARLOS.   I'll go right away, Doña Pepita. As soon as I finish a little matter with Ignacio.

DOÑA PEPITA.   And what about you, Ignacio? Don't you want to skate? When are you going to decide to give up that cane?

IGNACIO.   I don't dare, Doña Pepita. Anyhow, why should I?

DOÑA PEPITA. Well, my boy, don't you see how your schoolmates come and go without it?

IGNACIO. No, Doña Pepita, I don't *see* anything.

DOÑA PEPITA. Of course not. Forgive me. It's just a way of speaking that we have. . . . Shall we go, girls?

JUANA. Whenever you wish.

DOÑA PEPITA. [*Putting an arm around each of the girls*] We'll leave you to yourselves. [*Affectionately*] Don't forget to talk with my husband, Carlos.

CARLOS. Don't worry. I'll go right away.

[DOÑA PEPITA *and the girls walk to the edge of the terrace where they stop.* DOÑA PEPITA, *with quick gestures, explains to the blind girls what is happening on the skating rink.* IGNACIO *sits down again. A pause.*]

IGNACIO. Your turn.

[CARLOS *says nothing. He goes to the small table, picks it up, and with deliberate noise moves it to its original position. Then he confronts* IGNACIO.]

CARLOS. [*Sharply*] Where have you put the ashtray?

IGNACIO. [*Smiling*] Ah, yes. I was about to forget. Here. [*He holds it out in his hand.* CARLOS *gropes in the emptiness and grabs it brusquely.*]

CARLOS. I don't know if you realize it, but I'm on the verge of giving you a good beating.

IGNACIO. It wouldn't make you any more right if you did.

[CARLOS *controls himself. Then he replaces the ashtray with a loud thud and returns to* IGNACIO's *side.*]

CARLOS. [*Showing his emotion*] Listen, Ignacio. Let's talk man to man and make every effort to understand each other.

IGNACIO. I believe I understand you quite well.

CARLOS. I'm talking about putting our understanding into practice.

IGNACIO. That won't be so easy.

CARLOS. Agreed. But don't you think it's necessary to make the effort?

IGNACIO. Why?

CARLOS. [*With repressed impatience*] I'll try to explain myself. Since you don't seem inclined to give up your pessimism, I will respect your right to your own attitudes. But I find it wrong for you to try to infect the other students with your ideas. What right do you have to do that?

IGNACIO. I'm not trying to sell my ideas to anybody. I'm simply being sincere, and that infection you're speaking of is nothing more than the awakening of sincerity in the others. Since there was so little to be found here when I arrived, I find it completely proper. Now will you tell me what right you have to constantly recommend happiness, optimism, and all that drivel?

CARLOS. Ignacio, you know that these things aren't what you're mak-

ing them seem. My words of encouragement can help our fellow
students achieve a relatively happy life. Your negative ideas can
only destroy them, lead them to desperation, make them give up
their studies.

[DOÑA PEPITA *calls from the terrace to the students who are skating
on the rink.* IGNACIO *and* CARLOS *interrupt their exchange to listen.*]

DOÑA PEPITA.   Miguel, that's twice you've fallen down! That's not
good. And you, Andrés, what's come over you? Why don't you
put your heart into it? . . . Come on, now. You've all lost your
confidence.

CARLOS.   Do you hear that?

IGNACIO.   So?

CARLOS.   You are to blame.

IGNACIO.   I?

CARLOS.   Yes, you, Ignacio! And I want you to think about it . . . and
to cooperate in keeping this school free of problems. I believe it
is the concern of us all.

IGNACIO.   It doesn't concern me. This school is built on a lie.

[DOÑA PEPITA *places her hands on the shoulders of each girl and
kisses them before exiting from the terrace left.* JUANA *and* ELISA *join
hands.*]

CARLOS.   What lie?

IGNACIO.   That we are normal human beings.

CARLOS.   We won't discuss that now!

IGNACIO. [*Standing up*]   We'll never discuss anything! There's no
understanding possible between you and me. I'll say what I please
and I'll not renounce any conquest that comes my way. None!

CARLOS. [*He clenches his fists and then gains control of himself.*]   All
right. Goodbye.

[*He exits rapidly left.* IGNACIO *remains alone. He whistles sadly a few
notes of the* Moonlight *Sonata. After a moment, he rests his hands on
his cane and leans back. Brief pause.* LOLA *enters from the terrace. A
moment later,* ESPERANZA *enters from the left. Their expressions
brighten when they hear each other's footsteps. They continue toward
the place where* IGNACIO *is seated, and almost at the same instant
they exclaim:*]

LOLA.   Ignacio!

ESPERANZA.   Ignacio!

[IGNACIO *does not move or respond. The girls laugh embarrassedly at
their mistake.*]

LOLA.   He's not here.

ESPERANZA. [*Sadly*]   He's avoiding us.

LOLA.   Do you think so?

ESPERANZA.   Oh, he speaks to us out of courtesy, only because we
speak to him. But he despises us. He knows that we don't understand him.

LOLA. Couldn't it be . . . another girl?

ESPERANZA. We would have noticed something.

LOLA. Don't be so sure. He's very secretive. There just might be a girl involved.

ESPERANZA. Maybe we'll find him in the study hall.

LOLA. Let's try.

[*They exit right calling him. Pause.* JUANA *and* ELISA *are discussing something on the terrace.* ELISA *is visibly upset; she attempts to pull away from* JUANA *to enter the lounge, and* JUANA *tries to restrain her.*]

ELISA. [*From the terrace*]   Let me go! I'm fed up with Ignacio. [*She pulls free and crosses to the entrance to the lounge;* IGNACIO *looks up.*]

JUANA. [*Close behind her*]   Be sensible, Elisa. Let's sit and talk for a few minutes.

ELISA. I don't want to.

JUANA. Sit down . . . [*She forces* ELISA *to sit on the sofa and then sits beside her.*]

ELISA. I hate him! I hate him!

JUANA. Try to be calm for a moment, Elisa. [*Raising her voice*] Is there someone here?

[IGNACIO *does not respond.* JUANA *takes her friend's hand.*]

ELISA. Oh, how I hate him!

JUANA. It isn't good to hate.

ELISA. He's taken Miguel away from me, and he's going to destroy our lives. My Miguel!

JUANA. He'll come back. Don't worry about that. He loves you. Why, actually, nothing has happened at all! Perhaps he's a little indifferent . . . because Miguel was always carried away by a new interest. But Ignacio is only a passing distraction for him. And, after all, Ignacio is a boy. If you had to worry about some other girl and Miguel . . . and even that wouldn't mean that he'd stopped loving you.

ELISA. I'd rather that he deceived me with another girl.

JUANA. Why do you say that?

ELISA. This is worse. That boy has taken over his mind, and I have no place in his thoughts.

JUANA. I think you're exaggerating.

ELISA. No. Listen . . . isn't there someone here?

JUANA. No . . . I don't think so.

ELISA. I was certain . . . [*Pause. Her intense tone returns.*] I told you so the first day, Juana. That boy is full of evil. I sensed it! And he puts on his act of a suffering Christ just to win disciples. Men are stupid. And Miguel is the stupidest of all. But I do love him! [*She begins to cry silently.*]

JUANA. I understand. Don't cry . . .

ELISA. [*Getting up to walk off her anguish*]   It's just that I love him, Juana!

JUANA.   What Miguel needs is a little indifference on your part. Don't
run after him so much.

ELISA.   I know that I make a fool of myself. But I can't help it. [*She
stops beside* IGNACIO *who holds his breath; she dries her eyes and
puts away her handkerchief.*]

JUANA.   Try it. He'll come back to you.

ELISA.   How do you expect me to try it with that man between us? His
being here frustrates me. . . . Oh! How I'd like to hit him! I wish I
knew what he's really up to! [*She clenches her hands in the air. But,
suddenly, she begins to turn slowly toward* IGNACIO, *without realizing
that she senses his presence.*]

JUANA.   He's not up to anything. He's suffering . . . and we don't know
how to cure him. But he does deserve our compassion.

[ELISA *turns her head in* JUANA'S *direction again. She has still not suspected anything.*]

ELISA. [*Moving toward* JUANA]   You've given him too much compassion. He's a selfish person. Let him suffer alone and not try to
make the rest of us miserable!

JUANA. [*Smiling*]   Sit down and control yourself. [*She gets up and goes
toward her.*] You accuse Ignacio of being selfish. And what else do
you expect him to be if he hurts inside. We could be a little less
selfish ourselves. People should be tolerant of the weaknesses of
others and help them . . . [*Brief pause*]

ELISA. [*Suddenly, with intensity, she grabs* JUANA *by the arms.*]   No, no,
Juana, not that!

JUANA. [*Alarmed*]   Not what?

ELISA.   Not that, not that!

JUANA.   Make sense! Not what?

ELISA.   Your sympathy for Ignacio.

JUANA.   What are you trying to say?

ELISA.   Promise me you'll be strong! For Carlos's sake, promise me!
[*Shaking her*] Promise me!

JUANA.   Don't be silly. I love Carlos and nothing's going to happen. I
don't know what you think could happen.

ELISA.   Everything! Everything could happen! He took Miguel from
me, and now you are in danger! Promise me you'll stay away
from him. Promise!

JUANA. [*Very upset*]   Elisa, shut up this very minute! I won't allow this
. . . [*She pulls away from her violently. Pause.*]

ELISA. [*Moving away slowly*]   Oh! I'm your best friend, and you won't
allow me to speak. He's won you over too. You're under his spell
and you don't realize it.

JUANA.   Elisa!

ELISA.   I feel sorry for you. And I feel sorry for Carlos too, because
he's going to be hurt the way I've been hurt.

JUANA. [*Raising her voice*]   Elisa! Either you shut up, or . . . ! [*She goes *toward her.*]

ELISA. Leave me alone. It's useless to resist. He's stronger than all of us. He's taking everything away from us! Everything! Even our friendship. I don't recognize you! I don't know you! . . . [*Crying, she goes upstage and exits.* JUANA, *upset and hurt, hesitates.* IGNACIO *stands up.*]

IGNACIO. Juana. [*She stifles a cry and turns toward* IGNACIO. *He goes to her side.*] I was here and I heard you. Poor Elisa! I have nothing against her.

JUANA. [*Trying to keep from trembling*] Why didn't you say something?

IGNACIO. I'm not sorry, Juana. [*He takes her hand.*] You've given me my first moment of happiness. Thank you! If you knew how beautiful it is to feel you're understood. And you've sensed what I feel. You're right. I do hurt inside. And that suffering drives me . . .

JUANA. Ignacio . . . why don't you try to control yourself? I know very well that you don't want to harm us, but you are doing just that.

IGNACIO. I can't keep it inside me. I can't lie to people when they question me. . . . The deceptions they invent for living disgust me.

JUANA. You've brought us only dissension when we wanted peace!

IGNACIO. I warned you there'd be a fight . . . In this very room. And I'm winning. Remember that you're the one who insisted that I stay. [*Brief pause*]

JUANA. And if I asked you now, for your own good, for mine, and for the good of us all, to leave?

IGNACIO. [*Slowly*] Do you really want that?

JUANA. [*Her voice very weak*] I beg you to go.

IGNACIO. No. You don't want me to. You want to ease my pain with your gentleness. And you're going to be kind to me! You're going to be kind! You, who've understood me and defended me. I love you, Juana.

JUANA. Hush!

IGNACIO. I love you and not one of those others. It's been you from the first day. I love you for your goodness, for the tenderness in your voice, for the soft touch of your hands. [*Transition*] I love you and I need you. You know that.

JUANA. Please! Don't talk like that! You've forgotten that Carlos . . .

IGNACIO. [*With irony*] Carlos? Carlos is a fool who would leave you for the first woman with sight who asked him. He thinks our world and theirs are the same. He'd love another Doña Pepita who'd look after him. He longs for a whole woman, and he loves you as a poor substitute. [*A change in tone*] But I love a blind girl—not one of the seers. A blind girl from my world of the blind, one who understands. You. Because only you can love me as I am – not a deluded optimist who thinks he's normal. It's me you love! You don't dare to say so, or confess it. You'd be breaking the rules. But I'll say it for you. Yes. You love me; you're only realizing it at this very moment. Your feelings show in your voice. You love me with all my anguish and sadness, enough to face the truth with me and turn your back on all the lies that mask and hide our misfortune! Because you're strong and because you're good! [*He embraces her passionately.*]

JUANA.   No!

[IGNACIO *seals her mouth with a prolonged kiss.* JUANA *hardly resists.* DON PABLO *and* CARLOS *have entered at left. They stop, surprised.*]

DON PABLO.   What's this!

[IGNACIO *steps back quickly without releasing* JUANA. *They listen nervously.*]

CARLOS.   I heard two people . . . kiss.

[JUANA *wrings her hands.*]

DON PABLO.   What disregard for propriety! Who are the lovebirds cooing in the corner? I'll have to have a talk with you!

[*No one answers.* JUANA *is on the verge of blurting out something.* IGNACIO *grasps her arm forcefully.*]

So you won't answer?

[IGNACIO, *with his cane held up from the floor, leads* JUANA *rapidly toward the terrace. His steps are sure; he seems possessed of a new and triumphant confidence. In her anguish,* JUANA *raises and lowers her head. Pulled along, almost running, she is seen passing across the terrace with* IGNACIO *who holds her arm tightly.* DON PABLO *in a joking tone:*]

They've gone! We made them ashamed.

CARLOS. [*Serious*]   Yes.

Curtain

ACT THREE

A sitting room in the dormitory. A wide window at the rear with the curtains drawn back. The sky is filled with stars. At left, placed diagonally, a curtained doorway; downstage right another door. Along the right wall, a radio set and a bookshelf with games and books for the blind. Downstage left, a chessboard is set up with all the chessmen in place; two chairs. A sofa centerstage in front of the large window; and a desk lamp near the radio. Only the central chandelier is lighted.

Note: This act may also be effectively played on the same set as ACTS ONE and TWO, with only slight modifications between the acts.

ELISA, *seated on the left side of the sofa, is crying.* CARLOS *is seated at the chessboard playing a game with himself and trying to keep his mind off other matters. His collar is unbuttoned and his tie loose.*

ELISA.   We're both so unhappy, Carlos! We're absolutely miserable! Why do people fall in love? I'd like to know that. [*Brief pause*] Now I realize that he didn't love me.

CARLOS.   He loved you and he still does. It's all Ignacio's fault. Miguel is very young. He's only seventeen, and . . .

ELISA.   You're right. I want to convince myself that he'll come back . . . but I don't believe it, Carlos. Not at all! [*She starts to cry again. Then she regains control.*] How selfish I am! You've been hurt, too, and I make you listen to my troubles. [*She gets up and goes to his side.*]

CARLOS.   I've not been hurt.

ELISA.   Yes, you have . . . and you're suffering because of Juana. [*A movement from* CARLOS] Because of that awful flirt.

CARLOS.   I wish it were only flirting.

ELISA.   And you say you haven't been hurt? [CARLOS *hides his face in his hands.*] Ignacio has ruined things for both of us.

CARLOS.   No one has ruined anything for me.

ELISA.   Don't pretend with me. . . . I understand your pain very well because it's like mine. Juana's desertion hurts you all the more because there's no real explanation. . . . It's frightening! It seems that nothing has happened, and yet we both know in our hearts that everything has changed.

CARLOS. [*Vehemently*] Nothing has changed! Nothing is going to change. I refuse to be hurt.

ELISA.   You frighten me.

CARLOS.   Yes. I refuse to be hurt. You say that I'm miserable. It's not true. Do you think I suffer because of Juana? She can't hurt me because she hasn't stopped loving me. Do you understand? She hasn't stopped loving me. It has to be that way and it is.

ELISA. [*Pitying him*] Pain without tears is the worst. If you could let yourself go like me.

CARLOS.   Don't expect me to cry. Go ahead and shed your own tears if you wish, but you're doing the wrong thing. You have no reason to. There won't be a reason. Miguel loves you and he'll come back. Juana hasn't stopped loving me.

ELISA.   You won't admit that things are as they really are. I've also wanted to delude myself at times. I still do, but . . .

CARLOS. [*Desperately*] But don't you understand that we can't let ourselves be defeated by Ignacio? If we let ourselves be hurt because of him, that hurt will be his victory. And we must not let him win! We mustn't!

ELISA. [*Frightened*] But in privacy we can at least share each other's pain.

CARLOS.   Not even in privacy. [*Pause. He slowly lowers his head again.* JUANA *enters from left.*]

JUANA.   Ignacio?

[ELISA *is about to speak but* CARLOS *presses her arm to keep her quiet.*]

He's not here. I wonder where he is . . . Poor boy . . .

[*She crosses and exits right.*]

ELISA.   Carlos!

CARLOS.   Be quiet.

ELISA.   Oh, what's wrong with you? You aren't acting normal . . . I couldn't have resisted.

CARLOS. [*Almost smiling*]   Why, nothing has happened at all. . . . Another . . . another girl who's looking for poor Ignacio. Just another one who wanders around calling his name. . . . Nothing at all.

ELISA.   I don't understand you. I don't know if you're desperate or crazy. . . .

CARLOS.   Neither. My mind was never clearer than it is now. [*He strikes one hand rapidly against the other.*] Cheer up, Elisa! Everything is going to be fixed.

[IGNACIO *and* MIGUEL *enter from left, talking animatedly.* ELISA *presses* CARLOS's *hand when she hears them.*]

IGNACIO.   Not all women are the same, although it's undeniable that blind girls are pretty much alike . . . with an occasional exception. I once knew a girl who could see . . .

MIGUEL. [*Interrupting impulsively*]   Girls who can see are very nice. I knew one who used to live next door to us. I didn't pay her any attention, but she was sold on me.

IGNACIO.   Do you know if she was ugly?

MIGUEL. [*With embarrassment*]   Well . . . no. I never managed to find out.

CARLOS.   Good evening, friends. Why don't you sit down?

MIGUEL. [*Nervously*]   Carlos! I want to have a talk with you. I don't know why we never seem to talk anymore. And it's the same with Elisa.

ELISA. [*With effort*]   Well, here we are.

MIGUEL. [*Showing little enthusiasm*]   Well, if it isn't Elisa with you! How are things, Elisa?

ELISA. [*Dryly*]   Fine, thank you.

MIGUEL. [*Casually*]   Good! I'm glad.

CARLOS. [*Articulating carefully*]   I believe that Juana was looking for you, Ignacio.

IGNACIO. [*Disturbed*]   Oh . . . maybe . . .

CARLOS.   Yes. No maybe about it. She was looking for you.

IGNACIO. [*Recovering his composure*]   It's possible. We were supposed to talk about something.

MIGUEL. Listen, Ignacio, why don't you go on and tell me about that girl who could see. Elisa and Carlos won't mind.

CARLOS. Not at all.

IGNACIO. Carlos and Elisa aren't interested in such matters. They're very abstract.

CARLOS. I don't see anything abstract about a girl of flesh and blood.

IGNACIO. But do you really want to get involved in these matters again?

ELISA. [*Violently*] Forgive me, but Ignacio is right. I can't stand any more talk. I'm going to bed.

CARLOS. As you wish. Do you mind if I don't walk with you? I'd like to continue this conversation with Ignacio. Miguel will go with you.

[MIGUEL *receives this suggestion with displeasure.*]

ELISA. [*In an unpleasant tone*] Don't bother about me. Miguel will surely prefer to stay and talk with you . . . and Ignacio.

MIGUEL. [*Without the slightest enthusiasm*] You can be very silly sometimes. . . . I'll be glad to walk with you.

ELISA. If you want to. Good night.

IGNACIO. Good night.

CARLOS. I'll see you tomorrow, Elisa. [*She exits right.* MIGUEL *follows her like an obedient dog.* CARLOS *and* IGNACIO *sit at right, but before they begin to speak,* DOÑA PEPITA *enters from left.*]

DOÑA PEPITA. Good evening, boys. Isn't it time to be going to your rooms?

[CARLOS *and* IGNACIO *stand up.*]

CARLOS. I don't think it's so late.

DOÑA PEPITA. Well, be seated, please. And you, man with the cane. Haven't you anything to say?

IGNACIO. Good evening.

DOÑA PEPITA. Perk up, my boy! I find you looking more depressed every day. Well, don't let me interfere with your talk. I'm going for a walk. I'll see you later.

CARLOS. Goodbye, Doña Pepita. [*She exits right. Pause.*]

IGNACIO. I guess you didn't stay with me to talk about the girl who could see.

CARLOS. You guessed correctly.

IGNACIO. We've already talked several times and always about the same topic. It is also going to be today's topic?

CARLOS. Same topic.

IGNACIO. Patience. Could you tell me how many times we're going to have to talk about the same things?

CARLOS. Not many more. . . . Maybe this will be the last time.

IGNACIO. I'm delighted. You can begin when you're ready.

CARLOS. Ignacio . . . the very day you came here you tried to leave. [*Bitterly*] I learned that when Juana still confided in me. It was a very good idea you had then, and I think the moment has come to put it into practice. Leave now!

IGNACIO. That sounds like an order . . .

CARLOS. The appropriateness of which I'm prepared to explain.

IGNACIO. Don Pablo sent you, didn't he?

CARLOS. No. But you must go away from here.

IGNACIO. Why?

CARLOS. You must leave because your influence is too strong in this place. And your influence is destructive. If you don't go, this house will collapse. But before that happens, I'll see that you leave.

IGNACIO. You're talking nonsense. Naturally I don't have any intention of leaving. Oh, I know that some of you would like that. Beginning with your director. But he doesn't dare to say so because he knows he has no real cause to. Aren't you speaking to me in his name?

CARLOS. I'm speaking for the best interests of this institution.

IGNACIO. More nonsense. You certainly are fond of clichés. Well, you listen to me. I'm certain that most of the students want me to stay. So I'm not going.

CARLOS. What do the other students mean to you?

[Brief pause]

IGNACIO. The greatest obstacle between you and me is that you refuse to understand me. [Ardently] The students, and you along with them, mean more to me than you think! Your blindness hurts me like a personal mutilation. I hurt for all of you! [Enraptured] Listen! Didn't you realize when you came along the terrace that it's dry and cold tonight? Do you know what that means? No, you don't, of course. Well, it means that the stars are shining in all their splendor and that seers can know the marvel of their presence. Those far-off worlds beyond the window. [He has gone to the window and is touching the panes.] Within reach of our sight . . . if we could see! [Brief pause] What does that matter to you? But I long for them, I want to see them, to feel their light on my face. And I think I do almost see them. [He is facing the window ecstatically. CARLOS has turned too, influenced by IGNACIO's words in spite of himself.] But I know that if I had vision, I would die from the pain of not being able to reach them! But at least I could see them! And not one of you sees them, Carlos. And you think these concerns are bad? You know that they can't be. Isn't it possible for you – even a little – to feel this too?

CARLOS. [Stubbornly] No! I don't feel any of that.

IGNACIO. You don't feel the presence of the stars? Well, that is your misfortune. Not to feel the hope I've brought you.

CARLOS. What hope?

IGNACIO. The hope of light.

CARLOS. Of light?

IGNACIO. Of light, yes! They say that we're incurable. But what do we know of that? No one knows what the world can hold for us — through scientific discovery, or even a miracle.

CARLOS. [*Scornfully*] Bah!

IGNACIO. Of course, I know that you reject it. You reject the faith that I bring you.

CARLOS. That's enough! Light, vision . . . empty words. We are blind men! Do you understand that?

IGNACIO. Some progress has been made when you recognize that fact . . . I thought we were only . . . non-seers.

CARLOS. Blind men, yes. So be it.

IGNACIO. And what is blindness?

CARLOS. [*Hesitating*] What is it? . . .

IGNACIO. The absence of light. Of something you crave to understand . . . although you deny it. [*A change of tone*] Listen: I know many things. I know that seers try at times to imagine our condition, and so they close their eyes. [*The stage lights begin to dim.*] Then they tremble at the horror of it. Once a man went crazy because he believed he was blind . . . only because they failed to open the window of his room on time. [*The stage is totally dark. Only the stars are still shining through the window.*] We are all immersed in that horror and that madness, without knowing what it is! [*Now the stars begin to go out.*] And that's why it's doubly terrible for me. [*Absolute darkness on the stage and in the theatre.*] Only our voices cross in the darkness. . . .

CARLOS. [*With a suggestion of apprehension in his voice*] Ignacio!

IGNACIO. Yes. It is a terrible word because it is so mysterious. You've made a start. You're beginning to understand. [*Brief pause*] I've sensed how men with sight are happy with the return of light in the mornings. [*The stars begin to shine again, as the stage lights slowly come up.*] They move about identifying objects, enjoying their shapes and . . . their colors. They are filled with the joy of light, which is for them a real gift from God. A gift so remarkable that they have been inspired to find ways to imitate it at night. But for us it's all the same. Light can go and come back; it can draw forms and colors from the darkness; it can show an object in the completeness of its creation. [*Now the lights are completely up again.*] Even the distant stars! Yet for us it doesn't matter. We see nothing.

CARLOS. [*Brusquely shaking off the involuntary influence of* IGNACIO's *words*] That's enough! I understand you. Yes, I do, but I can't excuse you. [*With the tone of a person who perceives a sudden revelation*] You think you're some kind of Messiah! And you're warped. I'll tell you what's wrong with you. You have a death wish. You say you want to see. . . . What you really want is to die!

IGNACIO.   Maybe . . . maybe. Perhaps death is the only way to obtain absolute vision. . . .

CARLOS.   Or absolute darkness. But it's all the same. Death is what you're seeking and you don't know it. Death for yourself and for other people. That's why you must leave. I stand for life! For the lives of my companions whom you threaten. Because I want to live completely, to find fulfillment, even though that doesn't mean a completely happy or peaceful life. Even if it's hard and bitter. But life is real, and it makes a claim on us. [*Brief pause*] All of us were fighting for life here . . . until you came. Just go!

IGNACIO.   You argue well for life. I'm not surprised. And you want me to leave for a reason that touches your life deeply: Juana.

[DOÑA PEPITA *appears at right and observes them.*]

CARLOS. [*Raising his fist threateningly*]   Ignacio!

DOÑA PEPITA. [*Quickly*]   You're still here. Your talk must be an interesting one. [CARLOS *lowers his arm.*] You look as if you were rehearsing a play, my dear Carlos.

CARLOS. [*Controlling himself*]   Almost, almost, Doña Pepita.

DOÑA PEPITA. [*Crossing to them*]   It would be better if you went to bed now. My husband is coming down to work a while. Good night.

CARLOS and IGNACIO.   Good night.

[*From the doorway at left,* DOÑA PEPITA *turns around and looks at them with an expression of hesitancy; then she exits.*]

CARLOS. [*Calmly*]   You've mentioned Juana. Juana has nothing to do with this. We can leave her out of it.

IGNACIO.   Did I hear you correctly? Twice you've brought her into your argument and now you say she has no connection with it. I didn't think you were such a hypocrite. Juana is the reason for your anger, my friend.

CARLOS.   I'm not angry.

IGNACIO.   Well, let's call it displeasure. The thought of Juana inspired that beautiful song to life you've just sung to me.

CARLOS.   I'm telling you again to leave Juana out of this. You and I had already talked about this before you . . . poisoned her mind.

IGNACIO.   Even then she didn't belong to you completely. All right: I do love her. That's a fact. And I too have some arguments on the side of life. And it's because of her that I'm staying. Just as it's because of her that you want me to leave. [*Brief pause*] I'll give you a small consolation: Juana isn't completely mine yet.

CARLOS. [*Calmly*]   With people like you there's always something low and dirty behind your actions. That's what really inspires your mysticism. I'm not going to speak of this again. You're leaving this school one way or another.

IGNACIO. [*Laughing*]   Dear Carlos, there's nothing you can do about me. I'm not going . . . one way or another. And even if I did think of suicide a few times, that's not in my mind any longer.

CARLOS. Maybe you're hoping that one of the boys you've led to despair will set an example.

IGNACIO. [*Tired of the duel*] Let's not discuss it further. You'll have to excuse my sarcasm. I don't like it, but you do get to me. I'm sorry. I'm going out for a while – but no farther than the playing field. It's a pleasant night, and I want to walk so that I can sleep. [*Serious*] The light from those fantastic stars will fall on me even if I don't see it. [*He goes toward the door.*] Would you like to go with me?

CARLOS. No.

IGNACIO. Then good night.

CARLOS. Good night. [IGNACIO *exits right.* CARLOS *drops down on one of the chairs beside the chessboard and begins to run his fingers over the chessmen absentmindedly. He starts to talk to himself, holding back his rage.*] No! I don't want to go with you! I'll never go to hell with you! Let the others do it!

[*A few moments later,* DOÑA PEPITA *and* DON PABLO *enter from left. She is carrying a leather briefcase.*]

DOÑA PEPITA. Still here?

CARLOS. [*Looking up*] Yes. I'm not sleepy.

DON PABLO. [*Who has been led by* DOÑA PEPITA *to the sofa*] Good evening, Carlos.

CARLOS. Good evening, sir.

DOÑA PEPITA. Did Ignacio go off to bed?

CARLOS. Yes . . . I think so.

DON PABLO. [*Serious*] I'm glad to find you here, Carlos. It's Ignacio that I'd like to talk to you about. May I have a cigarette, my dear? [DOÑA PEPITA *takes a pack from her briefcase, puts a cigarette in his mouth, and lights it for him.*] Thank you, my dear. Yes, Carlos, I think this has gone beyond the ordinary. [DOÑA PEPITA *sits down at the desk, takes some papers from the briefcase, and begins to write comments on them.*] It's become a serious threat to this institution. Is it possible that one boy can demoralize a hundred students? I really don't understand it.

DOÑA PEPITA. There is at least one detail that you're not aware of. Many of the students have become careless in their dress.

DON PABLO. Is that so!

DOÑA PEPITA. They neglect to send their clothes to the laundry . . . or they stop wearing their ties, like Ignacio. [*Brief pause.* CARLOS *involuntarily feels his own tie.*] Even so, I wonder how he affects so many.

DON PABLO. I suppose he works on them all day long, talking to them. What do you think about all this, Carlos? [*Pause*] Eh?

[DOÑA PEPITA *looks at* CARLOS.]

CARLOS. I'm sorry. What were you saying?

DON PABLO. How is it possible for Ignacio to affect so many of the non-seers in this school. What do they know of light?

CARLOS. [*Gravely*] Perhaps it's what they don't know that bothers them.

DON PABLO. [*Smiling*] Oh, that's very subtle, my boy. [*He stands up.*]

CARLOS. But it's true. They're fascinated by anything mysterious. It's a pity. Furthermore, Ignacio isn't alone. He sowed the seed and now he has a group of unconscious helpers. [*Brief pause. Sadly*] Especially among the girls.

DOÑA PEPITA. [*Gently*] I don't think his helpers are that important. If Ignacio should leave, the harmful influence he's had would disappear with him.

DON PABLO. If Ignacio left, everything would return to normal. We could expel him, of course, but that would be harmful to the reputation of the institution. Couldn't you suggest to him under some pretext or other – and very kindly, of course – the advisability of his leaving us? [*Pause*] Are you listening to me, Carlos?

CARLOS. I'm sorry. My mind was wandering. I didn't quite understand what you said. . . .

DOÑA PEPITA. You're acting very strange tonight. My husband was saying that you might suggest to Ignacio that he leave the school.

DON PABLO. Unless you have a better idea . . .

[*Brief pause*]

CARLOS. I've already talked with him.

DON PABLO. Yes? And what happened?

CARLOS. Nothing at all. He says he won't leave.

DON PABLO. I suppose you spoke to him in an appropriate manner, tactfully. . . .

CARLOS. The most appropriate manner. Don't worry about that.

DON PABLO. And why doesn't he want to leave?

[*Pause.* DOÑA PEPITA *looks at* CARLOS *curiously.*]

CARLOS. I don't know.

DON PABLO. Well! One way or another he has to go!

CARLOS. Yes. He must!

DON PABLO. [*Worried*] He really has to go. He's the most disrupting enemy of our educational mission that we've ever encountered. We can do nothing for him. He's an incorrigible troublemaker. [*Impulsively*] Carlos, think of a solution. I have great confidence in you.

DOÑA PEPITA. We'll have to give it careful thought. But not tonight. It's getting late. I think you both should get some rest.

DON PABLO. You're probably right. But I doubt that I'll sleep tonight. Are you coming with me, Pepita?

DOÑA PEPITA. Not yet. I'm going to finish these papers.

DON PABLO. Good night, my dear. Don't forget our problem, Carlos. [CARLOS *does not answer.*]

DOÑA PEPITA. Good night. Rest well. [DON PABLO *exits right.* DOÑA PEPITA *gets up and goes over to* CARLOS. *As always, she speaks to him affectionately.*] Don't you intend to go to bed tonight?

CARLOS. [*Startled*]   What's that?

DOÑA PEPITA.   But what's come over you, my boy?

CARLOS. [*Trying to smile*]   Nothing.

DOÑA PEPITA.   Off to bed. You need some sleep.

CARLOS.   Yes. My head hurts. But I'm not sleepy.

DOÑA PEPITA.   As you wish . . . [*She switches on a lamp and walks to the doorway to turn off the central light. She sits down again and begins to murmur as she goes over her notes; she writes something. Suddenly she stops and looks at* CARLOS *who is starting to get up.*] Were you telling Ignacio to leave when I saw you talking to him? [CARLOS *doesn't respond. His expression is strangely rigid. Slowly he moves toward the door.* DOÑA PEPITA *reacts with surprise.*] Are you going outside?

CARLOS. [*Controlling himself*]   I'm going to get some air to clear my head. I hope you rest well. Good night. [*He exits.*]

DOÑA PEPITA.   Good night. I'll be going in a moment. [*She watches him leave and makes a gesture of commiseration. Then she goes on with her work. After a moment, she stretches and looks at her wristwatch.*] Midnight. [*She gets up to turn on the radio. A fragment of "Aase's Death" from Grieg's music for* Peer Gynt *is heard softly. She listens for a few moments. She glances disinterestedly at the sheets of paper. She goes slowly toward the window and looks out at the night with her face close to the glass. Suddenly she is intrigued by something she sees.*] What's that? [*She makes a shade with her hands to see better. With a tone of extraordinary surprise.*] What are they doing? [*Her hands grasp the window frame. Then she steps back as if she had been struck and utters a stifled cry. She turns around, her face contracted with horror. Her hands go to her mouth. She gasps and hesitates. Finally she runs to the door and exits. For several moments the melody is heard from the empty stage. Then, far-off cries and shouts.* MIGUEL *and* ANDRES *enter rapidly from right.*]

ANDRES.   What's happening?

MIGUEL. [*Still walking*]   I don't know. They're calling for help from the sports field. They want three or four of us. Go tell the others in the dormitory.

[*They exit left. A pause.* ESPERANZA *appears at right, trembling and groping the air. A moment later,* LOLA *follows her. Both are in pajamas and bathrobe.*]

ESPERANZA.   Who . . . who is it?

LOLA. [*Moving closer to her*]   Esperanza!

[*They embrace from fear.*]

ESPERANZA.   Did you hear them calling?

LOLA.   Yes.

ESPERANZA.   What's happening?

LOLA.   I don't know! . . .

[*They separate for a moment and listen.*]

ESPERANZA.   Don't leave me alone! I'm afraid.

LOLA. [*Embracing her again*]   I can't hear a thing. It's awful.

ESPERANZA.   Dear God, help us! I have the feeling that something terrible has happened. . . .

LOLA.   Be quiet!

ESPERANZA.   It's as if we'd made a great mistake. I feel empty . . . and
alone.

LOLA.   I hear footsteps. [*She faces the doorway.*] Let's go!

ESPERANZA. [*Grabbing her by the hand*]   Don't leave me, Lola! I'm
afraid. Sleep in my room tonight.

LOLA.   They're coming in here.

ESPERANZA.   Come to my room! I can't stand to be alone!

LOLA.   All right, I will. . . . I feel so cold. . . .

[*They hurry off at right, very distressed. Pause. Voices are heard, and
in a moment* DOÑA PEPITA *enters and turns on the central light. Close
behind her are* ALBERTO *and* ANDRES *who are carrying the body of*
IGNACIO *whose head hangs limply, swaying back and forth. Then*
MIGUEL, PEDRO *and* CARLOS *appear. They are all pale with emotion.*]

DOÑA PEPITA.   Put him there, on the sofa. Hurry! Miguel, turn off that
radio, please. [MIGUEL *complies and remains near the radio set.*
DOÑA PEPITA *touches* ANDRES'S *arm.*] Andrés, go inform Don Pablo
immediately.

ANDRES.   This very minute. [*He exits right.*]

DOÑA PEPITA. [*Kneeling down, she takes* IGNACIO'S *wrist and places her
ear against his chest.*]   He's dead! [*Incredulous, she looks at*
CARLOS *who does not react.* DON PABLO *enters hurriedly from right.
He is half-dressed and without his dark glasses.* ANDRES *appears
behind him.*]

DON PABLO.   What's wrong? What's happened to Ignacio? Are you
there, Pepita?

DOÑA PEPITA.   Ignacio has been killed. He's here, on the sofa.

DON PABLO.   Killed? . . . I don't understand! [*He advances toward the
sofa, kneels down and feels.*] How did it happen? Where?

DOÑA PEPITA.   On the sports field. I really don't know. . . . I arrived
afterwards.

DON PABLO.   Doesn't anyone know how it happened? Who got to him
first?

CARLOS.   I did.

[DOÑA PEPITA *doesn't take her eyes off* CARLOS.]

DON PABLO.   Ah! Tell us, tell us, Carlos.

CARLOS.   There's not much to tell. I'd gone out to get some air because
my head hurt. I thought I heard sounds near the toboggan slide. I
started over and then I heard a thud, very strong. And a movement in the air. I understood immediately that it was some kind
of accident. I got there and felt around. I thought it was Ignacio.
He had fallen from the tower, and beside him was one of the

mats we use for the descent. Doña Pepita came at once, and we called for help. . . . Then we brought him here.

[*While he has been speaking,* DOÑA PEPITA *has covered the dead boy with the cloth from one of the tables.*]

DON PABLO.   How is it possible? Now I understand it even less! I can't imagine what Ignacio was doing on the toboggan run at this time of night.

ANDRES.   Maybe it was suicide, Don Pablo.

ALBERTO.   Then why did he have the mat? Ignacio must have killed himself trying to slide down the toboggan. That's obvious. We all know that he was clumsy in everything he tried.

DON PABLO.   But he wasn't interested in such activities. What did a toboggan slide matter to him? Because of his clumsiness he always refused to take part in any sports.

MIGUEL.   Sir, would you permit me to respectfully suggest a reason you haven't thought of. [*Expectation*] I knew Ignacio very well. [*Sorrowfully*] Precisely because his shortcomings tortured him so much he probably tried to overcome them in secret, pretending indifference in front of us. I believe that tonight and many other nights, when he was late in getting to our room, he was trying to improve his skill without running the risk of ridicule. You know how sensitive he was. . . .

DON PABLO. [*Eagerly accepting this explanation*]   Instead of learning at the proper time, he brings us this complication because of his stubbornness. I hope that this will serve as a lesson to all of you.
. . .

[*Brief pause. Shamed, the students turn their heads away.*]

Yes. Surely that is what happened. Isn't it likely, Pepita?

DOÑA PEPITA. [*With her eyes still on* CARLOS]   It's very possible. . . .

DON PABLO.   What do you think, Carlos?

CARLOS.   I think Miguel has hit on the explanation.

DON PABLO.   Thank goodness. The suicide hypothesis was very disagreeable to me. It would have reflected badly on the morale of the institution.

DOÑA PEPITA.   Shall I telephone the authorities?

DON PABLO.   It's better that I do it. I'll also have to break the news to his father . . . poor man! I recall how he spoke to me of his fear of accidents . . . but an accident can happen to anyone, and we can show ample evidence that the toboggan and other sports have a place in a well-rounded educational program. We can, can't we, Pepita?

DOÑA PEPITA.   Yes. Don't worry about that now. I'll stay here.

DON PABLO.   That clumsy boy! He was trying to . . . Of course! [*He exits.* ELISA *enters from right, still dressed. She stops near the door.*]

ELISA.   What's happened? They're saying that Ignacio . . .

MIGUEL.   Ignacio has been killed. His body is in this room.

ELISA. [*With surprise but no real emotion*]   Oh! [*Instinctively she moves
   closer to* MIGUEL *until she touches him. She slips her hands around
   his waist in an expressive gesture of taking repossession.* MIGUEL *puts
   his arm around her tightly. Little by little,* ELISA *lets her head fall until
   it is resting on his shoulder.*]
DOÑA PEPITA.   I think you all should leave now. Thank you for your
   help, and try not to discuss this too much with the other students. Good night. [*She sends* PEDRO *and* ALBERTO *off with pats on
   the shoulder.*] No one else is to come into this room.
   [ANDRES *also exits; behind him* MIGUEL *and* ELISA, *arm in arm. He
   looks serious, but* ELISA *cannot restrain a smile of happiness.*]
ELISA.   Maybe it's better for him after all. . . . He wasn't suited for a
   normal life, was he, Miguel?
MIGUEL. [*Affectionately*]   No. He's better off now. Everything he tried
   turned out wrong.
   [JUANA'S *voice is heard from right. She enters immediately in bath-
   robe, crossing in front of them.* MIGUEL *tries to stop her, but* ELISA
   takes possession again and leads him gently through the doorway.]
JUANA.   Carlos! Carlos! Are you here?
CARLOS.   I'm here, Juana. [*She reaches him downstage and throws herself
   into his arms sobbing.*]
JUANA.   Carlos!
   [CARLOS *reaches out to her with a smile that betrays his disenchant-
   ment.* DOÑA PEPITA *watches them sorrowfully.*]
JUANA.   Poor Ignacio!
CARLOS.   He's at peace now.
JUANA.   Yes. He must be happier now. [*She cries.*] Will you forgive
   me? I know I've hurt you. . . .
CARLOS.   I have nothing to forgive, my dearest.
JUANA.   Yes, you do! I have to confess many things to you . . . they
   weigh on me terribly. But my intentions were good. I swear it! I
   never stopped loving you, Carlos!
CARLOS.   I know that, Juana. I know that.
JUANA.   Will you forgive me? I'll tell you everything.
CARLOS.   It's not necessary, for it couldn't matter now. I forgive you
   without knowing.
JUANA.   Carlos! [*She kisses him impulsively.*]
DOÑA PEPITA. [*Somberly*]   My friends, you have forgotten that there is
   a dead boy here.
CARLOS.   You're right. Come, Juana. We should go now.
   [*Arm in arm, they start off right—he melancholy and she trembling
   with emotion.*]
DOÑA PEPITA. [*With effort*]   You stay, Carlos. I want to talk with you.
CARLOS. [*Bowing his head*]   All right. Goodnight, Juana.
JUANA.   Until tomorrow, Carlos. And thank you!
   [*Their hands separate slowly.* JUANA *exits.* CARLOS *stands waiting.*

DOÑA PEPITA *looks at him sorrowfully. A long pause.*]

DOÑA PEPITA.   It was terrible, wasn't it?

CARLOS.   Yes. [*Pause*]

DOÑA PEPITA. [*She goes closer to him; her eyes study him.*]   It would be useless to deny that the school has been freed from its greatest threat . . . that all of us are going to relax and live normally again. The solution my husband was looking for has been found. [*With reproach*] But no one expected . . . such a thing as this.

CARLOS. [*Firmly*]   However it may have happened, the danger was eliminated in time.

DOÑA PEPITA. [*Bitterly*]   Do you think so?

CARLOS. [*Contemptuously*]   Didn't you notice? Now that he's dead his best friends abandon him. They whisper over his body. Ah, the blind, the blind! They think they have the right to feel sorry for him, but they are so little and insignificant! Miguel and Elisa are reconciled. The others are relieved. Happiness is returning! Everything's all right again.

DOÑA PEPITA.   It hurts me to hear you talk like that.

CARLOS. [*Violently*]   Why? [*Brief pause*]

DOÑA PEPITA. [*In an outburst*]   Because of what you have done!

CARLOS. [*Suddenly becoming rigid*]   I don't know what you mean.

DOÑA PEPITA.   Sometimes, Carlos, we believe that we're doing the right thing, and we commit a grave error. . . .

CARLOS.   I don't know what you're talking about.

DOÑA PEPITA.   And we fail to recognize that the words which disturbed us have been meant to console us. People touch our lives, love us, and suffer when they see us suffer. And we refuse to see this. . . . We reject them when we most desperately need their friendship. . . .

CARLOS. [*Coldly*]   Many thanks for your interest . . . but it's unnecessary now.

DOÑA PEPITA. [*Taking his hands*]   My boy!

CARLOS. [*Freeing himself*]   I'm no fool, Doña Pepita. I know very well what you're insinuating. Ignacio and I, at the same time, on the sports field. . . . Your supposition is false.

DOÑA PEPITA.   But, of course! False! I never said otherwise. [*Slowly*] Nor do I intend to say otherwise.

CARLOS.   I can't express my gratitude for that. I've done nothing.

DOÑA PEPITA. [*With a fleeting glance at the dead boy*]   And poor Ignacio can no longer speak. But rest easy, Carlos. Supposing it were true . . . [*A movement from* CARLOS] Yes, yes, I know it isn't. But if it were, my speaking out would help no one. . . . And the good name of the school comes before everything else.

CARLOS.   I agree.

DOÑA PEPITA.   And all our acts must serve the interest of the institution, don't you agree?

CARLOS. [*Ironically*]   Of course they must. I know what you're think-
  ing. Don't waste your energy.
DOÑA PEPITA.   Or serve our own interests.
CARLOS.   What?
DOÑA PEPITA.   This institution can have enemies . . . and people,
  rivals in love.
  [*Pause.* CARLOS *turns around and starts tiredly toward the left. He
  stumbles over one of the chairs beside the chessboard and sinks down
  on it.*]
  Don't you want to confide in me?
CARLOS. [*Stubbornly*]   I repeat that what you are thinking is false!
DOÑA PEPITA. [*Going up to him from behind and resting her hands on his
  shoulders*]   Well . . . I was wrong. No crime was committed, not
  even a crime of passion. You don't want anyone's pity. Not even
  Juana's?
CARLOS. [*Fiercely*]   Juana should learn to avoid that dangerous senti-
  ment!
  [*Pause. His hand toys with the chessmen on the board.*]
DOÑA PEPITA.   Carlos . . .
CARLOS.   What?
DOÑA PEPITA.   It would do you so much good to let yourself go. . . .
CARLOS. [*Standing up abruptly*]   Enough! Stop trying to obtain an
  impossible confession! What are you up to? Do you want to show
  off your wisdom? Play the role of a mother with me because you
  have no sons of your own?
DOÑA PEPITA. [*Ashen*]   You are a cruel person . . . I could never go so
  far. Because, half an hour ago, I was working here, and it might
  have occurred to me to get up and look out the window. I didn't.
  Perhaps, if I had, I would have seen someone climbing the toboggan stairs, carrying Ignacio—unconscious, or even already dead!
  [*Pause*] Then, from up there, he pushes the body off . . . Without
  taking the precaution of thinking about the eyes of others. We
  always forget that others can see. Only Ignacio thought of that.
  [*Pause*] But I saw nothing, for I stayed at my desk. [*She waits,
  watching his face.*]
CARLOS.   No! You didn't see anything! And even if you had gotten up
  and you thought you saw something . . . [*With deep scorn*] What
  is sight? Sight doesn't exist here! How can you presume to invoke
  the testimony of your eyes? Your eyes! Bah!
DOÑA PEPITA. [*Tearfully*]   My son, it isn't good to be so hard.
CARLOS.   Leave me alone! And stop trying to win me over with your
  revolting feminine reasoning!
DOÑA PEPITA.   You're forgetting that I'm not a young woman.
CARLOS.   You're the one who seems to have forgotten it.
DOÑA PEPITA.   What? You're out of your mind, out of your mind! . . .
CARLOS. [*Desperately*]   Yes, I am. So get out! [*Pause*]

DOÑA PEPITA.   Yes, I'm going. . . . It seems that my husband should have been back before now. [*She starts away and stops.*] You don't want friendship . . . or peace. You don't want peace now. And you think you've won, that it will be enough. But you haven't won, Carlos. Remember what I'm saying. You haven't won. [*She encompasses in a final, sad glance the murderer and his victim and exits at left.* CARLOS *sinks down on the chair. His head loses its former rigidity and falls to his breast. His breathing becomes progressively more agitated; finally he can endure it no longer. He pulls open his shirt collar and removes his tie with a gesture that indicates his choking sensation and also his indifference. Then he turns his head toward the window as if responding to some inaudible call. He gets up hesitatingly and accidentally overturns the chessmen on the board with his arm. It makes a discordant noise, adding a bitter and brutal note at that moment. He stops a second, frightened by the mishap, and sadly gropes for the scattered chessmen. Then he advances toward the dead body of* IGNACIO. *When he is beside him, in the supreme bitterness of his irremediable loneliness, he falls to his knees and uncovers the pale face of the dead boy. He touches him with the despair of one who touches a sleeping person who can no longer be awakened. Then he stands up, as if drawn by a mysterious force and walks with his hands outstretched to the window. There he remains motionless facing the starlight. He begins to speak in a low voice which suddenly breaks forth with deep passion.*]

CARLOS.   . . . And now the stars are shining in all their splendor, and men with sight know their marvelous presence. Those far-off worlds, beyond the window. [*His hands, like the wings of a wounded bird, tremble and beat against the mysterious prison of glass*] Within reach of our sight! . . . if we could see . . .

The curtain slowly falls.